A NEW VOLUME IN AMERICA'S WAR HERITAGE

For the first time in modern history, the United States Army had to adapt to guerrilla warfare where front lines did not exist and to terrain where coastal rice paddies gave way to thick jungle and steep mountains.

Leading the way in adapting to the new environment were the members of the Long Range Reconnaissance Patrols.

They may have been an innovation in Vietnam, but they were following in the proud footsteps of many Rangers who had gone before them. Whatever their designation, LRRP or Ranger, their lineage is a long and courageous history of unsurpassed fighting spirit.

Also by Michael Lee Lanning
Published by Ivy Books:

THE ONLY WAR WE HAD

VIETNAM 1969–1970: A Company Commander's
Journal

INSIDE THE LRRPS
Rangers in Vietnam

MICHAEL LEE LANNING

IVY BOOKS • NEW YORK

Ivy Books
Published by Ballantine Books
Copyright © 1988 by Michael Lee Lanning

Library of Congress Catalog Card Number: 87-92141

ISBN-0-8041-0166-3

Manufactured in the United States of America

First Edition: August 1988

Cover photo: Co Rentmeester, LIFE magazine © Time Inc.

CONTENTS

●━●━●━●━●

INTRODUCTION   1

CHAPTER 1   All in a Day's Work   5

CHAPTER 2   Past Wars, Past Rangers:
             The Early Years   13

CHAPTER 3   Past Wars, Past Rangers:
             World War II to Vietnam   30

CHAPTER 4   A Different War, Different Rangers:
             The Beginnings   43

CHAPTER 5   A Different War, Different Rangers:
             Formation of the LRRPs   50

CHAPTER 6   The Men with Painted Faces   76

CHAPTER 7   Training   98

CHAPTER 8   Equipment   111

CHAPTER 9   Operations   134

CHAPTER 10   Results and Accolades   160

CHAPTER 11   The Nonbelievers   171

v

CHAPTER 12 Legacy of the LRRP/Rangers   176

CHAPTER 13 Conclusions   187

APPENDIX A Tactical Standard Operating
            Procedures, LRRP Company   189

APPENDIX B Standing Orders—Rogers's Rangers,
            1759   220

APPENDIX C LRRP and Ranger Units in Vietnam   222

APPENDIX D LRRP Medal of Honor Recipients   226

APPENDIX E Unit Awards, Citations, and
            Commendations   228

APPENDIX F LRRP Unit Replacement Training
            Schedule   235

APPENDIX G Ranger Creed   238

BIBLIOGRAPHY   240

ACKNOWLEDGMENTS

In writing this book, I am indebted to
Owen Lock, for the idea;
Bill and Palmer Morrow, for assistance and support;
Al and Barbara Call, for believing;
Linda, for everything;
Reveilee and Meridith, because they are ours.

INTRODUCTION

●◇●◇●◇●◇●◇●

THE LRRP veteran spoke quietly yet proudly of his days in Vietnam as he occasionally adjusted the metal and leather leg prosthesis that had become necessary as a result of his last recon mission. "It's about time someone wrote about us. We did what others only dream about and walked where others didn't dare. We accomplished and gave too much for our story not to be known."

Those words were spoken by a former recon man in one of the first interviews I conducted in preparation of this book. It would ultimately summarize the purpose of my putting pen to paper.

Despite the fact that the LRRPs have become almost legendary for their exploits in Vietnam, there has as yet been no definitive history of their feats. Except for a few sketchy articles in military journals, the LRRP reputation has been one spread more by word of mouth than by the printed page.

Three somewhat romanticized novels, *Tiger the Lurp Dog* by Kenn Miller, and *Charlie Mike* and *The Last Run*, both by Leonard B. Scott, added to the legend but contributed little to the history.* In his comprehensive *Vietnam Order of Battle*, Shelby Stanton records virtually the

*All three titles are available from Ballantine Books.

only facts in print to this time on LRRP history. Stanton adds a bit more on the formation of the LRRPs, but only a few pages, in *Green Berets at War*, his study of Special Forces in Vietnam.

In preparation of this book, I drew on detailed research and personal experience to tell the complete story of the LRRPs. Writing from an understanding based upon on-the-ground experience as an infantry platoon leader, reconnaissance platoon leader, and company commander in Vietnam,* I have both an understanding of and an appreciation for the LRRPs. Upon my return from Vietnam, I spent two years as an instructor in the U.S. Army Infantry Center's Ranger School, followed by continued active service in the Army for a total of twenty years. This reinforced my admiration for the recon men.

Research for the text included file searches in the National Archives in Suitland, Maryland; the U.S. Army Center of Military History in Washington, D.C.; the Office of the Adjutant General of the U.S. Army in Washington, D.C.; the Combat Studies Institute at Fort Leavenworth, Kansas; the U.S. Army Military History Institute at Carlisle Barracks, Pennsylvania; and the various museums across the United States that house the historical records of the units that fought in Vietnam. A majority of the records uncovered were still classified and were downgraded and released for the first time at my request.

Interviews were conducted with over fifty general officers who commanded units that had LRRPs assigned to them or who were responsible for their formation, and over two hundred LRRP veterans. Many of these individuals shared their personal papers as well as their memories of the war.

Other special units, including U.S. Marine Corps Force Recon, U.S. Navy SEALS, and Australian and New Zealander special air services, operated similarly to the LRRPs and with equal bravery and success. However, their stories

---

*See *The Only War We Had, a Platoon Leader's Vietnam Journal* (Ivy Books, 1987) and *Vietnam 1969–1970, A Company Commander's Journal* (Ivy Books, 1988).

are not included in this work as they deserve their own studies.

For the reader who is unfamiliar with the missions and operational procedures of the long range reconnaissance patrols, the Tactical Standard Operating Procedures (Tac SOP) in Appendix A will provide useful insights for better understanding this book.

CHAPTER 1
●○●○●○●

All in a Day's Work

V_{IETNAM} was a different kind of war from America's previous conflicts, one that required different tactics and a different kind of soldier. One of the most successful innovations of the war was the formation of Long Range Reconnaissance Patrols—LRRPs, pronounced "Lurps," which were redesignated Rangers in 1969.

Operating for a week at a time in six-man teams deep within enemy territory, often beyond range of friendly artillery fire or other support, they were the eyes and ears of the units they served. While best known for the timely intelligence provided by their reconnaissance, their enemy body count often rivaled or exceeded combat units of far greater numbers. When a live prisoner was needed for interrogation, it was the LRRPs who were assigned this most difficult, hazardous mission. To state it quite simply, the LRRPs may very well have been the most effective use of manpower in the war.

Although their designation changed several times, only thirteen LRRP units saw action in Southeast Asia. Each of the recon units was similarly manned and equipped, and each followed the same basic tactical procedures. However, there was no centralized command or control of the total LRRP force. Each LRRP unit operated independently of the others, answering only to the command to which it was assigned.

This command relationship, combined with the vastly different areas of operation—which varied from river deltas and lowland rice paddies to mountain jungles—made each LRRP unit unique. The only constant was the men who volunteered for this exceptional duty—the valorous thread of humanity that bound all LRRP units together as brothers of the same cloth.

LRRP missions were characterized by extreme hardship, extraordinary attention to detail, absolute professionalism, and uncommon bravery. The following three stories are typical of the accomplishments of the recon men in Vietnam.

Thomas P. Dineen, Jr., from Annapolis, Maryland, was a Specialist 4 in E Company, 50th Infantry (LRP)* of the 9th Infantry Division, working out of Tan An in the Delta in 1968. Dineen recalls, "Early one morning at the company base camp in September, the team leader called us together to issue his warning order for the next mission. He included a detailed schedule of what we would do in preparation and told each of us exactly what weapons and equipment we should pack. He concluded that the assistant team leader would conduct an inspection as soon as we were ready to ensure we had followed his orders.

"Returning to the team hooch, I gathered my pistol belt, web-carrying harness, first-aid pouch, knife, strobe light, six frag grenades, three smoke grenades, two white phosphorous grenades, two Claymore mines, compass, canteens, map, thirty loaded magazines, and my M-16 rifle. I then carefully assembled the gear and taped all parts that might reflect light, or rattle, with flat, black tape. Disassembling my rifle, I cleaned it and lubricated each part as I put it back together. After again oiling the bolt, I placed a magazine of rounds into the weapon and manually

*The chapters to follow contain more information on the designations LRRP and LRP than most people will ever need to know.

pumped the cartridges through the breech. It worked properly, so I reloaded the magazine and taped it end-to-end with another magazine so I could reload quickly if things got hot.

"When I was satisfied that everything was in order, I emptied my pockets of all mission nonessential items, put on all the gear, and with weapon in hand jumped up and down to be sure I didn't make any noise. After adding a little more tape to items that rubbed together, I took a camouflage stick and covered all exposed skin with the black and green greasepaint.

"The assistant team leader soon arrived to inspect me and the other three LRRPs. Afterwards we met the team leader at the operations bunker where a sergeant from the division intelligence section briefed us on the upcoming mission. He explained that an infantry battalion had been sweeping an area about twelve kilometers to our west for several days with scattered resistance—the enemy was in the area, but the large infantry unit could not get them to stand and fight. Our mission was to go in with the helicopters that pulled them out and conduct a 'stay behind' ambush. We were all aware that the VC and NVA frequently checked LZs after Americans were extracted to recover any lost or discarded food or supplies they might find useful. The intel briefers also gave us a complete rundown on the number and identification of enemy units in the area. They even had pictures of several of the local VC leaders that we might encounter.

"We spent the remainder of the afternoon under control of our team leader rehearsing our insertion and extraction plans, procedures during movement, and the various ambush formations we might use. The team leader and his assistant repeatedly asked the rest of us questions about our duties and radio call signs and frequencies. A final inspection of our equipment was followed by a test firing of our weapons, after which we headed to the helipad for pickup.

"We were soon airborne and joined up with the seven other choppers that were going in to pick up the infantry unit. The LZ was a large, open area of rice paddies surrounded by tree lines. We offloaded while those on the ground climbed aboard. There were several more lifts inbound to pick up the remaining grunts, so we had ample time to mingle with them and disappear into the tree line. By the time the last birds lifted off, we had our Claymores out and were well camouflaged in the edge of a canal overlooking a trail that snaked from the woods to the LZ. All there was left to do was wait.

"Less than an hour later, as the sun began to set, we heard a single rifle shot about a half-kilometer away. It was quickly followed by another shot from about the same location. By the sounds of the rifles, I knew they were AK-47s. The enemy frequently used such shots as a means of communications so elements could link up.

"A short time later we could hear the dinks noisily moving down the trail toward us. They must have thought all Americans had pulled out on the choppers as they were making little effort to be quiet. We had picked our position well, as twelve VC and NVA were soon in our kill zone.

"The nearest man was only three feet from our hidden positions when the team leader sprung the ambush by blowing the Claymores. We poured M-16 rounds and hand grenades into the screaming mass of dying men. In less than a minute the fight was over—twelve dead bodies lay before us. They had not been able to fire a single shot in return.

"As several of us gathered up the weapons and searched for documents, the radio operator called for an extraction chopper. We moved back onto the LZ and within minutes were airborne on our way back to the base. It had been a textbook mission—a perfect ambush—one where all the shots had been one-sided.

"I spent a total of two years with the LRRPs, but the events, impressions, and emotions of that stay-behind ambush on the LZ are as vivid today as they were then. You see, that was my first mission as a LRRP. There would be many more, but that first one is the most memorable."

* * *

Lee Roy Pipkin, from San Jose, California, was a twenty-two-year-old sergeant in the 74th Infantry Detachment (LRP) of the 173rd Airborne Brigade. Pipkin remembers, "In late November 1967 my team was inserted into a recon zone near the Laotian border west of Dak To. On a pre-mission overflight the day before we had spotted a trail along a streambed. We were inserted by helicopter early in the morning into a landing zone about a kilometer from the trail. Moving as quietly as possible, we took several hours to reach the stream. After checking the jungle along the trail, we found a bend in the stream that gave us good observation in both directions. We set up about seventy-five meters off the trail and carefully camouflaged our positions.

"A few hours later we spotted two figures slowly moving down the narrow pathway. A short distance behind them came more and more soldiers. As they reached the bend just in front of us they stopped for a break. We remained calm as we knew we were well hidden despite the fact that we could now see sixty or more of the well-armed enemy. I was a little surprised to see that they were not particularly concerned with security. Several even had transistor radios which they turned on and tuned in to a station playing Vietnamese music. As they removed their packs, we could see that ten or twelve of them were women. Male and female alike varied from as young as fifteen to as old as forty or so—it is hard to tell the exact age of the gooks even after months in country.

"Several of the enemy took advantage of the break to take a quick bath in the stream. They acted like they owned the jungle and were not at all worried about being detected. Maybe they thought they were still in Laos, or maybe they just did not think Americans would venture so far from our bases.

"We were a long way out—so far, in fact, that we were out of radio contact. An air force spotter plane was to overfly our position three times a day to receive our reports. He was not due for another two hours, so all we could do was wait and watch.

"There was plenty to see. Each gook carried either an AK-47 or SKS* and a few were armed with RPG [Rocket Propelled Grenade] launchers. All had heavy packs and some had large wooden 'A' frames on which were heavy 122-millimeter rockets or mortar rounds. Their uniforms were a mixture of green and khaki and everyone, including the women, was wearing the standard NVA pith helmet.

"The only time our observation of the group got a bit hairy was when one of the dinks wandered toward our position. He opened his fly and urinated so near us that the splashing piss landed on the back of one of my men. We were so well camouflaged that the gook finished his business and returned to his friends without spotting us.

"We kept hoping that they would stay around long enough for the spotter plane to arrive so we could call in an air strike on them—we were out of range of any friendly artillery. They moved out before he arrived, but by following the direction of their movement that we gave him, he was able to find them. The air strikes he called in on them certainly ended their party—and any idea they might have had that any area in Vietnam was safe for them when LRRPs were in the field."

Jerry R. Ballantyne, from Tacoma, Washington, was a staff sergeant and team leader in the LRRPs of the 1st Cavalry Division. According to Ballantyne, "For most of 1967 we were a provisional unit with no official designation. It was not until the end of December [December 20] that we became an authorized unit—Company E, 52nd Infantry (LRP). All of that meant little to us at the time because LRRPs had been an important part of the Cav since shortly after the division's arrival in Vietnam in '65.

"In October of '67, my team—composed of myself, four other Americans, and a Montagnard mercenary scout—

---

*A semiautomatic rifle of Soviet design, the SKS was much favored as a war trophy by American soldiers because it could be legally imported into the United States (unlike the fully automatic AK-47, which qualified as a machine gun).

was inserted by helicopter into the south end of the A Shau Valley to conduct a zone reconnaissance. Everyone on the team was well experienced, with many missions under their belts. The Yard scout had fought the VC and NVA for years and knew every sound in the jungle. His only problem was that he hated the enemy so badly that he was much more interested in killing than reconnaissance.

"The area we were assigned was covered in head-high elephant grass spotted with dense patches of jungle. We moved very cautiously and slowly for about an hour when we came to a well-used trail about two feet across. After watching the trail for a half hour or so, I ordered the team to cross it and move out of the grass into a nearby wood-line. Three of the team members were across and my radio operator, myself, and the Yard were about to rise up out of the grass when a khaki-clad NVA suddenly appeared walking down the path. Our camouflage was good and, although we were only feet from the trail, he did not see us. We were far from being out of trouble, however, as right behind the first gook came more. Since my team was split on both sides of the trail, all we could do was wait—and count the enemy as they passed. If we had tried to pull out, they would have seen the grass move. They were too close to call for help on the radio—so close, in fact, that the radio operator turned the set off so an incoming message would not reveal our position.

"As I counted more and more soldiers pass I began to fear that my pounding heart would make so much noise it would give us away. Over the next hour I counted three hundred and thirty well-armed enemy—all fit-looking in nearly new uniforms and carrying packs.

"My plan was to call in artillery and air support as soon as the end of the formation passed our position. The Yard mercenary had other ideas. We knew from experience that the dinks would have a rear guard several hundred meters behind the tail of the group. When the lone enemy appeared, the Yard, despite my lunge to stop him, sprang from the grass behind the rear sentry. With a stab and slash of his knife he soundlessly took the guy's head nearly off. We drug the body off the trail and headed for the nearest pickup zone at a dead run as I called for artillery and air.

"Seconds later gunships had the dinks in their sights and began to shred their formation. Unfortunately, in their retreat, they found their comrade with the cut throat and picked up our trail. With over three hundred of them after us, the thought of stopping to make a fight of it never crossed my mind. We were still far from an LZ when the lead dinks closed near enough to put fire on us. More gunships and artillery kept them somewhat at bay as we continued to run.

"Things were looking pretty bad when a chopper hovered above the brush that surrounded us and kicked out flexible ladders. In seconds all six of us were climbing up the rungs, halting only to fire a magazine from our CAR-15s as the bird gained altitude. Not only were we able to escape, but the dinks in their pursuit of us made a good target for the arty and air. Other units of the Cav piled on, sweeping the area both on the ground and from the air. By day's end over two hundred enemy dead littered the area.

"I had a few words with the Yard when the chopper finally got us back to the company base camp. He had made a mistake in taking out the rear security man, but all in all everything had worked out pretty well."

CHAPTER 2

◻◻◻◻◻◻◻

Past Wars, Past Rangers: The Early Years

*W*ARFARE is by no means an exact science. Military strategists from Clausewitz and Jomini to present-day tacticians have sought principles and theories by which to fight. While their philosophies may have been beneficial to the classroom student and war-room planner, the combat soldier has long known the reality that the only constant on the actual battlefield is change.

What may have been successful in past battles or wars—or for that matter, the fire fight yesterday—may not work in the next engagement. Combat in Vietnam did not conform to any of our previous conflicts. There was no book. The new edition of conflict added an entirely new, bloody, and heartbreaking volume to America's war heritage. For the first time in modern history the United States Army had to adapt to guerrilla warfare where front lines did not exist and to terrain where coastal rice paddies gave way to thick jungle and steep mountains.

Leading the way in adapting to the new environment were the members of the Long Range Reconnaissance Patrols. In one of the first "Vietnam Studies," published by the Department of the Army in 1974, Lieutenant General John H. Hay, Jr., wrote, "The way in which the long-range patrols were used was one of the most significant innovations of the war." Hay, former commander of the

1st Infantry Division, did not, however, point out that the LRRPs were more evolutionary in concept than revolutionary. Vietnam LRRPs may have been an innovation, but they were following in the proud footsteps of many Rangers who had gone before them. Whatever their designation, LRRP or Ranger, their lineage is a long and courageous history of unsurpassed fighting spirit.

As Vietnam required new kinds of tactics, so had colonial American battles of the seventeenth century. Warfare on the European plain had been standardized into a near art form with long lines of troops facing each other across open fields. Soldier had fought soldier with little damage inflicted—or intended—upon the surrounding populus.

America was different. The vast countryside, covered in thick, virgin forest, had only game trails and occasional Indian pathways penetrating the green foliage. Roads capable of accommodating marching armies were nearly nonexistent.

The enemy was different as well. Indians struck from ambush and rarely stood to fight a direct battle. Operating throughout wide areas, and usually working from temporary bases, the Indian struck hard against any white—soldier or settler, man, woman, or child. To survive and conquer, the colonist had to determine how to out-Indian the Indian.

Small groups of frontiersmen soon were scouting the woods using the same tactics as their enemy. Reports of those patrols often included such phrases as "ranged five miles down river in pursuit of the enemy." From these reports the soldiers became known as "Rangers"—and the beginning of a legend was born on the American frontier.

The earliest unit formally called Rangers was that of the Massachusetts militiamen known as Church's Rangers. Under the command of Captain Benjamin Church, the Rangers fought in King Philip's War of 1675–1676. "King Philip" (Metecomet to his Indian allies), chief of the Wampanoags occupying the area that is now Rhode Island

and Massachusetts, led a revolt in 1675 against enforcement of a treaty limiting hunting and fishing rights ar-
ranged by his father and the original Mayflower colonists.
Philip and his allies, with no comprehension of land own-
ership or boundaries, destroyed twelve towns and killed
over a thousand colonists.

The Indians suffered as well when their principal village
near Kingstown, Rhode Island, was overwhelmed on December 19, 1675. After continued skirmishes, on August
12, 1676 Church's Rangers tracked Philip to his swampy
refuge near present-day Bristol, Rhode Island. During a
short battle, Philip was shot and killed by one of Church's
scouts. The war was over. Rangers had won their first
victory.

For the next three-quarters of a century, Rangers, such
as Gorham's Rangers, continued to develop their small
unit tactics and skills. However, it was not until the French
and Indian War of 1754–1763 that early Rangers gained
the reputation that lives today.

Although others had preceded him, the title of "Father
of the American Rangers" belongs by all rights to Major
Robert Rogers. Born on November 7, 1731, in Methuen,
Massachusetts, Rogers spent his youth in New Hampshire
learning the skills of the woods from Indians and hunters
rather than the more formal classroom scholastics. In 1755
Rogers was charged with counterfeiting. His solution to
the problem was one adopted by many Rangers of future
generations. He volunteered to join a dangerous military
mission instead of facing punishment by the courts.

Serving as a scout, Rogers participated in an expedition
under General William Johnson against the French at
Crown Point, New York. Rogers so impressed his superiors with his daring and scouting skills that he was promoted to captain and given command of a company of
Rangers in March 1756. In two short years he was advanced to major in command of nine Ranger companies.

Rogers recruited his own men, developed new training
programs, and published a list of commonsense rules of
operations, security, and tactics. He was one of the first

commanders to conduct live-fire training exercises and his Standing Orders, which include such wisdom as "don't forget nothing," "don't march home the same way. . . ." and ". . . finish them off with your hatchet" are still appropriate for today's Ranger operations.*

Rogers was as innovative in his methods of operation as he was in training. His use of scouting patrols, ambushes, and deep penetrations into enemy-held territory rivaled the skills of the Indians whom he copied. When campaigns by regular troops virtually ceased during the cold and the deep snowfalls of winter, Rogers's Rangers continued their scouting and raids, sometimes operating on snowshoes, and occasionally on ice skates to cross lakes. The enemy, whether French or Indian, never knew where the Rangers would strike next. At a time when little was going well for the English colonists, the success of Rogers's Rangers was one of the few sources of good news. Known nearly as much for their rowdy behavior and practical jokes as for their daring and bravery, they became heroes of the frontier.

Rogers's Rangers participated in many of the principal campaigns of the French and Indian War, including Halifax in 1757, Ticonderoga and Lake George in 1758, and Crown Point in 1759. Prior to the fights, they were deployed in small scout teams to gather intelligence on the enemy and the terrain. When the battles actually began, they often assembled into full companies to fight as regular infantry.

The best-known victory of the Rangers was their raid on the Abenaki Indian camp at St. Francis, about forty miles south of Montreal. The Abenakis, a part of the Algonquin tribe, were fierce raiders, and their lodge poles were hung with hundreds of colonists' scalps.

Rogers's force, composed of 180 or so men, traveled from Crown Point by boat and on foot to cover the four

---

*Rogers's Standing Orders were originally quite lengthy and have appeared in various forms. The nineteen orders, listed in their entirety in Appendix B, are the most commonly accepted and still found in Ranger Standard Operating Procedures and framed on barracks' walls today.

hundred miles in a little over six weeks. Disease and frequent skirmishes along the way reduced the force to 142. Through stealth the Rangers were able to remain undetected during the last miles of the expedition as they neared the Abenakis' stronghold. On October 5, 1759, they attacked, catching the Indians completely by surprise and killing well over two hundred warriors, destroying the village, and burning the scalp poles with their bloody trophies. Never again were the Abenakis able to field an effective fighting force.

Other Indians and the harsh elements further thinned the Rangers on their long withdrawal back across enemy territory to Crown Point. Only ninety-three returned. The Rangers were welcomed back by celebrations throughout the colonies, accompanied by tales that members of the expedition had resorted to cannibalism either from a lack of provisions or because of sheer bravado. Although the rumor was very likely false, it added another page to the book of Ranger legends that would grow with each succeeding conflict.

In November of 1760 Rogers left the Rangers to journey to Detroit in order to accept the surrender of the French forts on the western frontier. At the conclusion of the war he filled several administrative positions in the colonial governments of New York and South Carolina.

Unfortunately, Rogers was about as inept a peacetime administrator as he had been a success as a wartime leader. Financial problems, many a direct result of using his own funds to raise his Ranger companies, combined with some illicit trading with the Indians, required him to flee to England in 1765 with the law close behind. There he published two books and a play about his adventures on the frontier. Although the manuscripts lacked accuracy, they did help regain his reputation as a hero of the recent conflict. As a result he was able to secure a commission in the 60th Foot Regiment (The Royal Americans) and in 1766 was posted back to the colonies as the commander of Fort Maclanec in present-day Michigan.

Rogers again had trouble as a peacetime administrator

and was accused of dishonesty. By the time he was arrested by General Thomas Gage, the vague charges had escalated to include treason. Although he was eventually cleared of all charges, Rogers was removed from command. Shortly after his return to England, his financial difficulties became so acute that he was jailed in debtor's prison.

With the beginning of the American Revolution in 1775, Rogers was able to secure his freedom and departed England by dead of night to return to the colonies in order to offer his services to General George Washington. Washington so distrusted the former Ranger that he had him arrested. Apparently Rogers was more interested in the fight itself than in patriotism, as he soon escaped and approached the English. Touting his former fame in the French and Indian War, he talked his way into a commission as a lieutenant colonel in command of two Loyalist companies known as the "Queen's Rangers." In several battles near White Plains during the New York campaign he failed to achieve any success and was once again removed from command.

Rogers had turned against his American birthplace. With few remaining options, he returned to England, where by 1780 he was back in debtor's prison. Two years later his wife left him and Rogers's only remaining battle was with the bottle. He lost. On May 18, 1795, he died, in poverty and obscurity in London.

Rogers's life did not end well; however, his brilliant years of out-Indianing the Indian left a standard for future Rangers to emulate. Many would study his Standing Orders and learn much. Perhaps a few would also understand that a Ranger's value in war did not necessarily bring him fortune in peace.

Early Ranger tactics were further developed during the revolutionary war. Techniques learned in fighting the Indians worked equally well against the regiments of the king.

Colonel Daniel Morgan organized a unit of five hundred

frontiersmen known as Morgan's Rifles, or by many, including General George Washington, "The Corps of Rangers." Morgan's men, combining Ranger tactics with expert marksmanship, fought in most of the major campaigns between 1775 and 1781, including Freeman's Farm and Cowpens. In 1777, his troops were so important to the defeat of General John Burgoyne at Saratoga that the British general remarked, "Morgan's men were the most famous Corps of the Continental Army. All of them [were] crack shots."

At the Battle of Cowpens on January 16, 1781, Morgan displayed rhetoric the equal of his fighting abilities. On his arrival at the battle site, Morgan stated, "On this ground, I will defeat the British or lay down my bones."

Morgan also had advice for the North and South Carolinian militiamen attached to his force. To build their morale he said, "Just hold up your head, boys, three fires [musket shots], and you are free, and then when you return to your homes, how the folks will bless you, and the girls will kiss you for your gallant conduct."

The battle lasted but one hour. Morgan lost 12 killed and 60 wounded as opposed to British losses of 100 killed, 230 wounded, and 830 taken prisoner. Morgan attributed his success "to the justice of our cause and the bravery of our troops."*

Ranger units were invaluable to the revolution but were not always blessed with total success on the battlefield. Major Thomas Knowlton organized a group of about 120 volunteers into Knowlton's Rangers in August 1776. General Washington used the unit for long-range patrols behind enemy lines and as a means of capturing prisoners for intelligence purposes. On September 16, 1776, Wash-

*Morgan's aggressiveness against the British may not have reflected revolutionary zeal alone. In 1756, while working for the British as a teamster, he had struck a British officer during an argument. As a result he had been horsewhipped. According to some accounts, before the Battle of Cowpens, Morgan went to each of his Rangers, displaying the whip scars on his back as he asked their assistance in gaining revenge. His instructions to the Rangers reflected sound military judgment, as well as the possible existence of a revenge motive: "Shoot for the epaulettes [officers], boys."

ington ordered the Rangers to circle the British positions at Harlem Heights, New York, so that they could attack from the rear. During the movement, however, they were detected by a far superior force, resulting in many Ranger deaths, including that of Knowlton himself.

A more successful and much better-known Ranger unit was Marion's Partisans. Organized by Francis Marion, the "Swamp Fox," this group operated out of the South Carolina lowlands from 1775 to 1781, harassing the British by raids on communications and supply points. Adopting Rogers's Standing Orders as his guide, Marion also occasionally massed his troops to attack British and Loyalist strongholds. Marion's Partisans were a classic example of a small force being able to disrupt a much larger and better-supported army.

Also worth mention are brigadier generals John Stark and Israel Putnam, who commanded at Bunker Hill and other major engagements. Although they led regular Continental forces rather than Rangers, both had learned their war-fighting skills with Rogers's Rangers during the 1750s.

Ranger units, along with most of the rest of the army, were disbanded after the British surrender at Yorktown in 1781. Communities and states occasionally formed militia units that adopted Ranger tactics to fight Indian uprisings but stood them down as soon as the local threat was over.

Six companies of Rangers were organized for one year's service by congressional directive on January 2, 1812. Between that date and March 3, 1815, eleven other companies were authorized for similar periods of time. According to the Official Army Register published by the War Department in 1880, ten captains and forty-one lieutenants were on the rolls as "Ranger" officers—the senior man being Captain Andre Piere. There is no record of these Ranger companies making any significant contributions to the War of 1812 or in the Indian skirmishes that immediately followed.

In May 1818, two companies of Rangers were formed from volunteers from the Georgia and Tennessee militias at the direction of General Andrew Jackson. The companies, commanded by Captains McGirt and Boyle, were to combat hostile Seminole Indians in the panhandle of present-day Florida between the Mobile and Appalachicola rivers.

Boyle's Rangers, attached to the 4th U.S. Infantry Regiment at Pensacola, conducted a water-borne patrol up the Yellow River and then went overland to a Seminole camp on Choctawhatchy Bay. Skirmishes on October 8 and 9 yielded seven hostiles killed and sixteen prisoners.

Both of the Ranger companies were disbanded the following November. The significance of the campaign of Boyle's Rangers is not in their results but rather in the locations of their actions. Their patrol and fights took place within what is now Eglin Air Base—home of the Florida Ranger Camp. Modern Ranger students train on the same waterways and in the woodlands where Boyle's men fought nearly a century and a half ago.

As the American frontier expanded westward, the techniques of early Rangers such as Rogers, Morgan, and Marion continued to be successful in facing the numerically superior Indians. America's frontiersmen, just like their warrior progeny in Vietnam, found that the best way to fight was to carry the battle to the enemy with aggressive patrolling and swift attacks.

In the Spanish colony of Texas, Stephen F. Austin established "ranging companies" of part-time soldiers to defend the settlements as early as 1823. By 1836 these Texas Rangers had won a place in folklore and fact with their effective warfare against Mexicans and Indians alike. Until Texas joined the Union in 1845, its history was little more than the story of the Rangers protecting the lives and sovereignty of the Lone Star State.

T. E. Fehrenbach, in his masterful book *Lone Star*, said of the Rangers, "Throughout his whole existence as a fighting man, the Texas Ranger was outnumbered by his foes. This produced not caution but canniness and an almost incredible aggressiveness. The Ranger found his best defense was to attack, dominate, subdue." Fehrenbach could just have easily been writing of the Rangers of a future war thousands of miles away in Southeast Asia.

Texas Rangers were known for their innovativeness, as would the LRRPs in Vietnam. When U.S. Army ordinance experts rejected Sam Colt's six-shot revolver, the Texans adopted it as their major armament, allowing mounted Rangers six times the firepower of their Commanche foes.

After statehood, the Texas Rangers remained as a military force of the governor. Over the years they have evolved into a law enforcement agency, and although today they number only sixty strong, their abilities to solve crimes and maintain the peace still receive the highest respect.

Texas Rangers, not unlike Rangers of other eras and the Vietnam LRRPs, are known for their toughness, lack of respect for bureaucracy, and at times for plain old meanness. Perhaps the best example of these characteristics was during major labor riots by Mexicans in the Rio Grande Valley during the early part of this century. Local authorities requested that the governor send the National Guard to put down the disturbance. When the officials anxiously met the train carrying promised reinforcements, only one individual got off. In answer to the local officials' surprise and anger, the lone Texas Ranger responded, ''One riot, one Ranger.''

The Ranger then proceeded directly to the headquarters of the riot organizer, pistol-whipped him, placed him under arrest, and departed with his prisoner on the next train. The riot was over—one Ranger had indeed been sufficient.*

The American Civil War found Rangers fighting for both the Blue and the Gray. In a war where both sides spoke the same language and were of similar ethnic origins, Ranger units could operate with ease behind enemy lines.

''Rangers'' was an extremely popular name on both

---

*A monument to the ''one Ranger'' stands today in the lobby of Dallas's Love Field airport.

sides of the conflict, with over four hundred units so designated. However, most of these had only the name in common with true Ranger units.

John S. Mosby, the Gray Ghost, led the most famous of the Confederate Rangers. The war was not the first trouble Mosby had found. While enrolled at the University of Virginia he had shot and wounded a fellow student during an argument. Only an act of the state legislature prevented his serving six months in jail and paying a $1,000 fine. Mosby recovered well from those difficulties, graduating in 1852 and being admitted to the state bar three years later.

Mosby enlisted in the Confederate Army in 1861 and saw action at the First Battle of Bull Run. He later served as a scout for General Jeb Stuart's cavalry and participated in the famous ride around McClellan's army during the Peninsula Campaign of June 1862.

In February 1863, Mosby was commissioned a lieutenant in charge of partisan Rangers that were to bring terror, death, and destruction to the Union army for three years. Operating initially with only nine men in occupied northern Virginia, Mosby's Rangers, who copied many of the tactics of Francis Marion of the Revolutionary War, harassed isolated Union outposts, cut supply and communication lines, and gathered intelligence on troop movements. Mosby's Rangers took great pride that they were mounted on the finest thoroughbreds in Virginia—fleet horseflesh that allowed the Rangers to disperse after raids and later reassemble in friendly territory.*

Mosby's Rangers most spectacular raid occurred on March 9, 1863, when his force of twenty-nine men slipped through the Union lines at Fairfax Court House. Entering the enemy camp in a driving rainstorm, the Rangers caught the Yankee soldiers sleeping in confidence that they were far from the battlefront. Mosby himself crept into the

---

*Selection of good equipment was not the only trait of Mosby's adaptability that would be duplicated by future LRRPs in Vietnam. He also was one of the first American commanders to move and fight at night, trusting darkness as a friend rather than a foe.

quarters of General Edwin H. Stoughton, commander of the 5th New York Cavalry, and awoke the gentleman, asking, "General, did you ever hear tell of Mosby?"

Stoughton sleepily replied, "Have you caught him?"

With a laugh the Gray Ghost answered, "Sir, he has caught you."

At daybreak Mosby's Rangers recrossed the lines and turned Stoughton and one hundred of his cavalrymen over to the Confederate commander at Culpepper, Virginia. Their mission accomplished, the Rangers once again melted into the countryside.

Mosby's Rangers captured not only prisoners but also supplies—on one occasion a payroll of over $173,000. When Mosby was asked how he supplied his force, he often responded, "By the courtesy of the United States Army Quartermaster General."

The actions of Mosby's Rangers were so successful that in February 1864, General U. S. Grant declared them outlaws on the pretext that they had confiscated private as well as military supplies. Several Rangers were captured over the next few months and, on Grant's personal orders, were hanged as bandits. Mosby responded by executing an equal number of Union prisoners, causing Grant to rescind his orders and to recognize the Rangers as a formal Confederate unit.

By war's end Mosby was a full colonel in charge of eight Ranger companies and was one of the best-known heroes of the lost cause. His final raid was conducted on the same day of Lee's surrender at Appomattox Court House. Several days later he conferred with Union officers but refused to surrender his Rangers. Stealing away, he assembled his force one last time and addressed his men, stating, "I disband your organization in preference to surrendering. . . . I part from you with pride in the fame of your achievements and grateful recollections of your generous kindness to myself. . . ."*

*Mosby was as successful in later years as he had been as a warrior. After reestablishing his law practice, he entered politics and even supported his old enemy,

Other Confederate Rangers conducted operations similar to Mosby's throughout the war with, if not the fame, at least much of the same success. Colonel Turner Ashby, another Virginian, led a group of Rangers feared throughout the Union army for their raids and interdiction of supply lines.

Union Ranger units were not as successful or as well known as their rebel brothers. Perhaps it was because of the Union's lack of danger-loving risk-takers who seemed attracted to bands like Mosby's and Ashby's. A better explanation, however, is that most of the war was conducted on the rebels' home ground. Rangers who fought on land they had grown up on and who had support of the local populace had obvious advantages. Another reason was the simple fact that the Union forces had far more manpower, supplies, and an industrial base that much better supported conventional warfare.

Whatever the reason, few Union Ranger units gained any particular fame. Mean's Rangers were best known, primarily for their capture of Longstreet's ammunition trains and their counteroperations against Mosby in northern Virginia.

Another Confederate who deserves mention, even though his tactics more resembled an outlaw's than a soldier's, is William C. Quantrill. Operating as an independent guerrilla early in the war, Quantrill was commissioned a captain and his band mustered into the Confederate army after they assisted in the capture of Independence, Missouri, on August 11, 1862.

Quantrill, a former schoolteacher from Ohio, rarely answered to senior commanders. Most of his operations seemed more directed to settling old scores from the antislavery skirmishes in Kansas and Missouri before the war

Grant, for the presidency in 1872. Old conflicts were put aside, resulting in Mosby's appointment as U. S. Consul General to Hong Kong from 1878 to 1885. In addition to publishing two books on his wartime experiences, he went on to serve as an assistant attorney in the Department of Justice from 1904 to 1910. Mosby died on May 30, 1916, still revered as the Gray Ghost of the Confederacy—and as one of the great role models for future Rangers.

than to helping the cause of the South. Despite their ten-
dencies to loot towns, shoot unarmed civilians, and exe-
cute prisoners, Quantrill's Raiders did follow Ranger
tactics, moving at night and penetrating far behind enemy
lines. Although known as "the bloodiest man in American
history" after his sacking of Lawrence, Kansas, and killing 180 men, women, and children, Quantrill was a successful Ranger, as he avoided heavy concentrations of
Union patrols in slipping well over sixty miles behind enemy lines—and escaping virtually unscathed.

Quantrill won a conventional fight against Union troops
at Baxter Springs, Kansas, on October 6, 1863, but the
victory was tarnished by the execution of the surrendered
force. Soon after, due to internal command disagree-
ments, Quantrill's Raiders broke up into several groups
and ceased to be an effective fighting force.*

At the conclusion of the Civil War the re–United States
again faced an old enemy. This time it was not the foot-
mobile Indian tribes of the east but the great red horsemen
of the plains. For the next thirty years soldiers of the
U. S. Army would fight a war that more than any of the
United States' other conflicts would most resemble the operations in Vietnam.

Although the terrain of the vast western plains and the
desert Southwest little resembled Vietnam, the Indian and
the VC/NVA were similar. The Indian fought on land he
had been born to and where no stream or ridge line was a
stranger. He fought only when the opportunity and the
odds were in his favor. Time was no factor; the Indian was
a patient enemy.

Initial operations by the U.S. Army against the various

*On May 10, 1865, Quantrill was surprised by Union troops near Taylorsville,
Kentucky, and was severely wounded in the resulting fight. A few weeks later he
died in a prison hospital.

Quantrill's guerrilla band produced several notable, if infamous, characters—
none of whom went on to any success as soldiers. Frank and Jesse James, Cole
Younger, and, according to some accounts, Belle Starr, rode under the black flag
of Quantrill's Raiders. A copy of that simple black pennant with stitched letters
spelling out "Quantrill" hangs today on the wall of the boyhood home of the
James brothers, which is now a museum near Kearney, Missouri.

Indian tribes also resembled early actions in Vietnam. Frontier forts were established at critical points, and cavalry and infantry patrols were sent out in pursuit of the hostiles; the Indians slipped away in small groups and reassembled to attack isolated outposts or unprotected civilians.

In the early years of the Indian wars, the army was led and manned by soldiers with years of combat experience in the Civil War. However, the huge clashes of infantry and artillery at bloody battlefields such as Gettysburg, Bull Run, and Antietam did little to prepare soldiers for the hit-and-run tactics of the Native American guerrillas.

The need for the army to employ men who understood the enemy as well as the terrain was apparent. Indian scouts, both white and red, soon rode in front of the regular troops. Whites such as Bill Cody, Al Sieber, Tom Horn, and many others whose names have become linked with the myths and legends of the winning of the American West earned much of their fame as scouts for the army. Red scouts were even easier to find and stepped forward to war against tribes that had been traditional enemies for decades.

The use of Indian scouts was formalized in 1868 when Major George A. Forsyth presented a plan to General Phil Sheridan that would harass the Indians without using the already-shorthanded garrisons. Forsyth proposed that a small, highly mobile group of scouts be formed that would take the field using the tactics of the Indians. They would track, attack when possible, and keep the enemy from the safety of his sanctuaries.

Sheridan approved the plan, authorizing Forsyth to recruit a force of fifty volunteers. Forsyth, who had risen from private to brevet brigadier general in the Civil War, had no trouble finding willing scouts. The promise of a dollar a day to pursue Indians without formally being in the army was attractive to the frontiersmen. After all, they had been fighting for a long time for no reward at all except keeping the hair on their heads.

A month after Forsyth's Scouts had been formed, they

were involved in their first and last action. On September 17, 1868, they were surprised by a band of over a thousand Cheyennes, Sioux, and Arapahoes near the Arickaree fork of the Republican River. Retreating to an island in the river, the scouts held off the Indians under Roman Nose for four days before being rescued by black soldiers of the 10th Cavalry. Several of the scouts were killed, including Lieutenant F. H. Beecher, second in command of the expedition. Forsyth was seriously wounded, as was the concept of the scouts.

Sheridan began looking for new ways to battle the hostiles. The first was to campaign in the dead of winter when the Indians were less mobile and more restricted to their camps. With the assistance of the emerging rail system and the rapid communication provided by the telegraph, as well as some victories—better described as massacres of Indian villages—the Indians were slowly pushed onto reservations. More and more red scouts joined the men in blue to fight their hostile brethren.

In the last major campaign in the Southwest, General George Crook used Indian scouts to the utmost effectiveness. Pursuing 150 Apaches under Geronimo into the Sierra Madre of northern Mexico, Crook had 250 troops— 193 of whom were Indian scouts. The expedition was an unqualified success in defeating the renegade band and returning the survivors to the reservation. War cries of the Apaches were never to be heard again.

Captain John G. Bourke of the 3rd U.S. Cavalry accompanied Crook's expedition. In a book of his adventures, titled *An Apache Campaign in the Sierra Madre*, Bourke wrote of the Indian scouts, "The two great points of superiority of the native or savage soldier over the representative of civilized discipline are his absolute knowledge of the country and his perfect ability to take care of himself at all times and under all circumstances. . . . Every track in the trail, mark in the grass, scratch on the bark of a tree, explains itself. . . . He can tell to an hour, almost, when the man or animal making them passed by, and, like a hound, will keep on the scent until he catches up with the object of his pursuit. . . . Approaching the enemy his vigilance is a curious thing to witness. He avoids appearing suddenly upon the crest of a hill, knowing his figure projected against the sky can at such time be discerned from a great distance. . . . [He] has no false ideas about courage; he would prefer to skulk like the coyote for hours, and then kill his enemy, or capture his herd, rather than, by injudicious exposure, receive a wound, fatal or otherwise. But he is no coward; on the contrary, he is entitled to rank among the bravest.''*

*Bourke's description of Indian scouts could easily have been used nearly a century later to define LRRPs in Vietnam. Skills and bravery were not the only link between the scouts and the LRRPs. Crook had contacted General José Carbo of the Mexican army for permission to cross the international boundary in his pursuit of Geronimo. Carbo had agreed, stipulating that the scouts wear a red headband to distinguish them from the hostiles. Although the Vietnam LRRPs were more interested in a head cover that camouflaged their light complexions and kept the sweat from their eyes than any historical significance, a headband of olive-drab cloth was common in all LRRP units.

CHAPTER 3

◄○○○○○○►

Past Wars, Past Rangers: World War II to Vietnam

*A*FTER the conclusion of the Indian wars in the early 1890s, no formal or informal Ranger units existed in the U.S. Army for nearly a half century. Trench warfare of World War I offered no requirements for long-range patrols. Although not involved in ''the war to end all wars,'' Rangers were not to be denied when the everlasting peace ended with the beginning of World War II.

In the spring of 1942, armed forces of the United States were streaming into England and Northern Ireland, preparing to assist our allies in meeting the Nazi onslaught. Brigadier General Lucian Truscott was posted as the army chief of staff's official representative to General Mountbatten's Combined Operations Staff. Truscott's instructions from Chief of Staff George C. Marshall were to initiate American troops into conventional and commando-type operations as soon as possible.

Truscott responded on May 26, 1942, requesting formation of a commando unit along the lines of the British Commando Special Service Brigade. Marshall's reply was immediate in authorizing formation of the 1st Ranger Battalion. Truscott would later explain that the name ''Rangers'' was selected because ''the name Commandos rightfully belonged to the British and we sought a name that was more typically American. It was therefore fit that the organization destined to be the first of American ground forces to battle Germans on the European continent should have been called Rangers in compliment to those in American history who exemplified such high standards of individual courage, initiative, determination, ruggedness, fighting ability and achievement.''

It is interesting to note that early American Rangers, including Church and Rogers, had fought against the Indians and the French *for* the British—confusing the issue of who were the ''rightful heirs'' to the name. There is no evidence that the British considered naming their special operations units Rangers rather than Commandos. What is known is that Commando was the personal choice of Winston Churchill as an adaptation of the title used by mounted Boer bands the prime minister had fought as a young man in South Africa. Oddly, both the British and the Americans adopted names for their elite units from former enemies.

Truscott's next move was to direct Major General Russell P. Hartle, commander of U.S. forces in Northern Ireland, to secure volunteers for the new Ranger battalion. Hartle had to look only as far as his own aide-de-camp, Major William O. Darby, for his first volunteer and commander of the 1st Ranger Battalion. Darby, a thirty-one-year-old graduate of West Point and an artillery officer, may have seemed a strange choice coming from the position of a ''horse holder'' for a general. But Darby was the right man for the job—and would more than earn the title of ''Founder of the Modern Rangers'' over the next three years.

Darby was given carte blanche in manning, arming, supplying, and training his force. He personally interviewed each volunteer, selecting only the most physically and mentally fit. Darby blithely warned soldiers not to join his outfit, telling them there would be no privileged individuals and that no unit would have it tougher. Of the two thousand men who stepped forward, only seven hundred were initially accepted. With Darby in the lead, the seven hundred then went through the British Commando course and completed the usual seven-week school in only thirty-one days. At the conclusion of the training only five hundred twenty Rangers remained. On June 19, 1942, the 1st Ranger Battalion was officially activated at Garrick-Fergus, Northern Ireland.

Darby's Rangers received their battle baptism when a group of forty-two under command of Captain Roy Murray accompanied the disastrous British and Canadian raid on Dieppe the following August. Although their role was minor and their casualties few in comparison to their Commando allies, the American press—desperate for some good news—reported the Ranger participation as larger and more heroic than it actually was.

The Rangers' first action as a battalion was in North Africa, where Darby, then a lieutenant colonel, led the initial landings at Arzew, Algeria. Hard-fought battles followed in Tunisia, where the Rangers conducted several night attacks behind the lines. At the critical battle of El Guettar, the 1st Battalion won a Presidential Unit Citation for distinguished action. Near the end of the North African campaign, Darby formed two more battalions, the 3rd and 4th, combining them with the 1st into what was known as the Ranger Force.

Darby's Rangers spearheaded the Allied invasion of Sicily in July 1943, serving as a special task force in Patton's drive on Palermo. The rapid-hit-and-run tactics of the Rangers were highly successful, resulting in the capture of over four thousand prisoners in a single day—more than twice the size of the total Ranger Force.

By the time the Rangers went ashore near Salerno in the invasion of mainland Italy, they were known by ally and foe alike as furious fighters and dedicated soldiers. Their string of victories, however, was about to come to a violent end. More and more the Rangers were being deployed as conventional infantry by senior U.S. commanders. It was a role for which the lightly equipped Rangers were neither trained nor organized.

On the night of January 29, 1944, the 1st and 3rd battalions were ordered to lead the 3rd Infantry Division off the beachhead in their attack on Cisterna. Near the village, along a flooded irrigation ditch on the valley floor, the Rangers were caught in one of the most devastating ambushes in American military history.

German artillery, tanks, and machine guns fired pointblank into the Rangers from the surrounding hills. Darby, at the head of the 4th Battalion, moved immediately to reinforce but was turned back by fifty percent casualties and the deaths of all the company commanders. Of the 767 Rangers of the 1st and 3rd Battalions that advanced on Cisterna, only 6 returned. The Ranger Force had virtually ceased to exist.*

In addition to Darby's three Ranger battalions, three others were formed during the war. A task force made up of elements of the 2nd and the 5th Battalions, under command of Lieutenant Colonel Earl Rudder, landed on Omaha Beach in the D-Day invasion. They accomplished their mission of scaling the sheer two-hundred-foot cliffs at Point de Hoc but paid a high price for their success. Of the 355 Rangers, 197 were casualties.

It was on these bitterly-fought-for beaches that the Rangers earned their unofficial motto. When the main body of the invasion force was pinned down, Brigadier General Norman Cota, assistant commander of the 29th Infantry Division, realized that the invasion must advance inland or die at the water's edge. Cota turned to LTC (lieutenant colonel) Max Schneider, commander of the remainder of the 2nd and 5th Ranger Battalions and ordered, "Lead the way, Rangers." A breakthrough soon resulted, and the Rangers led the Allied advance into fortress Europe. From

*Darby survived and went on to command a regiment in the 45th Infantry Division. Later, as a colonel with the 10th Mountain Division, he was killed by German artillery at Torbole, Italy, on April 30, 1945, in one of the final actions of the war. At the time of his death, Darby was on the promotion list for brigadier general. On the recommendation of Secretary of War Stimson to President Truman, Darby was promoted posthumously to the one-star rank. Darby, only thirty-four years old, was dead, but he would live on in history books and Ranger tradition as one of the few modern military commanders, whose command was better known by its leader's name than its numerical designation.

that time Rangers have accompanied their salute to superiors with a proud, "Rangers lead the way, sir."*

One other Ranger battalion saw action in the European theater, although it was never officially recognized as an authorized unit. On December 20, 1942, the 29th Infantry Division formed a Ranger battalion at Tidworth Barracks, England, under the command of Major Randolph Millholland. The battalion, organized and trained in similar fashion to Darby's Rangers, participated in two raids and one recon on German positions in Norway while attached to the British Special Service Brigade.

Their final mission was to destroy a German radar station on the small island of Ile d'Ouessant just off the coast of the Brittany peninsula. After destroying the station and killing over twenty of its crew, the Rangers withdrew, but not before deliberately leaving behind a cartridge belt and helmet clearly marked "Maj. R. Millholland, U.S. Rangers." The Rangers wanted the Germans to know who had done the damage.

Despite the success of the 29th Rangers, all efforts to gain official recognition for the unit from the War Department failed. On October 15, 1943, the battalion was disbanded and its members returned to other elements of the 29th Division.

---

*The beaches of Normandy were not to be the last association between Cota and Rudder. By late 1944, Cota had been promoted to major general and was in command of the 28th Infantry Division. Rudder, still a lieutenant colonel, was in command of the Division's 109th Infantry Regiment. During the Battle of the Bulge, and in the weeks that followed, Cota and Rudder would again demonstrate that they demanded that their soldiers do their duty—be they Rangers or regular infantrymen.

On January 31, 1945, Private Eddie D. Slovik was executed by firing squad at St. Marie aux Mines in eastern France. Slovik was the first, and only, U.S. serviceman executed for desertion since the Civil War. Although the final decision was made by General Dwight D. Eisenhower, Cota convened Slovik's court-martial, approved the death sentence, and witnessed it being carried out. Rudder, who had been Slovik's commander in the 109th and who had recommended the court-martial, was also in attendance.

In a message to the soldiers of the 109th Infantry Regiment, sent on the day of the execution, Rudder stated, "I pray that this man's death will be a lesson to each of us who have any doubt at any time about the price that we must pay to win this war. The person that is not willing to fight and die, if need be, for his country has no right to live."

Rangers also led the way in the Pacific. The 6th Battalion played a key role in the retaking of the Philippines. Their most notable accomplishment was a thirty-five-mile penetration behind the Japanese lines in January 1945 to rescue over five hundred emaciated veterans of the Bataan Death March, who had been imprisoned at Cabanatuan for nearly three years. Attacking by night, the Rangers killed over two hundred Japanese before escaping back to friendly lines with the former POWs. General MacArthur would later say, "No incident of this war has given me greater satisfaction than the Ranger rescue of these Americans."

Of the six Ranger battalions, only the 6th was fortunate enough to be used exclusively for missions for which it had been trained. The successes of the 6th were directly attributable to the fact that it conducted long-range reconnaissance and hard-hitting combat patrols deep in the enemy rear rather than conventional infantry tasks.

Although the LRRP/Rangers of Vietnam would certainly be the heirs to the traditions of the six Ranger battalions, their official lineage would come from still another elite World War II organization. The 5307th Composite Unit (Provisional) was organized on October 3, 1943, for combat in the Chinese-Burmese-Indian theater. Composed of experienced jungle fighters from veteran infantry regiments throughout the Pacific, the 5307th was commanded by Brigadier General Frank D. Merrill.

The 5307th was the first American ground combat force to meet the enemy on the Asian continent. Shortly thereafter, the 5307th was dubbed "Merrill's Marauders" by *Time* correspondent James Shepley. Another chapter in the legend of the American Ranger was off to a good start.

On January 8, 1944, the Marauders were assigned to General Joe Stilwell's field command in northern Burma. From February to May, the 5307th worked closely with the Chinese 22nd and 38th divisions in the recovery of northern Burma and in clearing the way for the construction of the Ledo Road, which linked the Indian railhead at Ledo with the Burma Road to China.

The Marauders fought through dense jungle and rugged mountains from the Hukawny Valley in northwestern Burma to Myitkyina on the Irrawaddy River. In five major and thirty minor engagements, the Marauders virtually destroyed the veteran troops of the Japanese 18th Infantry Division. Using typical Ranger tactics, the Marauders operated deep within Japanese territory, disorganizing supply lines, destroying communications, and attacking unsuspecting rear echelons. In early August, the 5307th climaxed their operations with the capture at Myitkyina of the only all-weather airstrip in northern Burma.

The success of the Marauders gained them the Presidential Unit Citation; however, the action at Myitkyina was the last combat for the 5307th. Casualties from battling the Japanese and from jungle diseases had decimated its ranks. Only a provisional unit, the original intention had been for the Marauders to be committed for no more than ninety days. At Stilwell's insistence they had spent more than double that time in the world's harshest jungles against the best of the Japanese army.

Just like Ranger units in earlier wars, the Marauders were a hastily organized outfit of tough soldiers brought together for a difficult mission. During their entire existence they were treated as nearly expendable. Once they accomplished their purpose, they were disbanded.

On August 10, 1944, the 5307th was reorganized into the 475th Infantry Regiment under the 5332nd Brigade, which was also known as the "Mars Task Force." It continued actions in Burma until February 1945, when the remaining Japanese were finally defeated.

In March 1945 the 475th was airlifted to China, where it spent the remainder of the war training and equipping the Chinese army. The regiment was deactivated on July 1, 1945, remaining on the inactive list of regular army units until June 21, 1954. At that time it was redesignated the 75th Infantry Regiment and posted to duty on Okinawa. From this strange activation, deactivation, reorganization, and reactivation process ultimately came the lineage of the unit designation of the Vietnam LRRP/Rangers.

Unit insignia, or shoulder patches, of World War II Rangers are almost as confusing as the regimental lineage issue. The original authorized insignia was a blue and yellow diamond shape with "RANGERS" stitched across it. The patch closely resembled the logo worn on the uniform of Sunoco employees at gas stations across the United States. Needless to say, the patch was unpopular with the Rangers as well as a source of several brawls.

Another problem with the "blue diamond" patch was that it was officially recognized after the Rangers had already designed and worn a completely different insignia. Darby had sponsored a contest to design a patch long before the stateside bureaucracy had considered the matter. The winning design, submitted by Sergeant Anthony Rada of Flint, Michigan, was that of a scroll with a black background and red trim bearing "1st Ranger Battalion" in white letters. Little is known about the reasons for the color selection; however, the scroll was similar to the patch worn by the British Commandos who had assisted in the initial training of the Rangers.

In usual Ranger fashion, all five of the battalions in the European theater took matters into their own hands and wore the scroll rather than the diamond. The 6th Battalion in the Pacific, despite the fact there was no official link to the European battalions, learned of the scroll through the Ranger grapevine and also adopted it as their preferred insignia.

In Korea, and later in Vietnam, Rangers continued to wear the unauthorized scroll. Korean Rangers added "Airborne" above the Ranger lettering while Vietnam Rangers reversed the two so that "Ranger" was on top. Whatever the form, the scroll survived as the Rangers' patch of choice for over forty years before it was finally officially recognized by the Department of the Army on December 13, 1983. Time was not a factor in the scroll becoming official; once again the Rangers had won their honors—this time in their airborne assault on the island of Grenada.

Merrill's Marauders were also wearers of unauthorized insignia. Their blue, red, green, and white patch was in the shape of a shield adorned with a star, a sun, and a lightning bolt. After several changes over the years, two of which added and later deleted the Confederate flag in recognition of Mosby's Rangers, the Marauder patch was adopted as the official shield of the 75th Ranger Regiment. Although it took over four decades to become official, the Rangers of today proudly wear the patch of the Rangers and the shield of the Marauders of World War II.

While patches and shields are important to morale and history, the real business of Rangers is on the battlefield. It was only six years after the disbanding of the Ranger battalions at the end of World War II that once again our nation called upon its ultimate soldiers. This time it would be on the frozen mountainsides and mud-filled rice paddies of Korea.

Two months after the North Koreans invaded the South, Army Chief of Staff General J. Lawton Collins ordered the reestablishment of Ranger units with one company to be assigned to each infantry division. In a memorandum dated August 29, 1950, Collins outlined the mission of the Ranger companies: "to infiltrate through enemy lines and attack command posts, artillery, tank parks, and key communications centers or facilities."

General Collins also directed that the Rangers be formed and trained at Fort Benning, Georgia, under the command of Colonel John G. Van Houton. On September 29, 1950, Van Houton established his headquarters at the Harmony Church area of Benning and called for volunteers. Since airborne qualification was a requirement, most of the Ranger candidates came from the 82nd and 11th Airborne Divisions.

By mid-November the first four Ranger companies had completed their training. The 1st, 3rd, and 4th companies were listed on the official rolls as "white" while the 2nd was recorded as "black." The army—and the Rangers—of 1950 was still segregated, but for the first time black soldiers would have the opportunity to serve their country as Rangers. The 2nd Ranger Company would not only win honors for battlefield bravery but also would be recorded as the only all-black Ranger unit in U.S. military history.

While Rangers, black and white, were training at Fort Benning, the only Korean-era Ranger company to be formed outside the United States was being organized at Camp Drake, Japan. Manned by volunteers from divisions throughout the Far East, the 8213th Provisional Company was more frequently known as the 8th Army Ranger Company and on occasion simply as the "Raiders." The 8213th saw action with the 25th Infantry Division until their deactivation upon the arrival of the 5th Ranger Company from Fort Benning.

Of the fourteen Ranger companies organized and trained at Benning, only six arrived in Korea before the decision was made to stand down Ranger units once again. Although this particular chapter in Ranger history is short, it is characterized by typical Ranger daring. The six companies, assigned to the 8th U.S. Army and attached to the 1st Cavalry and the 2nd, 3rd, 7th, 24th, and 25th Infantry Divisions fought in almost every major battle of the war from their arrival in late 1950 until the fall of 1951. Suffering from forty to ninety percent wounded or killed, the Rangers conducted raids behind the lines, recon missions, and frequently fought as conventional infantry. Joseph Ulatoski, who served as a Ranger company-grade officer in Korea and later as a brigadier general in Vietnam, best summed it up in a 1986 interview when he said, "For the Ranger in Korea, fighting outnumbered and surrounded was routine."

Although no one doubted the fighting abilities of the Rangers, not all of the army's senior leadership in Korea and in the Pentagon was satisfied with the concept of Ranger companies. Many of the division commanders, who had Rangers attached, complained that the Ranger companies' organization was so austere that they could not supply or feed themselves, requiring support from other units. Another general criticism was that the com-

panies drained desperately needed elite soldiers from
other units and that the concentration of superior leaders
in a few units was a luxury the army as a whole could
not afford.

Still another comment was that the mostly white Rangers could not operate effectively behind the lines where
the enemy and the civilian populace was not caucasian.
Although this was accepted at the time, the Vietnam
LRRPs would prove it untrue.

The final blow to future operations by Rangers in Korea
was the stabilization of lines. For the first eighteen months
of the war each side took turns pushing the other up and
down the peninsula. When both sides became static in the
multiple belts of defenses along the future DMZ, there
was little opportunity for successful behind-the-lines
probes by the Rangers.

By July 1951 the Ranger companies began to deactivate.
On November 5, the last of the companies stood down.
Another era of Ranger valor had come to a close; however,
bringing down the curtain on one magnificent performance directly led to the opening of one of the most important phases of Ranger history—one that would make
the Ranger a permanent part of the army of the future.

Although the army chief of staff, General Collins, decided that Ranger companies were no longer needed in
Korea, he recognized that Rangers were not a concept that
the army could afford to place on the shelf until the next
war. On October 3, 1951, Collins directed "Ranger training be extended to all combat units of the Army in order
to develop the capability of carrying out Ranger type missions in all Infantry units of the Army."

The chief of staff's instructions also authorized the Infantry School to establish a Ranger Department capable of
training and maintaining one Ranger-qualified officer per
infantry company and one Ranger-qualified NCO per platoon.

On October 10 the Ranger Department was officially
established under the authority of General Order 113.
Members of the Ranger Training Command, who had

trained the Korean-era Ranger companies, were reassigned as instructors in the new school. The headquarters remained in the temporary wooden structures at Harmony Church that, with the exception of a few coats of paint, are still the same today.

The Ranger course of instruction has also remained fairly constant over the years. Basic conditioning, patrolling, and operations are taught at Fort Benning. Mountain training is conducted in northern Georgia near Dahlonega, and amphibious and jungle training in the Florida panhandle at Eglin Air Force Base. In more recent times, a desert training phase has been added at Dugway Proving Grounds, Utah.

From its beginning, the Ranger School has been the most physically and mentally demanding of all the army's courses. The school lasts eight weeks; however, the program of instruction is so intense that if the training were scheduled on the basis of a forty-hour week, it would take twenty-six weeks to complete.

Rangers of the past were not neglected in the preparation of Rangers of the future. Training camps at the different phases bear the names of Darby, Morgan, Merrill, and Rudder.

The symbol of graduates of the Ranger School was also based on history—with an unusual twist. Originally, the plan was for each man who successfully completed the course to be awarded a black and red tab with white letters reading ''Ranger.'' The design was an adaptation of the Ranger scroll and had originally been intended for those who completed the training for the Korean-era Ranger companies. By the time the tab was officially authorized by the Department of the Army, the colors had mysteriously changed to black and gold. Although no official explanation has ever been given, many Rangers noticed that the new colors closely resembled those of the U.S. Military Academy at West Point.

Whatever the source, the Ranger tab would soon become one of the most respected of uniform adornments.

By the time of the Vietnam conflict, the tab was proudly worn not only on the shoulders of many LRRP officers and NCOs, but also by leaders at all levels in all units.

# CHAPTER 4
o=o=o=o=o=o=o=

A Different War, Different Rangers: The Beginnings

*R*EESTABLISHMENT of Ranger units during the years following the Korean War was an issue that was often discussed; however, little occurred beyond talk. Graduates of the Ranger School returned to their regular units to train squads and platoons in the techniques of combat and recon patrolling. While most infantrymen developed a general knowledge of Ranger operations, no units were organized and trained for specific reconnaissance missions.

Commanders at all levels recognized the need for timely battlefield intelligence that could only be gathered by men on the ground. Despite this need, there were simply too many other skills that had to be taught to dedicate time and resources to develop ordinary infantrymen into teams capable of handling Ranger-type missions. Another problem was that, traditionally, the U.S. Army has always been prepared to fight the last war rather than planning new techniques for possible future conflicts, and since Rangers had generated so much controversy in Korea, few leaders were willing to advocate bringing back the elite units—especially in the limited-resource environment of post-Korean War America.

The army progressed, and in some instances regressed, through several reorganizations during the late 1950s. Unfortunately, none included adding any type of Ranger organization.

It was not until December 1960 that the seed was planted that would eventually give birth to the LRRPs of Vietnam. At that time the Department of the Army directed the Continental Army Command Headquarters (CONARC) at Fort Monroe, Virginia, "to re-evaluate the current organization and to make recommendations for necessary changes." The result of this review was a major armywide reorganization known as ROAD (Reorganization Objective Army Divisions). ROAD was soon renamed ROAD-65 to show its planned date of total implementation.

Under ROAD-65, each division had a common fixed base of support units with a varying number and type of infantry and armor battalions. Divisions could then be structured for particular missions, terrain, and tactical requirements. Although not originally intended for the type of war the army was about to face in Southeast Asia, ROAD-65 did provide the flexibility that allowed divisions to tailor their structure for the war without another armywide reorganization.

One of the more important characteristics of ROAD-65 was the recognition of the need for long-range reconnaissance units. Recognition was a long way from actual implementation, but it was at least the first step in the right direction.

The next step was small, albeit a significant one. Soon after the approval of ROAD-65, CONARC published a series of directives to assist "all USCONARC agencies in the timely preparation of official training literature for all aspects of the ROAD-65 reorganization." One of these documents, CONARC Directive 525-4, dated May 25, 1961, and titled "Combat Operations, ROAD-65 Training Literature, Long Range Reconnaissance Patrolling," presented the first official use of the term LRRP. This thin, five-page directive, classified confidential until three years after its publication and signed for the commander by

Brigadier General James R. Winn as acting chief of staff, is the "birth certificate" of the LRRPs.

CONARC Directive 525-4 stated in its "General Principle" paragraph that "long range reconnaissance patrols (LRRP) are small detachments of specially trained combat forces employed for extended periods to seek and report expeditiously detailed, accurate, and timely information concerning the enemy and the area of operations."

In its "Concept" paragraph the directive said that LRRPs should normally work in teams of four to six men, operate at night or under other conditions of limited visibility, and assume concealed positions during daylight to observe specific targets or routes. Possible missions included locating and identifying enemy formations and dispositions, adjusting air and artillery strikes on enemy positions, and performing bomb-damage assessments. Except for failing to mention the capture of prisoners, the authors of the directive listed the missions that would later be established for Vietnam LRRPs.

Other similarities were included in succeeding paragraphs. The directive recommended that previous Ranger or Special Forces training be a consideration for LRRP selection and that special equipment be provided LRRP units. An important difference between the directive and actual Vietnam LRRPs was the instruction that "normally, one company will be organic to each corps. . . ." rather than assigned to the division or lower level.

A year after the directive was published, it was redesignated CONARC Regulation 525-4. While there were no adjustments to its content beyond the name, the change was significant. What had been guidance for literature preparation was now a requirement for accomplishment. CONARC had succeeded in getting the process started that would lead to a field manual (FM) and a table of organization and equipment (TO&E) being written by the staff at the Infantry Center at Fort Benning. With its part completed, CONARC published CONARC Circular 310-19 on December 20, 1962, which rescinded 525-4.

On June 18, 1962, the Department of the Army published Field Manual Number 31-18, "Long Range Patrols, Divisions, Corps and Army." FM 31-18 expanded on CONARC Regulation 525-4 to include detailed instructions on missions, organization, training, and conduct of operations. While many of the concepts were applicable to any area of operations, the manual was written with a conventional war in mind. The army was still preparing for the last war instead of the next—though the next had already begun in Vietnam and was quickly escalating.

Along with the FM came TO&E 7-157, which called for an organization of two hundred enlisted men and nine officers organized into a company headquarters and three patrol platoons capable of fielding a total of twenty-four teams of five men each. Sections of transportation, communications, and operations were also included in the company organization. This TO&E would be modified several times in Vietnam but remained the basic organization, though the number of men and patrol teams varied for the entire war. (For the most common LRRP/Ranger company organization in Vietnam, see Annex I of Appendix A.)

On January 13, 1965, the Department of the Army published a new FM 31-18 that superceded the 1962 edition. Except for a new title of "Infantry Long Range Patrol Company," there were very few differences between the two manuals.

Everything was now in place for the formation of LRRP units—except for one major obstacle. FM 31-18 provided the hows and wheretos on establishing the LRRPs, but it also stated that authorization for the units could only come from "Headquarters, Department of the Army."

Whether or not the bureaucratic process would ever yield a LRRP unit grew moot as Vietnam became the center of the army's attention. Fighting a "different kind of war" from what the military had been preparing for demanded a "different kind of warrior."

General William C. Westmoreland assumed command of the Military Assistance Command–Vietnam (MACV) in June 1964. In a 1986 interview he stated that he became aware of the need for LRRPs "shortly after [he] arrived in Vietnam."

Although the need was apparent, the normal assets did not exist. Conventional U.S. infantry divisions were not yet in Vietnam, so Westmoreland turned to the Special Forces to organize the first LRRPs in Vietnam.

Special Forces had been "in country" since 1957, training the Vietnamese army (ARVN) and organizing paramilitary units of tribesmen such as the Montagnards. Special Forces teams also worked with the Central Intelligence Agency on cross-border missions in Laos and North Vietnam to conduct harassment and psychological warfare operations as early as 1961. These special operations were minor, however, in comparison to the overall commitment to teach the ARVN and other indigenous personnel to fight their own war. As a result, most of the Special Forces teams were stationed at static, austere camps throughout the country.

Westmoreland's directions for the Special Forces to form and conduct long-range reconnaissance patrols resulted in the organization of Project DELTA in October 1964. In June 1965, Detachment B-52 was formed as a control headquarters for the project. Along with the new control headquarters came Project DELTA's new commander, Major Charlie A. Beckwith.*

Beckwith found the Project DELTA team members living well and doing little in Nha Trang. "Charging Charlie" soon reduced the team from thirty to seven, keeping only those who preferred the jungle to the resort beaches of the South China Sea.

Within a month Beckwith had gathered volunteers from other detachments and was conducting long-range patrols. On occasion, such as the following October at Camp Plei Me, Beckwith consolidated his teams to reinforce outposts manned by Special Forces A Teams that were in danger of being overrun.

---

*Fifteen years later, Beckwith would organize and lead another unit known as DELTA Force in the unsuccessful raid to free U.S. hostages in Iran.

Project DELTA gained some experience from the only long-range patrol effort that had been fielded before the arrival of Westmoreland. Montagnard warriors of the Civilian Irregular Defense Group (CIDG), with Special Forces leadership, had begun conducting long-range recons as early as May 15, 1964, in classified operations codenamed LEAPING LENA.

Over the next five years Project DELTA fielded from six to sixteen teams at a time that ranged in size from six to ten men each. Team composition varied from all–Special Forces to all-Vietnamese, the most common mix being half and half. Missions included collecting information, adjusting artillery fire and air strikes, capturing prisoners for interrogation, and directing reaction forces to enemy concentrations.

Along with the recon teams, Project DELTA also organized eight teams (four indigenous personnel each) that traveled jungle trails dressed and equipped like the VC or NVA in the area. These teams, called "Roadrunners," had well-rehearsed cover stories that allowed them to link up with enemy forces and gather intelligence through casual conversation.

Project OMEGA (Detachment B-50) and Project SIGMA (Detachment B-56) were organized in August 1966, and were similar to Project DELTA except that each fielded only eight teams. Another long-range recon unit, Project GAMMA (Detachment B-57), conducted classified operations in Cambodia.

Projects OMEGA, SIGMA, and GAMMA would eventually be removed from the control of the Special Forces and placed under the MACV's Studies and Observation Group (SOG), which was formed on November 1, 1967. SOG also controlled elements of the other U.S. services, including on occasion Air Force Commandos, Navy SEALS, and Marine Force Recon. Project DELTA teams continued to operate as part of the Special Forces until their standdown on July 31, 1970.

With some notable exceptions, the "Greek" projects of the Special Forces operated much like the later LRRPs of the regular U.S. infantry. Special Forces recon teams rarely operated with only—or even a majority of—U.S. personnel. The units they worked for were nearly always Vietnamese. They also conducted cross-border operations into Cambodia, Laos, and North Vietnam. The infantry LRRPs seldom, and rarely with authorization, crossed international boundaries. While infantry LRRPs focused on tactical missions limited to their assigned corps, division, or brigade area of operations, the Special Forces projects were generally focused on strategic missions, gathering information from all across Southeast Asia.

Although Special Forces recon personnel numbered far fewer than their infantry LRRP brothers, their story of Vietnam service until now has been much better documented. Part of this is due to the ''mystique'' of the Green Berets, but even more it is a result of the ''Greek'' projects being under a central headquarters that could coordinate and record their performances;* while the infantry LRRPs were spread out under thirteen different commands with multiple reporting channels.

*For additional information concerning the Special Forces projects, see *Green Berets at War* by Shelby L. Stanton, Presidio Press, 1985, and *Vietnam Studies: US Army Special Forces, 1961–1971* by Colonel Francis J. Kelly, Department of the Army, 1973.

CHAPTER 5
●━●━●━●━●━●━●

A Different War, Different Rangers: Formation of the LRRPs

W_{HEN} regular infantry units began to arrive in Vietnam in 1965, the U.S. Army had not fought a guerrilla conflict of any significance since the Indian wars of the nineteenth century. The cease-fire in Korea was well over a decade in the past, and only a few senior officers and NCOs with combat experience were still on the active rolls.

For years the focus of the army had been training and equipping for conventional defensive wars. Offensive tactics were based on the ultimate combat multiplier—nuclear weapons.

The army's leadership had "won its spurs" on the plains of Europe or in the island-hopping campaigns of the Pacific in the Second World War or during the rapid advances—and retreats—in Korea before that conflict had settled into trench-line stalemates that more resembled World War I than a modern battlefield. Experienced guerrilla fighters, with the exception of the few Special Forces teams and MACV advisors, were few and far between. To put it bluntly, the U.S. Army was neither trained nor organized to face an irregular enemy.*

---

*Interestingly the term "guerrilla" was not originally a term for warriors but rather for conflict itself. From its Spanish origins, "guerrilla" literally translates as "little war."

When the U.S. Congress passed the Gulf of Tonkin Resolution on August 7, 1964, fewer than 24,000 American troops were in Vietnam. Under the provisions of the resolution that gave broad powers to President Lyndon Johnson to act in Southeast Asia, this number expanded to 184,000 by 1965 and to over 536,000 by 1968. Soon the ranks of the U.S. armed services were filled with draftees and volunteers whose only military experience was sixteen weeks of basic and advanced training before being thrown into the country's most unpopular war. Having inexperienced troops to fight the nation's battles was nothing new. But as a result of limiting draft eligibility to those twenty-six years old and below this group was different: Vietnam would be fought by the most youthful warriors in U.S. history, their average age being only nineteen.

The first troops to arrive in Vietnam wore uniforms and footgear suited more to the parade then to the battlefield. Fatigues were adorned with white name tapes and bright, multicolor shoulder and collar patches that looked more like decorated Christmas trees than battle dress. The basic weapon of the infantryman was the M-14, a bulky, long-barreled rifle with heavy ammunition that was designed for warfare on the European plains. In the jungle it would at best prove unsatisfactory. Helicopters and airmobile operations were still in their infancy.

From Rogers and Mosby to Merrill, American military history had proven the worth of small groups of dedicated fighters who used stealth, darkness, and minute attention to operational detail to destroy the enemy or to gain intelligence on his intentions. Ranger units had been a part of the U.S. Army since its birth in the colonies. From the use of patrols that adopted the tactics of their Indian enemies in King Philip's War to combined battalion operations in World War II, battlefield commanders had used Rangers to gather timely intelligence and to disrupt enemy communications and supply lines.

With these facts in mind, and the obvious fact that LRRP operations were best suited for the jungle environment of unconventional warfare, it is difficult to understand why no LRRP or Ranger units were on the army rolls at the beginning of the Vietnam War. As has been shown in previous chapters, the groundwork for the establishment of LRRPs had been accomplished. However, as with every other instance in Ranger history, it took actual combat before the army would take the LRRP concept off its dusty shelf and put it on the battlefield. Also, as in previous wars, the recognition of the requirement for LRRP units and their provisional formation by commanders in the field would precede the official authorization of their organization.

The reasons for these delays are many, yet, at the same time, almost inexplicable. Armies are reluctant to form elite units because elite units drain needed superior manpower from other units, and because the morale of the army as a whole decreases when some units are considered or treated better than others. Also, elite units tend to be too independent, preferring to do things their way rather than following the orders of higher commands.

Another reason for reluctance just may be that generals make their reputations and advancements based on their commands' overall performance. Generals like to maneuver battalions, brigades, and divisions in large-scale operations rather than field small, elite units that grab the headlines and the public's fancy.

Whatever the reasons, when the first regular U.S. troop units arrived in Vietnam in 1965, no official LRRP organizations existed in any brigade, division, or corps. Except for the embryonic Special Forces "Greek" teams and individual graduates of the Ranger School, soldiers experienced in LRRP operations were nonexistent.

Of the fifteen U.S. Army divisions and separate brigades that saw action in Vietnam, none arrived in-country with a LRRP unit structure already formed. Only one had even laid sufficient groundwork and conducted adequate training so LRRPs could be quickly organized. That was the 173rd Airborne Brigade, the first U.S. Army ground combat unit to arrive in Vietnam.

The 173rd had been formed two years before on Okinawa with the specific mission of being the army's "fire brigade" in the Pacific. Focusing on operations as diverse as rescuing a besieged embassy and taking part in large-scale land combat, the 173rd was one of the few units in the army that specifically trained for jungle operations.*

During its two years on Okinawa, before commitment to Vietnam on May 7, 1965, the 173rd used an island to the south, Irimoto, as a training area for small-unit patrolling and reconnaissance. Inserting groups ranging from three men to entire companies by parachute, by small boat, and from submarine, these training missions were carried out in the jungle for periods of up to a month with the only resupply coming by air drop.

Major General (Retired) Ellis W. Williamson, who commanded the 173rd on Okinawa and in Vietnam for three years as a brigadier general, states, "We had been in Vietnam only a few days when it became clear that small units could get out and get information much better than large search-and-destroy type operations."

Williamson continues, "I believe that I personally originated the LRRP [in Vietnam]; however, we did not call them by that name at the time. When we first started using them in Vietnam they were known as Delta Teams."*

Despite its previous training, the 173rd had many lessons to learn in deployment of its Delta Teams. Williamson says, "We immediately formalized the approach to small patrols by having each infantry battalion organize five special patrol units that were manned by specially selected personnel. We experimented quite a bit with re-

---

*The others were the 25th Infantry Division in Hawaii, which soon followed the 173rd to Vietnam, and the 193rd Infantry Brigade, which remained in Panama during the entire war to guard the Canal.

*The use of the term Delta Team by the 173rd had no link to the Special Forces Project Delta. Delta is a name that appears as the label for several special operations in Vietnam and other conflicts, yet extensive research has revealed no definitive source for it. A few veterans say that it merely was the fourth in a series of alphabetically named projects. Others claim it originated from the various cavalry troops that were attached to infantry units with the assigned mission of reconnaissance and were normally designated Delta Troop. Still others say Delta was the phonetic pronunciation for the letter "D," which stood for death teams.

spect to size, mission, armament, communications, and survival."

The 1st Brigade of the 101st Airborne Division (Airmobile) arrived in Vietnam soon after the 173rd, on July 29, 1965. Colonel (Retired) David H. Hackworth, of the brigade's 1st Battalion, 327th Airborne Infantry, and later Brigade S-3, states, "It was immediately obvious that we needed a LRRP-type unit when we arrived in-country. We formed two platoons of volunteers who were real 'studs' that we called the 'Tiger Force.' At the same time Hank Emerson [then lieutenant colonel and later lieutenant general] formed recon units he called 'Hatchet Teams' in the 2nd of the 502nd. The 2nd of the 327th [other battalions in the 1st Brigade] had teams called 'Hawks.' "

Hackworth, who was quite familiar with recon units based on his experiences as company commander of the 27th Raider Company in Korea, gives credit to Emerson for being the first Vietnam commander to name his recon units LRRPs. However, the decisions to change the name from "Hatchet Teams" to LRRPs was not exactly a traditional one. According to Hackworth, Emerson had issued his recon teams hatchets to go with their name. In December 1965 near Ben Cat one of the teams used their totems to "whack off a few heads." A reporter, Malcolm Brown, learned of the incident and it soon appeared in the papers back home. Complicating the incident was the fact that the Hatchet Teams were commanded by Captain Tommy Taylor, son of General (Retired) Maxwell Taylor, who was the U.S. ambassador to South Vietnam. Shortly after the "whacking" incident the 1st Brigade had its first LRRPs.*

While the 1st Brigade of the 101st was getting publicity, wanted or not, concerning its recon operations, the 173rd was doing everything possible to keep its Delta Teams confidential.

Williamson explains, "We did not want the enemy to

---

*The use of hatchets was both historical and practical. Robert Rogers had encouraged use of the weapon in his Standing Order 19. See Appendix B.

know that we were doing it, and certainly did not want him to know anything about our methods of operation. We did not even put accounts of our patrols in the operational reports. However, I did keep my higher headquarters informed and often got requests from there to investigate certain areas. We were able to keep it under wraps for several months.''

As more and more U.S. units arrived in-country, the number of LRRP-type units increased. The names varied at first, but as time passed LRRP became the preferred title. It is interesting to note that while there had been training directives, field manuals, and even an authorized table of organization and equipment (TO&E), there is no evidence of any of these publications being used in the initial establishment of the LRRPs in Vietnam by the units in the field. In every case, units arrived in-country, recognized the need for reconnaissance groups, and formed them to meet the need the ground commanders observed. All of this occurred with a complete lack of guidance from the Department of the Army (DA), MACV, or from the headquarters of the U.S. Army, Vietnam (USARV) beyond that found in FM 31–18.*

General Westmoreland continued his interest in and the recognition of the need for LRRPs. As new units arrived he sent leaders to the 173rd to observe and be briefed on how they were deploying patrol teams. Westmoreland's orders for establishing LRRP units, or formalizing those already in existence, came on July 8, 1966, in the form of a secret message released by the MACV operations officer, Major General John C. F. Tillson III. The message, ''Long Range Patrols,'' stated, ''COMUSMACV [Westmoreland] has directed that a comprehensive Long Range Patrol program be developed in SVN. In order to establish an interim MACV capability until sufficient TO&E Long Range Patrol units can be authorized, organized and be-

---

*USARV was formed on May 15, 1965, to command the rapidly increasing number of U.S. Army units. Westmoreland was ''dual hatted,'' as he commanded both MACV and the new headquarters.

come available in country, a provisional organization will be required from assets available in country. A Long Range Patrol (LRP) is defined as 'A specially trained military unit organized and equipped for the specific purpose of functioning as an information gathering agency responsive to the intelligence requirements of the tactical commander.' These patrols consist of specially trained personnel capable of performing reconnaissance, surveillance and target acquisition within the dispatching unit's area of interest.''

The message continued with instructions for major commands: ''A survey of in country assets and capabilities is required in order to establish a firm and sound program.''

With responses required within two weeks, the survey was to include LRP capabilities, assets, control level, training requirements, and types of missions visualized. It concluded with references to FM 31-18 and its accompanying TO&E 7-157-E, which provided information for allocation of patrol assets for the army. Although the manual focused on conventional warfare, the MACV staff officers recognized that it was the only doctrine on the subject available.

As indicated earlier, recon units were already operating in the Special Forces, the 173rd and 101st, as well as other units that had arrived early. While the message of July 8 provided authorization for what was already occurring, it also demonstrated Westmoreland's efforts to orchestrate all long-range patrol activities in Vietnam. Although the message focused on army efforts, including references to army publications, it was from Westmoreland and directed to all U.S. forces in his role as commander of MACV rather than wearing his ''army-only'' hat as the USARV commander. The message went to the navy and the Marine Corps as well as his subordinate army commanders.

This list of addressees explains part of, but not nearly all, the confusing subject title and repeated reference to ''Long Range Patrols'' rather than Long Range Reconnaissance Patrols. LRP was a generic term recognized by all services; however, the navy had already officially named their special patrol units SEALS, and Force Recon was a firmly established Marine term. LRRP, although not as well known, had been a part of official army documents since the CONARC directive of 1961. Despite all the official use of LRRP, when recon units finally received unit designations in 1967, they were named LRP companies.

So why LRP rather than LRRP? While the July 8 message clearly outlined that the purpose of the LRP was reconnaissance, the MACV staff officers who prepared it were true to their longtime army mission orientation of "closing with and destroying the enemy." The idea of forming units strictly for reconnaissance was foreign to their training. Giving them due credit, it should be noted that they were aware that the patrols would also have ambush and other combat missions as well as reconnaissance. Also, with a complete lack of doctrinal guidance on reconnaissance operations in an unconventional environment, the staff officers had to rely on what was in print—and that was FM 31–18, which conveniently offered the name LRP rather than LRRP.

LRP and LRRP would be used interchangeably for the rest of the war. Official documents would use both, often in the same paragraph. Company signs would have LRP while members of the same company had LRRP patches on their uniforms. LRRP had been the original designation and the one that has seemed to stand the test of time as the preferred designation by patrol veterans and historians alike. Adding to the confusion is the fact that the name for the patrols was *always* pronounced "Lurp" and on occasion was spelled phonetically, i.e., LURP, in official reports as well.

As with many issues concerning the war in Vietnam, LRRP versus LRP is confusing, unclear, and without complete explanation. Perhaps the best reason for the two names is given by a former NCO in the 9th Infantry Division LRRPs and current president of the Vietnam LRRP/Ranger Association, Mike Kentes. "Reconnaissance was just too long of a word and too hard to spell. It was much easier in written correspondence to write Long Range Patrol, but we always referred to and thought of ourselves as LRRPs.''

The July 8 MACV message was an important step in the recognition of LRRPs, but except to provide a survey of current assets, it yielded little results. LRRPs were progressing at a rapid rate on their own, and the army as a whole had many adjustments to make to the new environment of an unconventional war.

Units continued to experiment with recon teams attached at various levels as far down as battalion and brigade with a few consolidating LRRPs at the division. Size ranged from small detachments to large companies. Since no formal unit designations had been allocated for the LRRPs, they were attached as provisional units at various headquarters. A few units placed their LRRPs with the cavalry troop or squadron that had the traditional responsibility for reconnaissance.

The delay in authorization of LRRP units was not at all a lack of recognition of the need for them. LRRPs were only a part of the total combat effort and commanders had a war to fight on a daily basis. Time is always the most critical asset in combat—and often the one in shortest supply.

The foremost factor in the delay in official unit formation was the politics of the war itself. For the first time in the nation's history the services were fighting a war ''on the cheap.'' There had been no national mobilization of Army Reserve or National Guard forces. Monetary expenditures and the numbers of combat troops were being monitored by a Congress and a public that were far less than enthusiastically supporting the overall war effort.

If LRRP units were formally organized, given unit designations, and added to the roll of committed forces, their numbers would have added to the total numbers in Vietnam. By taking men from regular units, the army had LRRPs without paying the price in paper accountability of increased total troop strength. Of course, every soldier diverted to the LRRPs meant one less body in the regular infantry.

For the next step in the development of the LRRPs, Westmoreland again turned to the Special Forces. On September 15, 1966, Westmoreland directed Colonel Francis J. Kelly, commander of the 5th Special Forces Group, to establish the Recondo School at Nha Trang. Kelly placed the school under the responsibility of Detachment B-52, whose veterans of Project DELTA became the instructors.

LRRPs now had a place to learn their skills besides the jungle. While the course was not as deadly as actual patrols, it was in many ways every bit as tough. Many veterans would later remark that the course had been so physically and mentally demanding that it had rivaled combat.

"Recondo" was yet another addition to the list of names such as Delta, Hawk, Hatchet, LRP, and LRRP that represented recon teams. Its origins are more easily defined, however. Recondo, a combination of recon and commando, was the personal selection of Westmoreland and dated back to his prewar command of the 101st Airborne Division at Fort Campbell, Kentucky. During his tenure there, from April 1958 to July 1960, Westmoreland had established his first Recondo School for the purpose of teaching recon techniques and developing small-unit leadership skills.

The Recondo School of the 101st continued in operation after Westmoreland's command until the remainder of the division joined its 1st Brigade in Vietnam in December 1967. Many of the school's cadre became the nucleus of the division's LRRPs that were provisionally formed soon after their arrival in-country.

Another unit that led the way in the formation of LRRPs was the 4th Infantry Division. Arriving in-country from Fort Lewis, Washington, on September 25, 1966, the "Ivy" Division soon was fielding LRRP teams. A year later they were so proficient that Westmoreland invited the division commander, Major General William R. Peers, to address a Commanders' Conference on the use of LRRPs.

A secret briefing summary of Peers's verbal remarks was prepared by Westmoreland's staff. According to the summary, Peers opened his presentation by reviewing the history of the LRRP program in the 4th Infantry Division. Peers stated, "The program at its inception in the Fall of 1966 was small, with control exercised at the battalion level. In early 1967, the Division reviewed the patrolling concept. The review resulted in an increase in the size of the program, improved techniques, and raising the command and control level to division and brigade."

Peers outlined his LRRP organization, saying, "Each brigade has four LRRP platoons, one in each battalion and one in the Headquarters and Headquarters Company. The Division G-2 [intelligence officer] has OPCON [operational control] over the platoons as required."

The 4th Division's LRRP mission, according to Peers, was "to observe and/or conduct harassing activities." Capabilities included "observing and reporting enemy activities, analyzing terrain for future operations, checking enemy activity around potential LZs [landing zones], serving as stay-behinds near abandoned forward bases, conducting hit and run ambushes of small enemy bases, directing artillery and/or air strikes on enemy locations, serving as a surveillance force to screen front or flanks of an AO [area of operations] and causing the enemy to disclose himself or draw him to a given area."

Peers offered other excellent insights on the early days of Vietnam LRRPs. He stated, "There are no absolutes in 4th Division patrolling. For example, although the patrol size average is five, from three to eight personnel have been employed." He also described special LRRP teams called "Hawkeyes," primarily hunter-killer teams. Hawkeyes, usually armed with M-14s fitted with sniper scopes, were fielded in positions to overwatch large open areas and kill enemy soldiers with single, well-aimed shots.

Results of the 4th Infantry Division's LRRP operations, as reported by Peers, clearly show their impact. From February to September 1967, the LRRPs had conducted a total of 503 missions. On three hundred forty of those operations, they had sighted the enemy, initiating contact on seventy-three occasions. Twelve times the LRRP teams had had to be extracted under fire. With the loss of only one killed and fifteen wounded, the 4th Division's LRRPs had killed eighty-six of the enemy.

Peers also credited his LRRPs for the initial sighting of a large NVA force near the Cambodian border that directly led to Operation JUNCTION CITY, the largest operation in the war to that date. JUNCTION CITY ultimately involved twenty-two battalions from the 4th, 1st, and 25th Infantry Divisions; the 196th Infantry Brigade; the 11th Armored Cavalry Regiment; and the 173rd Airborne Brigade. Four ARVN battalions also participated. In eighty-three days of combat from February to May of 1967, JUNCTION CITY yielded a confirmed body count of 2,728 enemy troops.

The success of the 4th Division's LRRPs was a major topic of discussion at the Commanders' Conference. Peers's remarks were not a major revelation to the other commanders, however, because they were experiencing similar results with their own LRRPs. Organization, capabilities, and results were interesting, but what the commanders really wanted to know was when they would receive permission to replace their LRRPs' provisional status with authorized unit designations.

Westmoreland had the answers. LRRPs had more than proved their value. With the increase in troop authorizations for Vietnam, LRRP units could now be formalized. Westmoreland announced that over the next sixty days each division would receive a separate company designation for its LRRPs; separate brigades would be assigned a detachment organization.

Separate companies were a rarity in the army's structure and there were no common numerical designations or regiments or historical connections to draw from for long-range patrol units. No one voiced any complaints about the unusual unit designations because whatever they were called, at least they were, finally, official. Commanders could now fill the ranks of the LRRPs without depleting the regular infantry units. By the end of 1968 nearly half of all separate companies in the Active Army would be LRRPs. (For a complete listing of LRRP companies and detachments, see Appendix C.)

In addition to the formation of division LRRP companies that were authorized 118 men and the brigade detachments with 61, Westmoreland also announced that two new LRRP companies composed of 230 personnel would be formed and assigned to I and II Field Forces.*

The two new units were officially on the books the day following the Commanders' Conference—September 25, 1967. Company E, 20th Infantry (LRP), commanded by Major Danridge M. (Mike) Malone, in I Field Force, and Company F, 51st Infantry (LRP), commanded by Major William C. Maus, in II Field Force, were the first *authorized* Ranger-type units in the U.S. Army since the Korean War.

Although the two field-force LRRP companies earned the official honor of being first, they were by no means the leaders in organizing recon units. As has been shown, divisions and brigades throughout Vietnam had provisional LRRP units already integrated into their battle plans. The provisional units merely had to adopt their new designations as LRRP companies and detachments and continue operations as directed by their commanders. The field-force companies still had to recruit volunteers, locate equipment, and organize for combat. Malone noted in the E/20 daily staff journal on November 20, 1967, "Lack of operational A/C [aircraft] for both training and operations will probably postpone readiness date."

---

*I Field Force exercised operational control over U.S. and allied ground forces and provided assistance to ARVN units in the northern half of South Vietnam. II Field force had the same mission for the southern part of the country. The two field forces had the same basic responsibilities as a corps headquarters—to control divisions and separate brigades assigned under them. Because field forces operated in areas already designated as "corps zones" by the ARVNs, the field force concept had been adopted on March 15, 1966, to minimize confusion. The field forces, unlike a corps, had the additional responsibilities of supply, pacification, and advisory duties to the ARVN but did not command them. Also, the field force allowed for more flexibility in organizing subordinate units to meet the constantly changing battlefield conditions.

In other entries Malone noted difficulties in securing the release of qualified volunteers from other units and problems in finding needed equipment. Despite the difficulties, both Malone and Maus were able to begin patrol operations within sixty days of their companies' establishment.

Only three months after F/51 was formed, it participated in Operation UNIONTOWN III-BOXSPRINGS about thirty miles northeast of Saigon between Bien Hoa and Xuan Loc. In February and March 1968, while attached to the 199th Light Infantry Brigade, F/51 conducted one hundred seventeen patrols with no friendly casualties. They sighted the enemy on ninety-one occasions and made contact on thirty-three of them, resulting in forty-eight enemy killed, twenty-six more probable kills, and eighteen prisoners captured.

After Westmoreland had authorized the formal organization of LRRP units, neither he nor his staff provided further guidance for their use. LRRPs were entirely controlled by their parent field force, division, or separate brigade. No central command of LRRP units and no staff agency at MACV or USARV oversaw their operations.

This lack of command unity was not an inadvertent omission, but rather an intentional decentralization. Westmoreland gave great latitude to his subordinate commanders not only because he had confidence in their abilities but also because the nature of the war itself demanded it. Vietnam offered a vast variety of terrain and combat conditions. What worked for LRRPs in one area might prove deadly in another.

Lieutenant General (Retired) Julian J. Ewell, who commanded the 9th Infantry Division, and later the II Field Force from February 1968 to April 1970, best summed up this need for decentralization. "At any time in Vietnam there were ten or more different wars and they kept changing. Flexibility was the word."

This decentralization of LRRP control best fitted the different kind of war that had to be fought. At the same time, it offered little opportunity for sharing lessons learned among units, in-country policy makers, and the Department of the Army.

Despite the fact that LRRPs were playing a major role in every command in Vietnam, the rest of the army was still not forming similar units. No stateside or European divisions had authorization for the establishment of LRRPs.

As a result, on February 18, 1968, the 3rd Brigade of the 82nd Airborne Division, one of the last units to arrive in Vietnam, did so with no LRRP organization. Deployed from Fort Bragg, North Carolina, with only thirty hours' notice in President Johnson's Tet offensive response, the brigade was immediately committed to the battle for the imperial city of Hue.

The initial assembly area for the 3rd Brigade was a new, austere base that had no wire perimeter or even basic security system. Brigadier General A. R. Bolling, Jr., the brigade's commander, recognized the need for LRRPs as soon as he landed in Vietnam. With the inadequate security of the new base camp, a system for early warning of possible enemy attack was an immediate necessity. A means of gathering intelligence for the brigade's future operations was also critical. Bolling realized that LRRPs would fill the bill in both cases.

Volunteers were selected from throughout the brigade and assigned to Bolling's headquarters company as a provisional LRRP platoon. Within days after the lead elements of the 82nd were on the ground, LRRPs were in the jungle and paddies providing security and gathering critical information for future operations.

Bolling was fortunate in that eighty-five percent of his brigade were veterans of previous Vietnam tours. Many had been back in the States only a few months—in some cases, weeks. Some had experience with LRRPs while many were veteran combat infantrymen. LRRPs from Company F, 58th Infantry (LRP), assigned to the 101st, to whom the 82nd was initially attached, assisted in the newly formed LRRPs' organization and training. Even with this pool of experienced soldiers and the help from the 101st, the formation procedures and problems of the 82nd's LRRPs closely resembled that of units that had arrived in-country years before.

It is also noteworthy that Bolling states, "I received absolutely no guidance on LRRPs from DA or USARV. There simply was none." Official authorization for the brigade's 78th Infantry Detachment (LRP) did not come until December 15, 1968—ten months after they arrived in-country.

About the same time the 82nd was forming its LRRPs in Vietnam, the first efforts to establish stateside recon units were beginning. Oddly, rather than in the regular army, these efforts began in the National Guard. In December 1967, the 1st Battalion (Airborne), 151st Infantry of the Indiana National Guard was reorganized. Part of this reorganization was the formation of Company D, 151st Infantry (LRP).

Company D's principal recruiting area were the towns of Greenville and Evansville, Indiana. However, once word was out that a LRRP company was being formed, volunteers came from throughout the midwest. Only the most highly motivated were selected and each volunteer had to be airborne qualified.

As soon as the company reached its authorized strength of a little over two hundred men, an intensive training program was undertaken. In March 1968, Company D attended the Jungle Warfare School in the Canal Zone as a part of its annual training, and ninety-seven percent of the company successfully completed the course and were awarded the Jungle Expert badge, the best record of any reserve component unit since the course was initiated.

Without the Tet Offensive of 1968 the Indiana National Guard LRRPs would likely have sat out the war as citizen soldiers, meeting one weekend a month and two weeks each year for annual training. When the NVA and VC attacked every major city, including Saigon, during Tet the American people realized that there was no "light at the end of the tunnel" in the increasingly unpopular war. Although Tet proved to be a tremendous defeat on the battlefield for the enemy, it was also a victory in that it eroded the confidence of the American people in the war effort.

Johnson's call-up of 24,000 reserve component troops in response to the Tet offensive was as much a political decision as a tactical one. Before Tet, the president had limited units committed to the fighting in Vietnam to the regular forces. He had held off mobilizing the National Guard and reserves because he feared an already unhappy public would further turn against the war effort if their "citizen soldiers" were called to active duty. Congressman, always concerned with reelection, also did not support the idea of reserve or guard units in their districts being activated for such an unpopular conflict.

As a result of Tet, Johnson was forced to prove his resolve in continuing American involvement in Vietnam. Although the call-up of twenty-four thousand reservists and guardsmen made a minor impact on the total number of troops in Southeast Asia, it showed Congress and the public that Johnson intended to continue the Vietnam War.*

The orders for the mobilization caused much controversy in the active army and the reserve components. Some individuals, as well as whole units had no desire to be activated for Vietnam. The guard and reserve in many cases had become the lesser of two evils for young men of draft age not wanting to leave home for the regular army. In addition, most units were not trained, equipped, or motivated to be thrown into the war. Still, other units were anxious to be selected for activation and, along with their Congressmen's support, lobbied for mobilization. The common concern of civilian and military leaders was that only the best units be activated.

Ultimately, the decision was reached to activate units across the country from such diverse locations as Kansas, Kentucky, and Hawaii. However, rather than deploying the newly mobilized troops as units, they would be sent

*Johnson's nationally televised speech announcing the twenty-four thousand man call-up is much better remembered for the final few minutes, when he announced he would not seek reelection the following November.

to Vietnam as individual replacements. One of the few exceptions to this policy, and the only ground combat maneuver unit so selected, was Company D, 151st Infantry (LRP). When alerted for activation, Company D and the leadership of the Indiana National Guard welcomed the notification and made only one request—that the unit stay together and be deployed in its present organization.

In response to Company D's request, the secretary of the army, Stanley R. Resor, responded by letter to the state's adjutant general stating, "I appreciate very much the 'can do' attitude of this company and the spirit in which your request is made. The reason for mobilizing a unit of this type was to improve the long range capabilities of the Strategic Army Forces. Specifically, Company D was selected because of its overall readiness condition. Information available to me indicates we made a wise choice."

The key to Resor's decision was the "overall readiness condition." If an organization was to be sent as a unit, it had to be prepared. Although not mentioned, politics as well impacted on the company's selection. Senior National Guard officials, as well as some members of Congress, were anxious to prove that guardsmen could stand equal to the regular troops. The reputation of LRRPs as elite fighters had already been well established. If the Indiana LRRPs could stand beside the experienced recon men in Vietnam, the entire guard would benefit.

During its initial organization and training, Company D was commanded by Captain Kenneth W. Hemsel.* According to Hemsel, "D Company gained a lot of recognition when it did so well in the Jungle Warfare School. We had high morale and were well trained. That's why we were selected for mobilization."

Despite their high level of readiness, the company was not immediately sent to Vietnam. For twenty-three weeks they were assigned to Fort Benning, Georgia, for addi-

---

*Hemsel would remain in the guard after the war and at this writing in 1987 is a major general commanding the Indiana National Guard's 38th Infantry Division.

tional training. Much attention was being given the guard unit, for no one wanted it to fail. Hemsel remembers that they were welcomed to Benning by its commander, Major General John Wright, who told them that the entire assets of the Infantry Center were at their disposal.

During their time at Benning, twenty-six of D Company's LRRPs completed the Ranger Course and were awarded their tabs. In addition, the entire company went through modified Ranger training, spending two weeks at each of the school's phases. Near the end of the Benning training, Kenneth Hemsel was promoted to major and transferred to Vietnam as an individual replacement in the 4th Division. His replacement was his brother and former Company D executive officer, Captain Robert Hemsel.

Company D arrived in Vietnam on December 30, 1968, and after a brief in-country training period with the 199th Light Infantry Brigade, was assigned to II Field Force. In addition to being the only reserve component ground maneuver unit to be committed to the war, the company had the distinction of being the only preorganized, pretrained LRRP unit to serve in the war zone.

The assignment of D Company to Vietnam was a decision welcomed by commanders who recognized the importance of increased LRRP assets. However, when they arrived, each field force and every division and separate brigade already had an assigned LRRP company or detachment. The ultimate assignment of D Company caused little confusion in Vietnam at the time; however, the same cannot be said for historians who have tried to trace LRRP lineage since the war.

Varying accounts have been recorded as to where D Company, 151st Infantry (LRP), was assigned and its relationship with F Company, 51st Infantry (LRP), and the 71st Infantry Detachment (LRP). The situation is further complicated by the redesignation of all LRRP units to letter companies of the 75th Infantry (Ranger) while D Company was in-country. Information papers on file at the Ranger Department at Fort Benning and various listings of Vietnam LRRP unit orders of battle show F/51 being replaced at II Field Force by Company D and F/51 being transferred to the 199th Light Infantry Brigade to serve with the 199th's 71st Infantry Detachment (LRP). None of these accounts is completely accurate.

Much of this confusion comes from the fact that D Company did use the 199th's week-long, in-country orientation course upon its arrival. At the same time, F/51 was attached to the 199th from its regular assignment with II Field Force. During this period the 71st briefly operated with and assisted both units.

Shortly after D Company's arrival, it and F/51 returned to the control of II Field Force. There the two companies were combined under a provisional headquarters organization with the F/51 commander, Major George Heckman, being designated company commander and Captain Robert Hemsel the executive officer. In an unusual configuration, even for Vietnam, both company designations and both company guidons were maintained.

Initially, the LRRP teams of the two companies remained independent with all team members belonging to their parent company. As time passed, teams of the two companies integrated as replacements arrived to replace casualties or F/51 soldiers who rotated home. By the time D Company completed its tour, the two companies were virtually indistinguishable. However, they did submit separate morning reports and publish different orders for promotions, awards, and other formal documents. In front of the combined company headquarters flew three flags—the guidons of the two companies and the flag of the state of Indiana.

Shortly before D Company completed its tour, Kenneth Hemsel returned to the unit to assume command for its return home. On November 20, 1969, Company D was released from active duty and returned to the control of the Indiana National Guard. The company had represented the guard and the LRRPs well. Nineteen D Company LRRPs had received the Silver Star, the United States' third-highest award for valor, and one hundred seventy-five had been awarded the Bronze Star. Although one hundred ten Purple Hearts had been earned for combat wounds, only two of the Hoosier LRRPs had been killed in action. Two others had died from accidents that were not results of hostile action.

Before the transfer took place, guard officials received correspondence from the II Field Force commander, Lieutenant General Walter T. Kerwin, Jr., stating, "The purpose of this letter is to let you know how proud I am of the work being done by the officers and men of Company D (Ranger) 151st Infantry. I depend on your Rangers from the Indiana National Guard and I find them to be real professionals. The Long Range Reconnaissance Patrols of Company D are my 'eyes and ears' in many parts of the II Corps Tactical Zone, providing me with information that is vital to the success of our tactical operations. The Rangers have accepted each mission with eagerness. They have shown great courage, endurance and professional competence and I am proud to have officers and men from Greenville and Evansville as members of the II Field Force team."

Company D's return home was hailed as Unity Day across Indiana by Governor Edgar D. Whitcomb. At the official welcome ceremony in the National Guard Armory in Indianapolis, the building was filled to overflowing as bands played and the governor, mayor, congressmen, and senators made remarks. The ceremony added to the Vietnam honors of Company D. In addition to being the only reserve component combat maneuver unit to fight in the war, it was also the only LRRP company—and for that matter, one of the few units—to receive a welcome-home ceremony of any kind.

The next step in the historical development of the LRRPs was more an example of official doctrine attempting to catch up with the reality of recon operations in Vietnam than any actual guidance or impact. On August 23, 1968, a revised edition of FM 31-18 was published by the Department of the Army, superceding the 1965 manual. The new FM varied little from the previous two editions, with the exception of an added chapter, titled "Stability Operations,'' which was the military buzzword at the time for the type of warfare going on in Southeast Asia. Included were paragraphs on planning, preparation, support, and postmission activities that much more resembled actual operations in Vietnam than the remainder of the manual, which still focused on conventional operations.

At the back of the new FM were two appendixes that had not been included in the previous editions. A one-page appendix titled ''Patrol Steps'' was followed by two pages of a recommended Tactical SOP. Both of the additions were woefully inadequate.

While the revised FM was important in that it at least officially acknowledged, and somewhat clarified, LRRP operations in unconventional warfare, it added confusion to the question of whether LRP or LRRP was the designation of the recon men. The new manual had yet another title—''Long-Range Reconnaissance Patrol Company.'' No explanation was given for the reemergence of ''reconnaissance.'' Perhaps it was a final recognition of what the recon men had been calling themselves all along, or maybe the authors of the manual finally learned to spell the difficult word. Whatever the reason, the parenthetical (LRP) remained unchanged in the unit designations.

The final step in LRRP historical development was again partially military and partially political. By 1969 LRRPs shared a common organization and mission but were still identified as separate companies and detachments with no numerical sequence, relation, or historical lineage. Questions of unit designation mattered little to the LRRPs in Vietnam; they were proud of their work and of their reputation. A war was being fought against a real enemy and bureaucratic matters such as name changes were something they had neither time nor motivation to worry themselves about.

Back in the stateside army this ''attitude,'' that is, just fighting the war while overlooking bureaucratic detail, was not sufficient. After their wars, Ranger veterans of World War II and Korea had formed several large organizations that were greatly interested in seeing that Rangers be a part of the Vietnam conflict. The focus of the lobbying efforts of these organizations, as well as those of Ranger advocates within the active army staff, was that LRRPs were doing Ranger missions in Vietnam and should be so designated.

Ranger backers were supported by current army policy in addition to tradition. In 1957 the army had adopted the Combat Arms Regimental System (CARS) in an effort to maintain the continuity of the distinguished history of combat units and to provide a framework that would give stability to unit designations during fluctuations of strength and structure. CARS provided a system wherein regimental histories and traditions earned on battlefields since the country's beginnings could be passed on to and maintained by current generations of combat soldiers.

But there was a lot of seeming confusion built into the system. Often in Vietnam (and in the army of today) different battalions of a regiment were assigned to completely different headquarters at the next higher command level. In some cases one battalion might be fighting in Vietnam while another battalion with the same regimental number was stationed back in the States and still another was posted in Germany. Although the system was much maligned by critics, CARS did accomplish its purpose. Soldiers had to only to look to their battalion colors to see battle streamers representing campaigns fought in past wars by former members of the same regiment. Tradition was preserved and morale, it was hoped, influenced.*

The delay in designating a parent regiment for Vietnam LRRPs had two causes. First, a war was going on and more pressing matters had priority over name changes. Second, and most important, Ranger lineage and campaign participation credit from World War II and Korea had already been assigned to the Special Forces.

*It was not until 1984 that the army began another reorganization with the specific purpose of grouping battalions of the same regiment under the flag of a single brigade headquarters. Unit redesignations and moves to accomplish that goal continue.

Under CARS the Special Forces had not received the lineage of any infantry regiment but rather those of a variety of special warfare units including those of the Rangers. Finally, after much discussion and disagreement (and some very effective lobbying by former members of Merrill's Marauders), the 75th Infantry Regiment was selected as the Vietnam LRRP parent organization.

On January 16, 1969, the Department of the Army issued Message Number 893755, "Redesignation of Long Range Patrol (LRP) Units." The message stated that LRP units would be redesignated as letter companies of the 75th Infantry effective February 1, 1969, and that two new Ranger companies, A Company at Fort Benning and B Company at Fort Carson, would be formed.*

On March 7, 1969, the Department of the Army tied up the last loose end in the official transition of LRRPs to Rangers. Change number one to FM 31-18 was published, stating, "Title is changed to read Long Range Reconnaissance Ranger Company." A half-page of other changes consisting of typographical corrections and word additions or deletions for clarification of the original text followed. The use of LRRP throughout the manual was not changed to either LRRRP or Ranger.

The redesignation in Vietnam had little impact beyond cosmetics. Units changed names and began calling themselves Rangers. However, LRRP continued to be used interchangeably with Ranger unofficially and in some official documents as well. Messages followed stating that the new Rangers were to wear the patch of their parent unit, as no official Ranger patch was authorized. In the finest of Ranger traditions of past wars, the Vietnam Rangers ignored these directives and without exception adopted the black and red scroll of World War II and Korea veterans.

Along with the scroll, the LRRPs adopted the unofficial

---

*A Company would be moved to Fort Hood, Texas, shortly after formation. Neither company had future missions in Southeast Asia, as both were designated to deploy to Europe as corps support units in the event of hostilities there.

motto of the Rangers, "Rangers lead the way," that had been earned on the beaches of Normandy in World War II. The official motto of the 75th Infantry, "Sua sponte," also became a part of the LRRPs. The addition of the motto was quite appropriate for the volunteer recon men, as it means "of their own accord."

Although designation of the LRRPs as Rangers of the 75th Infantry was in compliance with tradition, the assignment of letters to each company was not. A and B were assigned to the two stateside companies while C through I and K through P were assigned to Vietnam. No explanation was given as to why J Company was not included, nor is there any record in any of the subsequent documents. The only speculation offered by veterans of the time is that the phonetic pronunciation of J is "Juliet," and that perhaps no one wanted a Ranger company with such a feminine designation. However, it should be noted that CARS had not included J companies because the army had traditionally avoided the letter since the nineteenth century; early telegraph operators and semaphore signalers confused J and I, so the former had been eliminated.

A simple system was followed in determining which of the thirteen LRRP companies and detachments received what specific 75th letter company designation. The two field force LRRP companies, E/20 and F/51, were designated C and D companies. The remaining companies and detachments were listed in numerical and alphabetical order and companies E through O (with J left out) were paired down the list. (See Appendix C.)

The only exception to these changes was that Company D, 151st Infantry (LRP), was not included in the 75th, as they would be returning to control of the Indiana National Guard. Their only change was the redesignation of the parenthetical "(LRP)" to "(Ranger)."

Although the formation of a parent regiment for the new Rangers created new company designations, no regimental headquarters was authorized. Ranger companies would continue to operate under the command of their parent field force, division, or separate brigade.*

General Westmoreland, who had returned from Vietnam to assume the duties of chief of staff of the army in July 1968, made the final decision on the redesignation of LRRPs to Rangers. Nearly two decades later he recalls little of the background involved in the change except to state, "DA wanted to give them [LRRPs] a parent organization. As far as I know there was no impact [on their operations]. I supported the action."

More insight is presented by Lieutenant Colonel B. J. Sutton, who was the principal action officer for the change within the Department of the Army's Office of the Assistant Chief of Staff for Force Development. In 1969, Sutton wrote to Captain George Paccerelli, commander of Company H 75th Infantry (Ranger), saying, "One of the reasons some of us at DA fought to get the 75th Infantry activated as the parent regiment for the Ranger/LRP units was to provide the members of the LRPs, and the rest of the Army for that matter, with a common regiment identifying an uncommon skill. I have made it a point to monitor the 75th Infantry because I believe in the concept behind the Ranger companies of the 75th Infantry, and I don't want to see the Army, for one reason or another, give them up in the post-Vietnam period."

Except for reduced strength in some companies when parts of their parent divisions rotated home near the end of the war, the final changes in LRRP/Ranger Vietnam history were complete. LRRPs were now adding to the long and illustrious history of Rangers as well as to their remarkable record already achieved across the war zone.

---

*Since there was no overall Ranger headquarters the Ranger Department at Fort Benning was designated by the Department of the Army as the custodian of the regimental colors of the 75th Infantry. This was a formality, as even the Ranger Department director, Colonel Y. Y. Phillips, acknowledged to his staff in a memo dated March 7, 1969: "The Department will not function as an 'active' headquarters."

CHAPTER 6
●□●□●□●

The Men with Painted Faces

*T*HE diversity of terrain in Vietnam required LRRP units to adapt their operational methods to their surroundings. Depending on the location, LRRPs might conduct their patrols in remote areas far from any population, or near large villages, or in a countryside with heavy concentrations of farmers and their families. At times the LRRPs faced Viet Cong, who were poorly equipped and less than enthusiastic to stand and fight. On other occasions the enemy were North Vietnamese regulars who were well organized and trained and who were fierce fighters.

LRRPs made whatever adjustments necessary in their patrol procedures and techniques to find, report, or eliminate whatever enemy they faced in all sorts of environments. LRRP units varied greatly, yet they shared many similarities. However, the greatest commonality was not organization, equipment, or mission. It was the men themselves.

The troops who volunteered for LRRP duty were a unique group in a unique war. They were not "super soldiers" any more than their brother infantrymen in the regular combat line units. Yet they performed "super feats" that earned the respect of ally and enemy alike. Even the media, which seldom had anything positive to report about U.S. operations, could find little fault with the recon soldiers. Of course, good news was seemingly not the priority of the correspondents. Little appeared in print or electronic media coverage of the war about LRRP operations. LRRPs did not seek publicity. Secrecy and stealth were not only their standard method of operation but also was the key to their longevity. Also, few reporters were invited to go along on hazardous missions far from friendly forces with a LRRP team of only six men. Fewer still accepted the opportunity when it was presented.

The VC and NVA had little trouble learning about the build-up of U.S. combat troops. Their agents reported arrivals at the ports and airfields, often confirming what the enemy had already learned from "friends" within the Saigon government. While American artillery, air assets, and the large numbers of U.S. troops were of great concern to enemy planners, they gave little thought to the possibility that the arriving GIs would attempt to out-guerrilla the guerrilla by using his own tactics.

They were to learn quickly, and most often the hard way, through casualties and loss of supplies, that the American soldier was very adaptable. The first formal record that the enemy was aware that LRRPs were seeking them out came during Operation AUSTIN II in April 1966. LRRPs from the 1st Brigade of the 101st operating near Phan Thiet surprised and overran a small VC training camp on April 16. The subject of the class, which the LRRPs rudely interrupted, was "Beware American Long Range Patrols."

As more months passed and additional LRRP teams took the field, the enemy became more sensitive to their presence. Captured documents and prisoner interrogations revealed that the enemy's common name for LRRPs was "the men with painted faces." This was in reference to the green and black camouflage greasepaint that the LRRPs applied to all uncovered areas of their skin while in the field.*

---

*Regular infantry units also used camouflage paint but with little regularity. Some credit this lack of camouflage use to poor discipline on the part of the line troops,

One characteristic of any elite group or organization is the small number of its members. The men with painted faces certainly met this requirement: of the 2.7 million men and women who served in Vietnam, fewer than 5,000 saw action as a LRRP or Ranger. Even at the height of U.S. involvement in the war, no more than 1,600 of the recon men were in-country at any one time.*

Elites often exist within elites. Infantrymen of all armies and time periods have considered themselves to be the "Queen of Battle" with other branches and sister services existing only to provide their support. LRRPs closely identified with their grunt brothers, as they were "of the infantry" themselves. With few exceptions (primarily communications specialists and a few from the ranks of armored reconnaissance or cavalry units) LRRPs held the military occupation specialty (MOS) of 11B (i.e., rifleman; technically infantry light weapons specialist). LRRPs were trained as infantry and recruited from the infantry, and to the infantry they returned after completion of their LRRP assignments. Infantryman and LRRP alike proudly referred to themselves as 11-bush or 11-bang-bang rather than the official 11-bravo.

Of course, not all infantrymen wanted to be LRRPs. One of the first lessons a soldier learns is never to volunteer for anything. To be a LRRP, one had to want to be a LRRP, and volunteering was the only way to become one.

Beyond the basic reluctance of soldiers to volunteer, other factors restricted LRRP commanders in manning their units. In the early months of the war, divisions and brigades arrived with cohesive units that had often lived

but this is not an accurate criticism. Regular infantry soldiers spent weeks and often months in the jungles and paddies while the LRRPs were rarely out for more than five to seven days before returning to a base camp. Lack of cleanliness, and the resulting skin infections and diseases, were a major problem to units that spent sustained periods in the field. Line infantry grunts had enough hygiene problems without compounding them with greasepaint.

*The Vietnam LRRP/Ranger Association published a letter in 1986 stating that, according to their calculations, 3,200 former recon men were eligible for membership. This number may be somewhat conservative even considering the combat casualties and those veterans who have died since the war.

and trained together for years. Loyalty to company and battalion was high, and many old troops who wanted to be LRRPs elected to remain with their comrades. Another important factor was that the LRRPs only accepted the very best, and commanders became downright belligerent at the idea of releasing their top soldiers.

When arriving units first organized provisional LRRPs, it often took influence from the highest commanders to secure the reassignment of volunteers. Problems of securing LRRPs in units such as the 4th Division and the 101st were minor, however, in comparison with the initial organization of the field force companies. When Major Mike Malone established the first authorized LRRP unit in Vietnam at I Field Force, he was told by the commander to secure volunteers. Subordinate commanders in the field force saw the request for volunteers as an excellent opportunity to cast off problem soldiers, malcontents, and poor performers. Major Bill Maus experienced similar problems in II Field Force.

On October 9, 1967, only days after the formal establishment of Company E, 20th Infantry (LRP), Malone recorded in the company's daily staff journal, "Interviewed five more men from forward area. Limited potential. Thus far have checked 27 from forward area and turned back 6 (Deserters; supply clerk with 9 years education and no experience; SP4 with 8 yrs in grade and four reductions, etc.). Advised thru grapevine that word forward is 'unload'."

The daily staff journal of E/20 reveals similar problems in securing platoon leaders and an executive officer. Although good lieutenants who wanted to be LRRPs could be found, their commanders refused to release them.

Malone eventually recorded in the daily staff journal two basic, but opposite, truths in recruiting LRRPs—experienced soldiers were needed, but inexperienced new arrivals were all that were available. Malone wrote, "Receiving personnel with combat experience very important." His next statement reflects the only course of action that was practical: "Began interviewing personnel from replacement streams."

Malone's route to secure men was the same one that, by necessity, was adopted by all other LRRP units. While they still actively recruited from the infantry units, most of their volunteers came from newly arriving soldiers.

Upon arrival in-country, replacements were assigned to the 22nd Replacement Battalion at Cam Ranh Bay or the 90th Replacement Battalion at Long Binh. After personnel processing that took twenty-four to forty-eight hours, replacements were reassigned to divisions or other headquarters. At the new station they were again processed and usually given five to seven days of orientation training.

To ensure an even and fair distribution of newly arrived soldiers to needy units, the 22nd and 90th were supposedly off-limits to LRRP and other commanders, but that did not prevent the recon commanders from scouring the ranks of new arrivals for NCOs wearing Ranger tabs or anyone else potentially interested in joining the LRRPs. Some volunteers were literally hi-jacked from the replacement centers with official orders requested only weeks later to formalize the "transfer." At nine-tenths of the law, possession was better odds than the LRRPs were used to, anyway. As replacement-center cadre caught on to the LRRP raids on the new arrivals, that technique became more difficult.

The authorized method came at the week-long division and separate-brigade orientation courses. Most commonly, representatives of the LRRP unit assigned to the organization sponsoring the orientation course gathered all newly arriving infantrymen and asked for volunteers.

William Gawthrop, a native of Huntsville, Texas, recalls being in the 1st Cavalry Division's orientation when 1st Sergeant Jerry L. Price of H Company, 75th Infantry (Ranger), gathered up all arriving infantrymen and gave a short speech in which he said, "What I'm looking for is a special kind of person. I want someone with the average of thirteen and a half years education, twenty to twenty-one years old, even tempered, likes the outdoors, is willing to undergo selective, intensive training, and can work in small groups." Gawthrop thought the pitch sounded pretty interesting and began to raise his hand when Price added, "And, preferably, orphans."

"It was too late to get my hand down," says Gawthrop. "I was 'volunteered' and spent the next year as a LRRP. . . . But I never regretted my decision."

The characteristics that Price was looking for were similar to those wanted by other LRRP units. However, these traits were often hard to find in the ranks of the draftees who filled the replacement centers. Gawthrop's future company commander in H Company, Captain George Paccerelli, was a bit more realistic. "As a rule we found the following characteristics to be true of our successful Ranger candidates: He was a high school graduate, twenty years of age, came from a small town, a team player, no prior combat experience, no police record, and unmarried. There were, of course, exceptions. In the same light, the following were the more obvious characteristics of those who failed to make the grade: The glory hunter, radicals, and eighteen-year-olds. As before, there were exceptions."

Everyone seems to have opinions as to what were desirable LRRP traits. General Ellis Williamson remembers what he looked for in the first 173rd Airborne Brigade recon men. "The most important element in recruitment was the selection of the recruiter. This individual had to know people. There was never any problem in getting volunteers for a unit that was to be relatively small and was considered to be a cut above the norm. The recruiter always had many more than he could use. His problem was to weed out the kooks. This type of activity was no place for a warped brain. He had to select the trainable, not necessarily the smartest or best educated. If not done initially, the psychologically unstable had to be eliminated in the early stages of training. People were by far the most important element of small-unit operations. Mutual trust among the individual members of the patrol was the glue that held them together; without it the patrol could not operate.''

Another general with definite opinions as to what made a good LRRP is Major General (Retired) Robert C. Forbes. Forbes, who commanded the 199th Light Infantry Brigade and its 71st Infantry Detachment (LRP) in 1967 as a brigadier, states that he looked for men who were ''alert, quick thinking, innovative, team players, resourceful, intelligent, well trained in basic fundamentals of soldiering, excellent health, dexterous, brave, steady under stress, capable of operating in unfriendly environments over extended periods, physically strong, and have a desire for dangerous and challenging assignments.''

Opinions of just what made a good LRRP vary greatly from source to source, with some of the most interesting coming from the LRRPs themselves. With few exceptions the first response of recon veterans when asked what made a good LRRP was the one word, ''crazy,'' followed by a pause before adding other characteristics.

William B. Bullen, from Lansdale, Pennsylvania, was an eighteen-year-old SP4 in the 4th Division's K Company Rangers in 1970. His description of the desired abilities of a LRRP include, ''A volunteer with balls, stamina, and a hell of a lot of team-oriented smarts.''

Also with an opinion is Walter D. Stock, another Pennsylvanian, who survived three tours in Vietnam, including one with E/20 LRRPs in 1967–68 as a staff sergeant. Stock remained in the army after the war, and his last assignment before retiring in 1982 was as command sergeant major of the 2nd Ranger Battalion at Fort Lewis, Washington. According to Stock, the traits of a good LRRP in Vietnam were the same thing he looked for in volunteers for the modern Ranger battalions. Stock's good LRRP possessed ''teamwork, enthusiasm, stamina, tenacity, initiative, courage, loyalty, excellence, and a sense of humor.'' Stock is obviously a believer in the last trait. The first letters of the characteristics form the acronym TESTICLES. Bullen and Stock obviously agree on the most important part of the LRRPs' anatomy. Stock also comments on the recruitment of LRRPs with a minimum of words. "Take who you can get. Look at them. Reject as required."

Still another profile of the LRRP is offered by Kregg P. J. Jorgenson, a veteran of H Company in 1969 when he was nineteen years old. Jorgenson, a native of Seattle, Washington, says, "For the most part LRRPs were young, cocky, foolishly brave, occasionally arrogant, and individualistic. Rank didn't seem to mean a damn thing except for the team leaders. We were extremely effective and little recognized."

Team leaders were the most critical element of the LRRP team and their orders were followed regardless of the rank of those accompanying the patrol. Despite this fact, the recruitment of noncommissioned officers was an even greater problem than securing enlisted volunteers.

As a result of the Army's expansion during the Vietnam years, NCOs were in short supply. Also, many of the older sergeants had been lost as casualties early in the war; many more had gained commissions as officers through battlefield appointments or Officers' Candidate School. As a result, in the Infantry, SP4s or corporals were often squad leaders with sergeants or staff sergeants acting as platoon sergeants. It was not uncommon by 1969 to find no NCOs with more than four years of service in either the LRRP or the infantry units except for 1st sergeants and operations sergeants.

The most common solution to this lack of NCOs in Vietnam was for units to "grow their own" sergeants. Arriving in-country as eighteen- or nineteen-year-old PFCs, soldiers who lived long enough and exhibited leadership potential often made sergeant E-5 by midtour.*

Another source of NCOs was the Fort Benning Non-Commissioned Officers' Candidate School (NCOC). Modeled after the Officers' Candidate School, NCOC al-

---

*There were no private E-1s or E-2s in Vietnam unless they had been reduced in rank for infractions of the Uniformed Code of Military Justice after their arrival. All soldiers were promoted to PFC immediately on arrival in the war zone.

lowed soldiers to continue training after the post-Induction basic and advanced courses and be promoted to sergeant E-5 upon completion. Another stripe was awarded, advancing the candidate to staff sergeant E-6 if he was an honor graduate of his class or volunteered to go to Ranger School and successfully completed the course. Rank that took six years or longer to earn in the peacetime army could be attained in less than twelve months of training. These "instant NCOs" or "shake and bakes," as they were known, filled many NCO leadership positions in Vietnam infantry and LRRP units soon after graduation.

Despite early promotion for proven combat leadership and the influx of instant NCOs from the stateside replacement pipeline, LRRPs and infantry units were always short of NCOs. A typical example was F Company, 52nd Infantry (LRP), later I Company (Ranger) of the 1st Infantry Division. The company's personnel status reports from 1968 to 1970 routinely showed the authorized number of officers on hand but reflected only twenty-seven to thirty of the authorized forty-four NCOs—this during a time when the company was at or occasionally above its total authorized strength. Shortages in NCOs were made up by assigning excess enlisted soldiers. PFCs and SP4s not only filled the vacant NCO slots in body but assumed their leadership roles as well.

Recruitment of officers for the LRRPs was not nearly as difficult as the securing of enlisted men and NCOs. With only one slot for either a major or captain and two to four for lieutenants in each of the thirteen companies, there were always more officer volunteers than positions available. Lieutenant Robert K. Suchke, a native of Dalonega, Georgia, and a member of L Company (Ranger) in the 101st, was typical of the LRRP officers. Suchke, still on active duty in 1987 as a lieutenant colonel in Special Forces, recalls, "I tried to get into the LRRPs from the time I arrived in-country. It was only after serving as an infantry platoon leader from July 1970 to February 1971 that I got my chance—and then it was only because the man I replaced had been killed and they needed a replacement 'fast.''

It was rare that officers were admitted into the LRRPs without previous combat experience. Most company commanders were on their second or third tours or specifically extended their current one for the chance to command the recon units.

Recruitment of officers was also assisted by the fact that infantry officers normally only spent six months in the field as platoon leaders or company commanders before being transferred to positions on their battalion or higher staff.*

Six months of field time was not enough for some officers, and many shunned the offer of rear jobs and sought to remain in action by transferring to the LRRPs. It was not uncommon in a LRRP company to find a commander on his second tour with all his platoon leaders (lieutenants) veterans of at least six months of combat before joining the unit.

LRRP officers took their jobs seriously. Captain George Paccerelli, while in command of H Company, received a letter from one soldier's father who was concerned about his son's welfare. Paccerelli responded, ''Rest assured I will do all I can for your son and insure that he has been properly trained and is being properly led. I have a keen interest in each and every one of my men. Due to the nature of our work, only the best remain in the company. Your son definitely receives close supervision. I demand, expect, and receive perfection in the execution of our duties. I promise that I will take good care of your son. He is a fine boy and a good soldier. Please don't overly worry about him; he has a good mind, pays attention to what he

---

*Although this practice added to the inconsistency of leadership caused by the one-year tour, the reasons for the policy were valid: experienced officers were needed on the rank-heavy staffs; most important, lieutenants and captains suffered the highest proportional casualties of the war. Of the 2,648 commissioned army officers killed by hostile action during the war, 2,433 were captains and lieutenants. Survival for six months as an officer in an infantry company was reason enough for transfer to a relatively safe staff job.

is told, and is a credit to his family, his country, and this company.''

LRRPs and those who were associated with them are as strong in their opinions today as they were efficient in their tasks in Vietnam. Unfortunately, there were neither studies made during the war nor statistics kept that give an overall picture of the LRRP. LRRPs and their leaders were never much for bureaucracy, and none were particularly concerned with the age, race, or background of the volunteers. No official summary of ages or other demographics was maintained on the LRRPs by DA, USARV, or any other agency. What statistics were kept, were maintained for the army as a whole.

It can be surmised from the characteristics of maturity, education, and experience as listed by the various LRRPs and their leaders that the recon men were older than their infantry counterparts. Although this is generally correct, the difference was not great—and there were many exceptions. LRRP recruiters sought volunteers who were mature in age and experience. However, they often had to settle for what was available, and Vietnam was by no means an old soldiers' war—especially in the infantry. LRRPs were older than the regular grunts, but by a matter of months rather than years.

In the LRRPs age was measured more by months in the field and in what a man had seen and done than by the date on a birth certificate. LRRPs were quite handy with rifles and grenades but had little use for pencils and paper. Even those LRRP commanders who did make the effort to record information beyond morning reports and operational summaries rarely passed them along to the various official archives or record centers.

One exception was Company E, 52nd Infantry (LRP), and the Ranger unit that evolved from it, H Company. Beginning in November 1968, Captain George Paccerelli published a newsletter several times a month for distribution to his troops. Paccerelli began the project ''because of the nature of our operations, that is, because it was rare that the full company could ever be assembled at any one time. I felt that it was important that all members be kept abreast of the Company's activities, lessons learned, and other information deemed necessary by myself, the 1st Sergeant or Operations.''

One of the few references to the actual ages of LRRPs appears in the H Company newsletter of July 21, 1969. A paragraph reporting recent praise for the company from the 1st Cavalry Division's chief of staff, Colonel R. M. Shoemaker, reads, ''Colonel Shoemaker later told the company commander that he hadn't realized how young the members of the company are; by their excellent accomplishments and professionalism he had expected much older men. (Average age of the company is 20.2 years.)''

By all accounts of LRRP veterans, the average age of H Company was typical of other units. While older than the average Vietnam soldier by half a year, few were old enough to order a beer legally back home. Perhaps the age of the LRRPs is best summed up by H Company veteran James W. Kraft, who would remain in the army after the war and, at this writing, is a sergeant major in the Washington, D.C., area. ''I arrived in Vietnam in December '68 as a PFC. I was nineteen years old, frightened, naive, with very little self-confidence. Twelve months later I would leave as a staff sergeant with a Silver Star, a Bronze Star for Valor, a Bronze Star for meritorious service, an Air Medal, and a Combat Infantryman Badge. I was a lot wiser and more confident, but still too young to vote.''

LRRP units wanted volunteers with above-average educational backgrounds because that was frequently an indicator of maturity as well as of intelligence. While the norm for volunteers was only a high school diploma, many LRRPs had completed a year or two of college, with a few having obtained degrees before enlisting or being drafted.

Officers in the LRRPs and other Vietnam units were generally graduates of colleges or from the U. S. Military Academy at West Point. Those who attended civilian universities had been commissioned through enrollment in ROTC while students or from OCS after graduation. A small minority had received direct or battlefield commissions. Still others had been commissioned through OCS with various amounts of college credits short of degree completion.

While colleges and universities were a prime source of officers for all of the services, they also were a haven for those more interested in maintaining their draft-exempt status than in education itself. The length of the Vietnam War and this draft loophole produced America's most-educated generation, as students stayed in college past undergraduate level to earn masters, doctorates, law degrees, or anything to remain deferred until the magical age of twenty-six, when a young man was no longer draft eligible.

Campuses were centers for war protest and dissent. Certainly, however, not every man enrolled in institutions of higher learning just to avoid the draft or to have a forum to protest the war. A majority were interested in furthering their educations. From the latter came a few who did not want their generation's war to pass while they were in the classroom. School could wait; the rites of passage offered only by serving one's country in time of conflict might not. For young men with strong enough convictions to leave the security of the campus and volunteer for Vietnam, the LRRPs offered the opportunity to join the best.

One distinction of the Vietnam War that is seldom mentioned is that it was the country's first conflict fought by a totally integrated army. Whites, blacks, Hispanics, and Asians fought side by side, with all races serving in all units and at all ranks—including the LRRPs.

Racial discord, particularly between blacks and whites, back home and in the war zone, was much in the news at the time. This portrayal, especially in the final years of the war, was to some degree accurate. However, it is rarely noted that racial problems were a characteristic of the rear areas and virtually nonexistent in the field combat units. Infantrymen in line or recon units, who depended on each other in day-to-day, life-threatening situations, did not fight among themselves. Men who shared the exhilaration and terror of combat formed a brotherhood far deeper than skin color. Racial prejudice and the resulting reactions

were generally for the rear-echelon types—not the warriors.

Due to their small numbers and volunteer status, LRRPs
were a minority themselves. If they harbored any preju-
dices, it was against the enemy in general and specifically
for anyone, regardless of side or cause, who was not a
LRRP. Color, creed, or religion mattered little to the men
with painted faces. Under the camouflage paint they might
be of different origins, but being in Vietnam and being
LRRPs made them all the same in their eyes and minds.

Again, no particular statistics were kept on LRRPs as
to racial background as compared to the rest of the army.
Memories of LRRP veterans and information gleaned by
studying morning reports and unit roster surnames reveal
that the racial makeup of LRRP units was similar to the
infantry with some exceptions—some explainable, others
not as much so. In general, LRRPs had a slightly higher
ratio of foreign-born soldiers, Hispanics, American Indians, and American Asians, but slightly fewer blacks than
found in the infantry and other units.

Refugees after World War II, and later escapees from
behind the Iron Curtain, particularly Hungary, Czechoslovakia, and Poland, were drawn to the U.S. Army to gain
their citizenship and to fight the communism that had en-
gulfed their countries. Because of their language skills,
these men often joined the Special Forces, and many later
transferred to the LRRPs.

One such was Staff Sergeant Laszlo Rabel, who was
born in Budapest, Hungary, in 1939. Rabel escaped Eastern Europe as a teenager, leading a blind friend through
a border minefield to freedom. Eventually making his way
to the United States, Rabel joined the army, as his friends
recall, "to fight communists."

Rabel must have believed communism was where one
found it because by 1968 he was fighting VC and NVA as
a team leader in the 74th Infantry Detachment (LRP) of
the 173rd Airborne Brigade. On November 13, in Binh
Dinh Province, Rabel threw himself on an enemy grenade
in order to save the other members of his team. He was

posthumously awarded the nation's highest recognition of valor, the Medal of Honor. (For the complete citation of Rabel's actions and those of other LRRP Medal of Honor recipients, see Appendix D.)

Another source of foreign-born LRRPs was Canada. Although it was often associated with being a refuge for those who fled the United States to avoid the draft and Vietnam service, Canada also provided many young men who shared and assisted in the U.S. war efforts. Canada was not officially involved in the war, and while it did not encourage draft dodgers to take up residence, neither did it discourage them. While many Canadians opposed our involvement in Southeast Asia, many others supported it— some with enough zeal to cross the border and volunteer for the U.S. armed forces. For a few, their purpose was solely to gain American citizenship, but for others their intentions were focused on helping friends. Another important reason, and perhaps the most common, was simply the spirit of adventure. After all, it was the only war available for an entire generation of North Americans.

Many of the over thirty thousand Canadians who served in Vietnam sought out the more challenging jobs, such as infantry, and some volunteered for the ultimate combat challenge—the LRRPs.

Hispanics, including Mexican-Americans, Cubans, and Puerto Ricans, also volunteered for the LRRPs in slightly larger numbers than were found in the rest of the army. Veteran Hispanics jokingly, but seriously, reflect that in addition to the usual motivations to be a recon soldier, the danger and independence of the LRRPs appealed to their macho sensibilities.

Many Cuban LRRPs had a more deliberate purpose in joining the LRRPs. Cuban-born, or sons of native Cubans who had emigrated or escaped from their island homeland, they looked to Vietnam as a means of fighting the same oppression that had overrun their homeland. If they could not fight the enemy just ninety miles off the Florida coastline, then the war in Vietnam over thirteen thousand miles away would have to do.

American Indians also seemed to be attracted to the LRRPs. Their numbers were not great, but nearly every LRRP veteran recalls at least one Indian in his company. Indian recon men made sense if for no other reason than historical perspective. Rangers had their beginnings in colonial America, learning how to out-Indian the Indian. In Vietnam, where the LRRPs worked to out-guerrilla the guerrilla, the idea of a Native American out-Indianing the guerrilla seemed most appropriate.

Don W. Dupont, originally from Rockford, Illinois, who served in the ranks of private through sergeant E-5 in the 9th Infantry Division's Company E, 50th Infantry (LRP), recalls an Indian from Oklahoma who not only out-Indianed the guerrilla but maintained his ancient tribal traditions as well.

Dupont says, "We had an Indian on our team by the name of Reddoor who was the son of a chief. Every time he got a body count, he had the company commander write his father confirming the kill so he would be authorized another feather in his ceremonial war bonnet when he got home."

Japanese-, Chinese-, Korean-, and Hawaiian-Americans were attracted to the LRRPs for much the same reasons as other soldiers. In addition, they were actively sought after because of their oriental appearance. Recon men who closely resembled the enemy they faced gave the LRRP teams an advantage of seconds while the VC and NVA decided whether a chance jungle encounter was with friend or foe. Some LRRP teams even dressed Asian-Americans in captured enemy uniforms and had them carry AK-47s to provide an added edge.

Blacks played an important role in the LRRPs, as they did in every other unit in Vietnam. Many blacks were LRRPs, but statistically fewer blacks served in LRRP units than were found in other units.

Many explanations for the smaller representation are difficult to credit, ranging from "there really was no reason" to "mathematically some type unit had to have fewer—others more" and "blacks as a whole were reluctant to be volunteers.'' The first two explanations are ambiguous at best and the latter reason is proven invalid by the fact that above-average numbers of blacks are found in other elite volunteer units such as the airborne.

A better explanation may lie in the sociological traits of blacks as a whole. Black soldiers usually came from gregarious homes and neighborhoods where there was extensive interaction between individuals. LRRP operations required extreme individualism where the ''loner'' type was much more comfortable than men who valued peer interaction.

Another probable cause, admittedly a bit farfetched but still having some validity, was the requirement of the Fort Benning Ranger School, since its formation in 1951, that all students should be able to swim. Public swimming pools before the 1960s were often for whites only. Also, few swimming areas were available in the large urban areas where many blacks grew up. It was not that blacks could not learn to swim; it was just that few had ever had the opportunity to learn.

A counter to this line of thinking, of course, is that there was no such requirement to be able to swim to join the Vietnam LRRPs. Still, LRRPs evolved from Rangers and Rangers they were to become again in 1969. Despite the fact that there had been an all-black Ranger company in the Korean War, relatively few black soldiers attended the Ranger School.*

LRRPs were little concerned about the reasons for the unit's ethnic makeup. It was the man, not the color, that made the difference. To be a LRRP was to be first and above all a LRRP. All other characteristics and past experiences were a distant second, if considered at all.

By the nature of the craft of reconnaissance, it would seem likely that LRRPs came from rural backgrounds. Experience gained from growing up on farms, ranches, or

---

*Even in today's army blacks are found in above-average numbers in the airborne units but in below-average numbers in Ranger battalions.

in the woods seemingly could be adapted to the requirements of stealth and independence required in recon work.

Once again the obvious did not prove accurate. LRRPs
came from every background—from the most isolated parts
of the country to the largest cities. If any trend at all can
be identified about the hometowns of the men who volunteered for the LRRPs, it is that a majority came from
medium-sized cities of fifty thousand to one hundred thousand. Of course, it must be realized that cities of this
population range dominate the country. As there was no
typical LRRP, neither was there a single type of hamlet
or upbringing that stands out as a principal characteristic.

It was not unusual to find in a single LRRP team men
from such diverse places as Sacramento, California; Ro-
tan, Texas; Rapid City, South Dakota; Roseville, Michigan; Mars Hill, Maine; and New York, New York. It was
the men themselves, not demographics, that made the
LRRPs unique.

One item that provides insight as to the type of man
drawn to the LRRPs is the nicknames that were bestowed
upon them by their fellow recon men. In a summary of
actions of L Company Rangers of the 101st during 1970,
nicknames were sprinkled throughout the report. Included
were "Mad Dog," "Paul Bunyon," "Termite," "Georgia Peach," "Mountain Man," "Kamikazie," "Under-
taker," "Gloves," and "Body Bag."

Vietnam, as other wars before it, caused men to turn to
or turn from religion. Battle has a way of making men
seek divine protection through prayer or giving up on religion altogether in a belief that no merciful God could
allow mankind to experience the horrors of warfare. Still
others evolved to believing that they themselves were more
powerful than any divine being.

LRRPs came from all kinds of religious backgrounds,
with varied degrees of devoutness and practice. Some of
the recon men held firm in their beliefs while others deep-
ened their religious convictions. However, the general tendency seemed to be that the longer they remained in the
recon units, the more the men believed in the reality of

themselves and their fellow LRRPs than in any superior being.

An old military axiom states, "There are no atheists in foxholes." While the theory is not accurate in itself, it was even less valid in the LRRPs—either figuratively or literally. LRRPs survived through silence. They did not dig foxholes. The recon men pretty well thought that God was on whichever side won—that was the way He remained God.

Many LRRPs recall that, after multiple successful missions of killing the enemy in numbers totaling ten, twenty, or even fifty for every LRRP lost, they developed a sense of cautious invulnerability. Don Dupont says of his days as a 9th Infantry Division LRRP, "After being shot at and missed so many times, you began to think that you could not be hit."

No chaplains were assigned to LRRP units. At a base camp, between missions, a chaplain might visit and hold services, but attendance was not heavy. Dupont does remember a time when his unit was an exception, filling a pew for every service.

Their attendance was not, however, entirely voluntary. It seems that, when the base chapel was being built, a group of LRRPs "appropriated" a truckload of plywood meant for the chapel walls and used it to build the LRRPs' private bar. When a chaplain discovered what his wood had become, it was too late to recover it. His reaction was to demand a pew full of LRRPs at every service or he would report the theft to the division commander.

It might be expected that the hazardous missions, which were routine for LRRP operations, would result in many individual valor awards. The men with painted faces certainly received their share, but few LRRPs were in the business for bits of medal and pieces of colored ribbon.

Nearly two decades after the war, LRRPs are still more inclined to talk about unit successes than personal accomplishments. Recon work was dangerous in itself, and since all were volunteers for the dangerous missions, no one expected any recognition other than being known as a

LRRP. Commanders often recommended their men for awards only to have the LRRP say not to bother, that he was only doing his job. In the same spirit, many LRRPs turned down recommendations for direct commissions or the opportunity to attend OCS so that they could remain recon men.

The LRRPs' general opinion of individual medals is perhaps best typified by Marshall C. Huckaby of Warner Robbins, Georgia. Huckaby, a July 1966 to April 1967 veteran of the provisional unit that preceded Company F (LRP) 50th Infantry in the 25th Infantry Division, recalls, "In the fall of '66 we were given the special mission of escorting a civilian scientist from the University of Montana deep into the jungle near the Cambodian border to study the effects of defoliation from what years later I learned was Agent Orange. The professor was a hell of a guy. After every mission he presented each member of the patrol a three-inch circular Junior Smokey the Bear Forest Ranger patch. We sewed them on our uniforms—they were a highly coveted item."

While individual awards were not of great interest, recognition of LRRP units was. LRRP, and later Ranger, companies were some of the most decorated units of the war. (For a complete listing of U.S. and foreign awards earned by the LRRPs and Rangers, see Appendix E.)

While LRRPs came from all kinds of background, locations, and experiences, their reasons for volunteering for the recon units were fairly similar. Most were attracted by the aspect of being in an elite unit doing what others could not or cared not to do. LRRP units provided all the excitement, intensity, challenge, and adventure that any soldier could desire.

In addition to the "super soldier" requirements and image of the LRRPs, the recon units offered other inducements for volunteers. LRRPs had a well-deserved reputation for sustaining relatively few casualties when compared to the "meatgrinder" of the infantry units. By design, LRRPs generally avoided enemy contact in accomplishing their principal mission, reconnaissance. When

LRRPs chose to fight, it was usually on their own terms with the odds heavily weighted in their favor. If a mission was compromised by enemy detection, LRRP teams were quickly extracted. If engaged by a superior force, their parent brigade or division piled on air, artillery, and ground assets in their support.

Some LRRP veterans offer an even more practical motivation behind their volunteering. The typical LRRP mission was three to seven days in length, and rarely more than nine days were passed in the boonies before the team was extracted and stood down at a base camp for three days or so to prepare for the next mission. Regular infantry units often spent weeks and even months in the field without breaks. Despite the dangers of conducting small patrols far from other friendly units, spending fewer days in the field had its own appeal.

Whatever was behind individuals' volunteering for LRRP duty, most sincerely liked being a man with a painted face. Few LRRPs requested transfers back to the regular infantry, and far more LRRPs than infantry grunts extended their one-year tours to remain in Vietnam. Extensions were normally granted in six-month increments and many LRRPs extended repeatedly rather than return to the States. It was not unusual to find LRRPs with two or more extensions and some with as many as three continuous years in the same LRRP unit.

Major General (Retired) Salve H. Matheson, who commanded the 1st Brigade of the 101st from February 1967 to February 1968, recalls, "During my period of command, two-thirds [of the LRRPs] extended."

The extension rate in Matheson's brigade was well above the average, which was between twelve and twenty percent in most LRRP units. When compared to the extension rate of less than five percent in the infantry units, it is apparent that LRRPs liked being LRRPs.

An excellent summation of the motivation to extend, as well as the reasons behind being a LRRP to begin with, is offered by Lee Roy Pipkin, a recon veteran of the 173rd Airborne Infantry Brigade's 74th Infantry Detachment

(LRP). Pipkin, who served as a team leader and was evacuated to the States after sustaining serious wounds while on a six-month extension, recalls, ''Part of the reason I extended was I had no real family back home. Both of my parents were dead. The primary reasons were not really that, though. I loved my work, I loved my job. There was a feeling in the LRRPs of comradery, closeness, and an intensity in living life—the extremes of life, and death. I wasn't ready to return to the false sense of values, the phoniness, of stateside. I did not want to leave Vietnam. I felt I would be abandoning a special fraternity, a brotherhood. We were doing something very special, very elite.''

CHAPTER 7

●━━━━━━●

Training

"Training must be a paramount consideration if LRRP
units are to accomplish their missions,"
—paragraph 2-6a, "Training," FM 31-18 (1968), *Long
Range Reconnaissance Patrol Company*.

THE paragraph continues: "Areas for train-
ing emphasis should include patrolling (with special focus
on point and area reconnaissance patrols), engineer terrain
reconnaissance, combat surveillance, airmobile and air-
landed operations, rough terrain parachute operations, target acquisition, forward observer procedures, use of night
vision devices, and other special technical aids for collection information. Members should be experts in evasion
escape, survival, communications security and procedures, and advanced first aid procedures including manual
transportation of the sick and wounded. In order to properly report their observations of the enemy, patrol members must be proficient in the principles of intelligence
information collection, land navigation, map reading, tactical terrain analysis, and spot reporting. They must also
be familiar with enemy tactics, organization, uniforms,
weapons, equipment, and logistical systems. Realistic
long-range reconnaissance, surveillance, and target acqui-

sition exercises should be incorporated into LRRP unit training to evaluate individual and unit proficiency and serve as the basis for further training. Training should be progressive rather than repetitive, with emphasis on practical application and cross training once basic and special skills have been learned.''

Paragraph 2-6b of the same manual states: ''Experience suggests that normally about eight months are required to produce an effectively trained and reliable LRRP unit.''

In stating training requirements, the 1968 version of FM 31-18 was an improvement over the 1962 and 1965 editions. A notable deletion from the first two manuals was the statement: ''Intensive specialized training conducted prior to the time the division or smaller unit is employed in active operations is mandatory if provisional LRPs are to accomplish long range reconnaissance operations.''

As has been illustrated in Chapter 5, LRRPs in Vietnam, with the exception of those in the 173rd and D Company, 151st Infantry (LRP) of the Indiana National Guard, did not have the luxury of intensive training or the eight months of preparatory time as outlined in the FMs. In the early years of the war, provisional LRRP units were hastily organized and committed to battle with a minimum of training. Training in the safe environs of a stateside post was an opportunity lost because LRRP units were not organized before their parent unit's deployment to Southeast Asia. LRRP training in Vietnam was strictly ''on the job,'' with a brief period of unit training in or near semi-secure fire bases.

The one-year tour policy caused a constant turnover of personnel in all units. In the first years of the war, deploying units were filled with experienced soldiers who could adapt quickly to LRRP techniques. As time passed and the numbers of units committed rapidly increased, experienced soldiers became few and far between.

With the exception of the LRRP officers, who were almost all graduates of the Fort Benning Ranger School, few LRRPs had any recon training before arriving in Vietnam.

Some NCOs had attended the Ranger School or the Jungle Warfare Course in Panama, but they were a minority.

The army had long claimed that sweat during peacetime training saves blood on the battlefield. Unfortunately, when a war actually begins, time is the commodity in shortest supply. While the sixteen weeks of basic infantry training may have been marginally adequate for conventional infantry replacements, it was woefully inadequate to prepare a replacement for the LRRPs. The skill required for a soldier to conduct effective recon operations were as difficult to acquire as any specialty in the war zone. Sweat and, all too often, blood had to be shed before the replacement could become a contributing member of the LRRPs. Leaders did their best to ensure that it was more of the former than the latter.

LRRP commanders recognized that volunteers—whether from the parent unit's one-week orientation course, veterans of a partial tour, or those returning for a second tour—required additional training before joining a team on patrol. Soon after the initial provisional LRRP units were formed, each company and detachment established its own training programs. There were two reasons for this: first, there were many skills to teach; second, the training offered an excellent opportunity to weed out those who were not capable or well-enough motivated to become recon soldiers.

Some commands established LRRP training courses concurrent with the formation of the provisional recon unit. A report to the Department of the Army (December 23, 1967) from the 9th Infantry Division stated, "The Long Range Patrol Detachment is presently organized under the provisions of General Order 3125, dated July 8, 1967. An intensive two-week training program was established to prepare new members in specialized skills and techniques of reconnaissance work. The program of instruction is based upon doctrine established by the MACV Recondo School and lessons learned from experienced LRRP leaders. Close supervision and intensive training are the instrumental factors for the successful preparation of graduates to be employed directly in operational long range patrols.''

The training for LRRP replacements lasted from seven to fourteen days, depending on the unit. Closely resembling a mini–Ranger School, the intense requirements and long hours made for a demanding training period. Physical fitness, weapons proficiency, land navigation, enemy organization, patrolling techniques, and artillery and air adjustment were priority subjects. Though compressing the recommended eight months of training into less than two weeks, the subjects taught closely paralleled the topics listed in FM 31-18. (For an example of the LRRP training schedule for replacements, see Appendix F.)

Initial LRRP training was conducted under the supervision of the operations NCO or a specially designated training NCO. Occasionally one of the platoon leaders had the additional duty of training officer if the unit commander so desired. Instructors came from the teams and LRRPs who were nearing the end of their tours. The training cadre was in constant change, as the best instructors were those with the most recent mission experience.

Upon completion of the training, the LRRP candidate was still not guaranteed a place on the unit's roster. Before that occurred, he had to complete from one to three patrols as a probationer. If a team leader found the probationer's performance to be satisfactory—which often meant accepting the new man as a member of his own team—the volunteer was awarded the black beret, the scroll shoulder patch, and full status of a LRRP. If not, or if the LRRP candidate chose to do so on his own, he was returned to the infantry replacement stream.

Another avenue open to further training of volunteers was the Recondo School operated by the Special Forces. Originally organized to train replacements for Detachment B-52, which ran recon missions for the Special Forces, the Recondo School trained LRRPs and other allied recon soldiers as well.

The Recondo School taught much the same program of instruction as the LRRP companies. Located at the west end of the Nha Trang airfield, the school primarily trained individuals except for a short period after it was established in September 1966. For several training cycles in the school's early months, each class was made up of entire teams from the various units. C. A. McDonald, Jr., an Omaha, Nebraska, native, attended one of the first Recondo classes with his team as a member of the 173rd's provisional LRRPs. He recalls, "It was a tough course, not so much in itself as in the competition with LRRPs from other units. Physical training was particularly rough. Each day it was led by a different team and each tried to outdo the other in running further and faster."

McDonald, who went on to extend his tour by six months to remain with the 173rd LRRPs and returned to Vietnam for a second tour four years later with the Americal Division's G Company Rangers, offers other insights on the three-week Recondo School and what it meant to be a LRRP. "I was an honor graduate of my Recondo class; received the dagger they gave you for being the best. But, you know, I never really did like it. I hated to run, was afraid of heights—all my life I had been working to overcome fears. Recondo and LRRPs made me feel like a professional and safe in any situation. I ended up staying in the army for twenty years because of those days in recon."

Spaces in the Recondo School were not always easy to secure and often LRRPs were veterans of many missions before getting the opportunity to attend. Part of the delay was intentional on the part of the LRRP units. They did not want anyone going to the school who would not do the unit proud.

Other units considered completion of the Recondo School critical to a LRRP volunteer before he was deployed on patrols. Some went so far as to focus their unit training strictly on preparation for the school at Nha Trang. A report (February 8, 1968) from the Americal Division states, "A program conducting training courses in long range patrol techniques commenced on December 4, 1967. The primary purpose of the course is to provide training for new members of the Division's Company E, 51st Infantry (LRP) prior to those personnel attending the MACV Recondo School. The training is conducted by the LRP company."

As a basis for instruction, the LRRP-unit training courses and the Recondo School relied heavily on lessons learned in actual combat, supplemented by army field and training manuals that filled shelf after shelf of wall space. The manuals were rarely used for more than casual reference, however, as they had been written almost entirely for conventional warfare. Beyond the company commander and the operations NCO, it was rare to find a LRRP who had ever heard of, much less seen or possessed, FM 31-18. Rather than any official publication, the bible of the LRRPs was a pocket-size, one-inch thick document with a tan cover, the *Ranger Handbook*.

The *Ranger Handbook* was published by the Infantry School at Fort Benning as the principal guide for Ranger students. Chapters detailed patrol planning and leading, steps and guides to the use of communications, fire support, demolitions, and aerial resupply. Other sections of the handbook gave particulars on such topics as how to tie knots for mountaineering, rope bridges, and stream crossings. First-aid and survival techniques were also included. Offering the most useful information gleaned from dozens of other manuals—mixed with checklists developed in training and combat—the handbook was as practical, or more so, as all the other army publications combined.

*Ranger Handbook*s were prized possessions, with their proud owners often covering the pages with waterproof acetate to protect them from the elements. Additional pages or notes were added with information more pertinent to the LRRP's area of operation or specialized mission.

The first copies of the handbook arrived in Vietnam in the jungle fatigue pockets of soldiers who were graduates of the Ranger course. Later, LRRP commanders and NCOs wrote back to Fort Benning to secure additional copies for their men. It became the bible not only for the individual LRRP but also the primary reference material for the orientation courses and unit refresher training.

Interestingly, like many items of LRRP and Ranger history, the *Ranger Handbook* was not an official army document. Some sources claim that the "to the point without any bullshit" focus of the handbook was counter to the usual verbosity of army literature. Others say that the booklet outlines the "Ranger way" of doing things and not necessarily the "army way."*

One aspect of LRRP training that is somewhat misunderstood is the fact that not all of the recon men were airborne-qualified. All of the editions of the FM 31-18 and the related tables of organization and equipment stated that parachute training was a prerequisite for becoming a LRRP. Originally, LRRPs were to be able to enter their recon zones by airborne means. The Korean War recon units were officially designated Airborne Ranger or Ranger Airborne companies. Also, Airborne and Ranger have long been synonymous, whether through association with unit-marching "jody calls" (risque marching songs), barroom reference, or the pages of official documents.

While the discipline, physical conditioning, and volunteer spirit of the airborne would have been positive attributes for the LRRP candidate, in reality the actual skill of reaching the battlefield by means of parachute in Vietnam was not. Helicopters offered a far safer and faster means of insertion. Even in areas where no landing zones were available, LRRPs could rappel down ropes from hovering aircraft into the jungle. Helicopters also offered a means

---

*In the more than a decade and a half since the war, the *Ranger Handbook* has changed little. The most noticeable differences in the current edition (June 1984) is the slightly smaller size and a new green-and-black, camouflage-pattern cover. Although now labeled a training circular, TC 21-76, it is still not an official army manual. On the inside a disclaimer reads: "This publication reflects the current thoughts of the United States Infantry School and conforms to published Department of the Army doctrine as closely as possible. It is not available through the USA Adjutant General Publication Center [the army's official distribution center]."

The key words in that paragraph are "conforms . . . as closely as possible." Getting Rangers of today or of yesterday to conform even closely is an ambitious objective.

of quick extraction not available to fixed-wing aircraft. If no pickup zone was available, LRRPs could climb rope ladders to hovering choppers or be "hooked out" at the end of a rope on a harness called a McGuire Rig.

The only two LRRP units to have all their personnel airborne-qualified for their entire stay in Vietnam were the 74th Infantry Detachment (LRP), later redesignated N Company, 75th Infantry (Ranger), of the 173rd Airborne Brigade and D Company, 151st Infantry, which served as both LRRPs and later Rangers. As the only brigade or larger unit to maintain its airborne status for the entire war, the 173rd accepted only jump-qualified replacements. The LRRP company from the Indiana National Guard had required that its original volunteers all be airborne or willing to attend the three-week school during their training before deployment to the war zone. Since the company was only in-country for a year, they were able to maintain their all-airborne status.

Two other companies, Company E, 20th Infantry (LRP), later Company C Rangers, and Company F, 51st Infantry (LRP), later Company D Rangers, of the I and II Field Forces, were originally organized as all-airborne. Although they both were able to maintain that status for part of the war, they, too, at times had non-jump-qualified members.

Other LRRP units made initial efforts to recruit airborne volunteers, but as the war went on, less and less emphasis was placed on jump experience. By the time LRRP units were redesignated Ranger companies, non-airborne personnel were assigned to most units.

There was one advantage to being airborne-qualified beyond the excellent Fort Benning training. Because all LRRP and Ranger units were authorized airborne personnel in their official manning documents, those who wore jump wings were authorized to received hazardous duty pay. Officers received an extra $110 a month while enlisted men received $55. The stateside requirement to jump at least once every three months to remain on jump status was waived in the combat zone.

Although not required to do so, under the pretext of training for future missions, many LRRPs did make parachute jumps in Vietnam. The real reason was, generally, just for the fun of it. Company E, 20th Infantry LRP, made its first jump with fourteen members of the new unit on November 11, 1967, just more than a month after its organization. According to the unit's daily staff journal, all the jump accomplished was to attract an inquiry from the MACV Public Information Office to cover the next drop.

When time was available between missions, other LRRPs journeyed to the ARVN Airborne School at Dalat to jump with the Vietnamese. The only purpose of the "training" was to be awarded the school's jump wings. Still other LRRPs would scrounge up any parachutes available and get a willing helicopter pilot to take them up. Such jumps were always accomplished in secure areas and had nothing to do with the LRRP mission.

The only actual combat parachute operation of the war was conducted by the 173rd on February 17, 1967, in War Zone C in Tay Ninh Province as a part of Operation JUNCTION CITY. Although the brigade's LRRPs did not participate in the actual drop, they did play an important role. Hours before the jump, LRRP teams were inserted by helicopter near the designated drop zone. By the time the parachute operation began, the LRRPs had thoroughly reconned the area and reported that no enemy ambush awaited the assault from the sky.*

The LRRP's training did not end with completion of the unit's orientation course or even after he was a veteran of multiple missions. Commanders conducted additional training for their troops between missions and on occasion—usually every three or four months—brought as many of the company together as operationally possible to teach new techniques or to reemphasize old ones.

---

*Stateside newspapers and magazines carried front-page coverage of the 173rd's airborne assault, headlining it as the first combat jump by American forces since the Korean War. Typically, no mention was made of the LRRPs.

Teams were also frequently called upon to attach themselves briefly to regular infantry units to teach ambush and recon techniques. The classes were held for any infantry unit requesting them, but the primary audiences were the members of the infantry battalion recon platoons.*

One division, the 101st, went so far as to formalize the training by LRRPs and to establish a school of its own. Run by Rangers of L Company, the school went even further after the MACV Recondo School ceased operations in early 1971. In May of that year, it reclaimed the name of Recondo School and opened its training to all personnel in the division in the grades of private first class to lieutenant. According to Robert Suchke, who, as a lieutenant in L Company, presented many of the school's classes, "It all seemed very appropriate for us to reclaim the Recondo School title since it had been the 101st that had established the first one back at Fort Campbell before the war in Vietnam began."†

Other sources of training were available to LRRPs with specific operational challenges. LRRPs from such units as the 9th Infantry Division and the 199th Light Infantry Brigade found much of their area of operations in the Delta region to be more water than land. Navy SEALS and Riv-

---

*These recon platoons are not to be confused with the LRRPs. Each infantry battalion was composed of three or four "line" companies and a headquarters company. Each battalion had an additional company composed of platoons of heavy 4.2-inch mortars, ground surveillance radar, and a scout or recon element. The recon platoons were comprised of twenty to thirty men under the command of a lieutenant and could operate as a unit or break down into squads or teams of six to ten men. Although the recon platoons operated similarly to the LRRPs, they did not venture far from supporting units. Their mission was to recon only in their parent battalion's area of operation. Another difference was that in many battalions, the recon elements were utilized more like a mini-company, conducting missions similar to those of the line companies rather than true reconnaissance work. Regardless of their mission, the recon platoons were generally the best of their battalion and, while they did not profess to be true LRRPs, were quite proud of their designation as "recon."

†Graduates of the MACV and original 101st Recondo Schools received awards for successful completion of the courses. The MACV school awarded an arrowhead patch that was black and white with "Recondo" spelled out at the top, a large "V" (for Vietnam) below. The 101st Recondo patch was the same color and shape with a "101" instead of a "V" and without "Recondo." Both patches were intended for wear on the upper-right shirt pocket of the uniform.

erine Assault forces offered training in the use of boats for transportation and fire support.

LRRPs also secured demolitions training from engineer units. Usually each team had at least one man who was an expert with explosives. LRRPs frequently captured more equipment than they could carry, and the easiest solution was to destroy the excess in place.

Since the key to the success of the LRRPs was in their ability to report what they found, communications training was also essential. The LRRPs could communicate with their support operations centers far into the no-man's-land in which they operated by learning how to use a variety of radios and to erect field-expedient antennas.

Additional medical training was also essential as no medics accompanied LRRP teams on patrol. Rapid evacuation of wounded by helicopter limited the requirement for medical knowledge, but the initial treatment on the battlefield was often the difference between life and death. Each individual carried a first-aid kit and was well versed in the traditional lifesaving steps: clearing the airway, stopping the bleeding, protecting and dressing the wound, and treating for shock. One team member, usually the assistant patrol leader, carried a larger aid bag containing more bandages and drugs for treatment of wounds and illnesses. (For a detailed listing of medical supplies carried on patrol, see Chapter 8, "Equipment.")

Specialized marksmanship training for LRRPs was available at the 25th Infantry Division's Sniper Course at Cu Chi. Primarily using the M-14 rifle fitted with either day or night scopes, the sniper school taught riflemen to make one-shot kills at up to eight hundred meters.

Although sniping was not a primary mission, LRRPs used the technique at times as a means of gaining body count and damaging the opponent's morale. A single, well-aimed shot from a long distance was difficult to defend against. The only sign that a sniper had been at work was the lifeless body of his target.

LRRPs maintained at least two or three sniper-qualified

individuals in each unit. Numbers varied depending upon the terrain. In the thick jungles there were rarely enough clearings and fields of fire for the sniper to be effective. In the relatively open Delta region, LRRPs frequently increased the number of sniper-trained individuals so that there was one per team.*

The men with painted faces had no lack of pride in their abilities to out-guerrilla the guerrilla. However, they were modest enough to seek out additional training regardless of the source. Individuals and teams cross-trained with Australian recon elements and ARVN Rangers.† They also visited the various ARVN schools. Good ideas were adopted from ally and enemy alike. LRRPs were no more hesitant to borrow techniques from any available source than they were to borrow needed supplies or equipment that was not properly secured.

The necessity of proper training for the recon men was recognized at command levels higher than just in the LRRP units. Westmoreland had the foresight to establish the Recondo School early in the war. General Peers emphasized the importance of intense training of the newly formed LRRP units in his presentation to the Commanders' Conference in September 1967 that had paved the way to official recognition of the recon units. General Bolling laments that the most critical problem in fielding his LRRPs upon the arrival of the 82nd in 1968 was the lack of training time. Perhaps the importance of training is best

---

*LRRP snipers and those in conventional infantry units were very effective. According to an Operations Report/Lessons Learned Report of the 9th Infantry Division dated February 28, 1969, a sergeant in the 3rd Battalion, 60th Infantry of the Division's Second Brigade, accounted for eighty-two sniper kills. Sniping was a very personal way of killing. Veteran marksmen state that the experienced sniper could place the telescopic crosshairs between a man's eyes from over a quarter of a mile away, pull the trigger, and readjust the sight picture after the weapon's recoil in time to see the bullet strike the target.

†The ARVN Rangers should not be confused with the U.S. LRRP/Rangers. Although they were the very best of the South Vietnamese military, the ARVN Rangers were organized into and fought as battalion-size units. They were used as a mobile strike force, transported to whatever was the "hot spot" of the time. Their missions were almost exclusively combat and very little reconnaissance was conducted.

summed up by Bolling when he says, ''LRRPs were the best of the best. There was nothing that they could not do—if properly trained.''

CHAPTER 8
○○○○○○○

Equipment

UNIFORMS, weapons, equipment, and supplies used by the LRRPs were as diversified—or more so—than those employed by warriors in any previous conflict. The LRRP philosophy was to use whatever was available, for whatever purpose was necessary. Great latitude was allowed and taken in clothing, weapons, communications gear, and anything deemed essential for a team of six men to operate in the enemy's backyard and, on occasion, in his living room.

If a needed item was in the normal supply channels, the LRRPs requested it. If an item was not available, or was thought to be unnecessary by the logistics "bean counters," the recon men "borrowed" it, using the same stealth and silent tactics that enabled them to succeed in the jungle. If the supply depots' security was tight, the LRRPs bartered, using trophies taken from fallen enemies. If an item of equipment made in North Vietnam, China, or the USSR seemed a necessary addition to the LRRP arsenal, all the recon man had to do was wait for the supply channel—a VC or NVA soldier—to walk down the trail.

Equipping themselves was a constantly changing, evolutionary process. Variations in equipment were based on areas of operation, preferences of LRRP commanders, and the individual desires of the team leaders and patrol members. Equipment varied from company to company, team to team, and individual to individual. What a LRRP wore and carried depended not on regulations or tradition but simply on what the LRRPs perceived as necessary to accomplish the assigned mission.

The basic uniform of all U.S. soldiers in Vietnam was the lightweight, olive-drab jungle fatigue. The cotton jungle fatigues were designed to dry rapidly when wet and to withstand the rigors of long-term wear in the field. The trousers had a big cargo pocket on each thigh capable of holding a map, a ration packet, or other large items. Two more pockets on the front at belt level and a couple over the buttocks offered still more carrying space. Drawstrings at the leg openings assisted in blousing the trousers at the boot tops to prevent insects from crawling up the soldier's legs. Additional protection could be provided by placing the bloused trouser legs inside the tops of the boots and lacing tightly.

The fatigue shirt was cut long to be worn outside the trousers rather than tucked in. Four large pockets were on the front of the shirt. Pockets on both shirt and trousers had a small, reinforced hole at the bottom of each so that water could drain after stream crossings or during monsoon rains. Tops of the shirt pockets slanted inward to assist in shedding water.*

Through the long years of the war, jungle fatigues were modified several times. Pocket placement was changed and draw tabs were added to the shirts and trousers to assist in their fit. The most practical modification was in replacing the ordinary cotton material with a cotton ripstop poplin that made the uniform much more durable.

Jungle fatigues were an excellent uniform for the ordinary American soldier. However, LRRPs were not ordi-

---

*It is interesting to note that in the stateside, peacetime army soldiers are never allowed to carry anything in their pockets where a bulge would detract from a sharp, parade-field appearance. In combat, practicality overrode spit and polish, and pockets were used for what they were intended.

nary—and ordinary uniforms were not always sufficient for their missions.

The major advantage of the jungle fatigue uniform for the LRRPs was that it made the recon men in the boonies look like any other infantryman. In a chance encounter, the enemy did not know if the jungle-fatigue-clad LRRP was a member of a small recon team or the lead element of a much larger unit. The disadvantage of jungle fatigues was that they did not offer sufficient camouflage for a team trying to blend in with its surroundings. As a result, many LRRP units secured—by requisition when able, and by trade and theft when necessary—various types of multi-colored and -patterned camouflage uniforms.

The primary camouflage uniform available through the official supply system was the khaki background, green-and-black spotted, "leopard" fatigues that dated to Korea and World War II. With the exception of defoliated areas and a few grassy regions, the "leopards" stood out rather than blended in with surrounding vegetation.

The uniform that was not in the supply system and proved over time to be the LRRP uniform of choice was "tiger fatigues." Composed of irregular green-and-black shadowy stripes, "tigers" blended well with jungle and grasslands alike. Tiger fatigues were available from the ARVNs but were made to Asian scale. Even the size large was barely big enough for the smallest LRRP. The Special Forces ordered some larger sizes made, and they became the principal source of the highly sought-after uniform. Some LRRP units contracted local seamstresses to have tiger-striped camouflage fatigues made.

Another uniform frequently worn by the LRRPs consisted of combinations of enemy gear. Depending on the opponent anticipated in an area, LRRPs might dress point men in black pajamas, olive green or khaki shirts, or NVA-issue dark blue sweatsuitlike sweaters. Some teams dressed all members in captured enemy uniforms. Usually these uniforms were carried to the field and changed into after insertion into the recon zone.

While wearing the attire of the enemy provided obvious

advantages, it also added to the danger of the LRRPs being fired on by friendly air or ground units. Despite the fact that LRRP recon zones were "no fire, no fly" areas for all allied forces, the risk of a pilot or unit off course was always a possibility. For that reason, LRRPs usually only wore enemy uniforms in regions far from other friendly units.

Another general practice required that LRRP field uniforms, regardless of type, be "sanitized": no unit patches, rank, or name tapes were worn on missions to deny the enemy any information about the recon units. Only upon return to his base camp did the LRRP don his jungle fatigues or specially tailored camouflage "tigers" with LRRP tab or Ranger scroll, name tapes, and badges of rank and skill qualifications. The rear-area uniforms were often called "club cammies" or "profile suits" as they were for show rather than practical use.

Underwear for the recon men was not a problem. Although the army issued olive-drab boxer shorts and T-shirts, field soldiers rarely wore any underwear—other than socks—to prevent rashes and jungle rot in the humid, damp climate. The body needed as much air circulation as possible.

One useful item of issue underwear that LRRPs in the cooler highland regions did wear was the jungle sweater. This long-sleeve, wool-polyester blend pullover was valuable in keeping the chill off a man waiting all night in a recon or ambush position.

Footwear for the LRRP was nearly exclusively the army issue black-leather-bottom and green-canvas-topped jungle boot. Designed with small holes just above the soles, the boot provided ventilation and drainage while the steel-plated bottom helped deflect punji stakes and other sharp objects.

Stories abound of LRRPs grinding off the distinctive sole design so the wearer would not leave behind a recognizable footprint. Some LRRPs experimented with wearing olive-drab tennis shoes and a variety of allied and enemy footgear, including the rubber-tire-soled "Ho Chi

Minh'' sandals. However, the jungle boot proved as effective as any.

Experimental boots from the Army Research Laboratory and various commercial enterprises were also tried. One of the more inane models was a normal jungle boot with a raised sole design of a bare foot. The few LRRPs who tried the ''barefoot boot'' laughingly recall that the boot left a print that looked exactly like a GI boot with a footprint design on the sole. It was even more distinctive than the regular pattern. Although many barroom stories are told about LRRP footwear, the truth is that the standard-issue jungle boot was worn by practically every LRRP unit on all missions.

Headgear for the LRRPs varied dramatically. One that was not used was the issue helmet, or ''steel pot,'' commonly worn by the infantry; the pot was too noisy, heavy, and distinctive for recon work. The most preferred headwear was the flop or ''boonie'' hat that came in various shades of olive-drab (OD) and camouflage patterns. Offering protection from sun and rain, the boonie hat's shapeless brim also assisted in blending with the environment as well as proving flexible. It could be wadded up and carried in a pocket or used as a pad to hold the barrel of a hot weapon or the handle of a canteen cup over a small fire made of burning C-4 plastic explosive.

Another popular hat was the Ranger-style patrol cap with a soft bill. Dating from the Korean War period, it was still issued to students at the Fort Benning Ranger School. Still other LRRPs adopted various soft caps that were secured from the Australians or other allied recon units.

Rivaling the boonie hat as the most popular headwear was no hat at all. Instead, some LRRPs wore headbands made of triangular OD bandages from the first-aid kits. These cotton cloths, intended for makeshift slings and tourniquets, were tied bandanna-fashion around the head with the tails hanging behind or to one side. Headbands were excellent for keeping sweat out of the eyes as well as obscuring light-colored skin. The cloths could also easily be converted into makeshift belts and trouser ties at the thighs to keep loose pant legs from becoming snagged on vines and thorns. Many LRRPs wore the same headband for their entire tour or until it rotted to pieces. Some recorded the number of missions or individual kills on the bands, while others bore "Kill Congs" or less polite phrases embroidered on them. One C Company Ranger wore the same cloth as a headband or belt for two years. It carried the legend "It don't mean nothing" to tell any enemy who killed him that he had no regrets.

Another headgear option, and the one most associated with the recon men by the general public, was the black beret. Although the beret was rarely, if ever, worn during field operations because it served no functional purpose in camouflage or protection from the elements, it was the standard headwear in base camp and garrison.

While the black beret was not the official headgear for Rangers until January 1975 (and the publication of Army Regulation 670-5), it had been around recon units long before Vietnam. As early as 1756 many of Rogers's Rangers had worn a Scottish cap, similar to a beret, known as a tam-o'-shanter. It was not until World War II, however, that the beret gained popularity when several of the airborne regiments adopted the British paratrooper's maroon beret for occasional wear.

Modern Rangers first began wearing berets during the Korean War while undergoing company training at Fort Benning. Colonel Van Houten, the Ranger Training Center commander, supported the beret, and members of his staff were the first to wear it. Soldiers assigned to the 10th Ranger Infantry Company (Airborne) attached to the 45th Infantry Division had the honor of being the first unit to wear the beret.

The black beret was popular among the Rangers, but until 1975 it was at best only tolerated by the army's leadership. During the years between Korea and Vietnam the only wearers of the black beret were the Ranger School instructors.

Despite the fact that the black beret was the accepted unofficial headgear of the LRRPs and later Rangers in Vietnam, not all units adopted it initially. Some recon units, particularly those that operated with Australian units, at times wore the Aussie tan beret. Others sometimes wore the maroon beret that is the international color of airborne units. Not until 1969, when LRRPs were redesignated as Rangers, did the black beret become standard.

A question that frequently arises is just why the LRRP/ Ranger beret was black to begin with. Maroon was fairly standard for airborne units around the world, including paratroopers in the army of South Vietnam. Commandos from Great Britain, France, and other European nations had long worn a green beret while their mechanized and armor units wore the black.

It would appear at first glance that green was not selected for the Rangers as it had already been awarded by President John F. Kennedy to his pet project, the Special Forces, in 1961. The fault in this theory, however, is that Rangers had selected black as their beret of choice as early as 1950 at the Ranger Training Command.

So why black? Although there are no confirmed sources or even a claimant to the idea of black, the color of the Ranger beret apparently comes from the color of the night in which recon men do their most efficient work. Whatever the reasons, the black beret became the symbol of the Ranger elite of Vietnam and of today.

Uniforms were only a part of the LRRPs total gear. To carry the equipment, ammunition, and rations required for five to seven days far from friendly lines and resupply, the LRRPs adopted a variety of U.S., enemy, and homemade carrying devices. The standard load-bearing equipment (LBE), known simply as web gear, provided a wide webbed canvas belt and shoulder harness. Ammo pouches, canteens, grenades, and other equipment could be clipped onto the belt and suspenders.*

Additional ammunition could be strung across the chest

*Web gear was also referred to as "LBJ" for load-bearing junk by those who did not care for the design. Still others called it "LBJ" in "honor" of the president who governed for much of the war.

in the cloth bandoleers that held seven loaded magazines. Canvas BAR (Browning Automatic Rifle) ammo belts dating to Korea were also popular, as were vestlike, Communist-manufactured AK-47 banana magazine pouches secured from captured stock.

For heavier gear, the LRRPs carried rucksacks of various manufacture. One was the green canvas GI-issue ruck with multiple pockets that strapped to a lightweight aluminum frame. Some LRRPs preferred the ARVN green or NVA tan canvas rucksacks that were made by the same manufacturers in Hong Kong and Korea and were virtually indentical except for the color. Still others preferred the U.S. frame with an ARVN or NVA ruck attached.

Regardless of type or origin, the most significant thing about a rucksack was its weight when packed for a mission. With all essential equipment and supplies, the ruck usually weighed seventy to eighty pounds, more for longer missions.

The common method of getting the burden of equipment on the LRRP's back was for him to crawl into the carrying straps while in a seated position, then roll over and pull himself up with the assistance of a buddy or tree trunk.

The necessity of carrying water added to the load. Amounts varied from three to eight quarts, depending on the terrain and season. During the monsoons, or when operating where there were numerous streams, the LRRPs carried fewer canteens. Iodine or halazone tablets allowed for the purification of water found in the field. In more arid areas, water had to be carried to sustain the LRRP for the entire mission.

The standard one-quart metal canteen—and its plastic replacement—presented problems, as it was noisy when struck by a branch or piece of equipment. A two-quart rubberized canteen was more popular with the recon men, because it was flexible enough to be rolled and stored in the rucksack when empty. Another sacklike container made of plastic and covered in thin canvas held five quarts and could be tied to the rucksack or placed in one of the large pouches.

The bulky weight of water was one burden that received no complaints from the LRRPs. Many individuals carried several canteens in addition to those called for by unit SOP. In the steamy jungles and paddies, water was one item no man could do without.

Rations for a seven-day patrol added more weight to the LRRP's pack—even with the standard practice of packing only one meal per day. Chow for all field troops in Vietnam, including the LRRPs in the early years, was C-rations. Consisting of twelve different canned-meat meals that included beef, pork, or poultry, C-rations were packaged in heavy OD cans. Each meal had a second can containing crackers and a tin of cheese, jelly, or peanut butter. A third can consisted of fruit—pears, apricots, peaches, or fruit cocktail—or a pound, fruit-, or pecan cake.

The fruits were prized because they quenched the thirst as well as tasted good. A pound cake with peaches or a sauce made from the cocoa beverage powder found in some of the rations was considered haute cuisine by many a grunt. However, it is unlikely that a single soldier ever consumed an entire fruitcake, much less more than one.

Rounding out the C-ration was a foil packet containing instant coffee, sugar, cream substitute, salt, chewing gum, a plastic spoon, toilet paper, matches, and a pack of four cigarettes. The coffee was strong, the smokes stale, and the chewing gum hard.

For units able to resupply every few days, C-rations were adequate, if monotonous. For LRRP operations, where the recon men were unable to resupply because of the risk of revealing their position by bringing in a chopper, C-rations were too heavy and bulky. Cans also had to be packed carefully so that they would not rattle, and the empties had to be buried or carried back out of the boonies so the enemy would not know Americans had been in the area.

The replacement for the Cs was not only lightweight and somewhat tasty but also received the name of the soldiers for whom they were developed. "LURPs," as they were known to all, were dehydrated rations packed in plastic bags. They could be eaten dry or reconstituted with cold or hot water. Originally designed exclusively for LRRPs, Special Forces, and other special units, they proved to be so popular that production was increased so that by 1970 they were available for all infantry units.

LURP meals included beef with rice, chicken with rice, beef stew, chicken stew, spaghetti with meat sauce, and chili with beans. Initially most of the meals, despite their labels, tasted mostly the same. This improved somewhat after the rations were freeze-dried rather than dehydrated.

Each LURP ration also included a chocolate, vanilla, or coconut candy wafer that was generally called a "John Wayne bar" by the troops. Some of the LURPs also included an orange-flavored cornflake bar that was supposed to be a good breakfast snack. The cornflake bar was about as popular as the C-ration fruitcake.

The same accessory packet that was in the C-ration was included in each LURP; however, the coffee packet was not often used. It was a rare LRRP mission where the recon men had the opportunity to heat water for a drink or to reconstitute their chow. If time and security permitted, heat tabs that looked like small blue bars of soap were available but not often used. Heat tabs were slow to heat and gave out a noxious odor that would gas the cook and alert any enemy with a sense of smell of the LRRPs' location.

A good field expedient for heating water was C-4. The plastic, claylike explosive burned intensely when touched with an open flame. A piece as small as a thumbnail would bring a canteen cup of water to a boil in less than a minute. There was little danger in burning C-4 as long as caution was taken not to attempt to smother the fire once it began to burn; that would cause it to explode. Caution also had to be taken not to get C-4 crumbs in the water or food as it was very harmful to the nervous system.

Regardless of the means available to heat rations, LRRPs nearly always had their chow cold. The inconvenience was preferable to the possibility of enemy detection. There were many more things for the recon men to worry about in the boonies than being hungry.

Another type of food consumed by the LRRPs, especially before the arrival of LURP rations, was a meal used by the ARVNs and mercenary forces trained by the Special Forces. These "indigenous rations" were packaged like LURPs, and they, too, required the addition of water before consumption. Rice was the basic ingredient of the small packets, which also contained dried lamb, beef, or minnowlike fish—complete with head and tail intact. Dried vegetables of undeterminable origin were included, along with a packet of dried peppers. The most interesting item in the "indigenous ration" was hard squares of peanut-flavored candy that could be eaten along with the sugar-based rice paper in which they were wrapped.

Medical supplies were essential to the LRRPs, not only to treat combat wounds, but also to fight the various infections and diseases common in the jungle. Types of medical equipment, and methods of carrying them, varied from unit to unit. The general policy was for each man to carry a small first-aid packet while the assistant team leader or another patrol member carried the larger team aid bag.

Individual packets contained a bandage compress complete with attached gauze wrapping that would protect a wound and help control bleeding. "Pill packets" to combat malaria and other diseases were also often included in the individual kit.

In the larger team aid bag were bandages, pills, and other gear that ranged from simple tourniquets to major lifesaving equipment. Bandages of various sizes and shapes came in sterile paper and foil containers. Slings, splints, and adhesive tape were included along with sturdy scissors for cutting away clothing and boots. The medical supplies were intended only for short-term treatment to stabilize the patient until a dust-off could evacuate the casualty.

The most sophisticated item for treating the wounded was serum albumin, which came in a gray metal container about the size of a beer can. Along with the serum was a

tube with a large needle that could transfer the liquid from
the can into a vein. Used only in the case of extreme blood
loss, serum albumin was not blood itself but an expander
that would assist the patient's remaining blood to keep him
alive until he could be evacuated to a better treatment fa-
cility.

Drugs in the LRRP medical bag included the usual ones
found in combat units and several that were unique to the
recon men. The common ones included chloroquine pri-
maquine, a large orange antimalaria tablet taken once a
week, and the daily small white antimalaria pill, dap-
sone.*

Other pills in the LRRP medical aid bag included dar-
von for minor pain relief, codeine for coughs and colds,
and tetracycline for minor infections such as jungle rot and
abrasions. Polymagna, an antidiarrheal, was useful for its
intended purpose, but was also taken to stop regular bowel
movements. No LRRP wanted to be caught with his pants
down, figuratively or literally, answering nature's call on
a mission. In addition to the obvious dangers, American
fecal matter smelled differently from that of the enemies'
and was a calling card announcing GIs had been in the
area. Various vitamin tablets and allergy remedies rounded
out the routine drug list.

LRRPs carried drugs that were normally not found in
combat units, including dextroamphetamine and other uppers that stimulated the central nervous system to assist
the LRRP in staying awake on extended missions. One of
the most common uppers was a capsule known as a
''greenie'' or ''green bomb'' because of its color. Uppers

*Many Vietnam vets, including LRRPs, still claim today that the antimalaria pills
did not prevent malaria but rather masked its symptoms. Medical authorities dis-
pute this theory; however, it must be considered that a unit's ''malaria rate'' was
of great concern to statistics-keeping staff officers. Many a soldier was hospitalized with all the symptoms of malaria only to be told—and have noted on his
medical records—that the illness was ''fever of unknown origin.'' Regardless of
the truth, many a vet had recurring bouts of malaria for years after returning from
the war zone. Also noteworthy is the fact that all hospitals, civilian and military
alike, refused to accept vets as blood donors until they had been home and ceased
taking the malaria pills for a minimum of twelve months.

had the added benefit of depressing appetite while increasing alertness. Team leaders closely monitored the consumption of greenies and allowed men to take them only in the case of extreme emergencies. There were few problems, as the LRRPs preferred to rely on their own senses without the influence of artificial stimulants.

Most important of the drugs carried by the LRRPs, as with any combat unit, was morphine. Packaged in quarter-grain Syrettes with a needle that could be placed on the nipple end, the drug could be quickly administered by rolling the Syrette down like a tube of toothpaste.

Morphine rapidly clouded pain and gave a sense of well-being. Control of the Syrettes was extremely close in all units, including the LRRPs. Trust among the recon men was so high, however, that frequently each LRRP was issued his own supply of morphine. Some wore the Syrette around their necks in a protective holder on their dog tag chains for quick access. Reports abound of LRRPs administering their own morphine after being wounded, bandaging themselves, and returning to the fire fight.

LRRP weapons covered the entire range of the allied and enemy inventories. It is likely that no firearm of any type available anywhere in the world during the war did not at one time or another find its way into the hands of the recon men.

The most common LRRP weapon was the standard infantry rifle of the war—the M-16. Capable of firing its twenty-round magazine (usually loaded with only eighteen rounds to reduce spring pressure and resultant jams) on semiautomatic or full automatic at the flip of a switch, the M-16 was light and small enough for recon operations. Its 5.56-mm projectile had an extremely high velocity that caused the bullet to tumble on impact, producing man-stopping wounds. The 5.56 cartridges were also small and lightweight enough so that each soldier could carry several hundred.

Although the M-16 was the most common LRRP weapon, the CAR-15 was the LRRP weapon of choice. Officially the XM-177E1, the CAR-15 was a shorter model of the M-16. Its original version, the Model E-1, had a ten-inch barrel while the later Model E-2 had a barrel of twelve inches. Labeled and stamped on the receiver by its manufacturer as the Colt Commando, the CAR-15 was reliable and nearly perfect in size and capability for recon operations.*

The major operational limitation of the CAR-15 was the increased noise and fireball produced by the short-barreled weapon. This was somewhat contained by a variety of different flash suppressors that were added.

The other major limitation of the rifle was one the LRRPs could not control. The CAR-15 was extremely popular with staff officers and other rear-echelon types who liked to look like the warriors they so avoided joining. As a result, CAR-15s were always in short supply, and the ones that were available were passed along from replacement to replacement. Many LRRPs who served in the final years of the war recall carrying nearly worn-out weapons with barrels so used that much of their accuracy had been lost.

Another popular rifle with the LRRPs was the enemy's own AK-47. Carried for its own merits of dependability and stopping power, the AK had the additional advantage of not sounding like an M-16 or a CAR-15 so its use did not automatically alert VC or NVA that LRRPs were in their area. On occasion, some teams were entirely armed with AK-47s—specially if they were donning enemy uniforms after reaching their recon zones. Still other teams, with the exception of newly assigned soldiers, carried only AKs by choice, regardless of the uniform they wore. New troops had to earn the right to carry the communist-made rifle, as the general rule was that an AK had to be a "blood" weapon—one taken from an enemy soldier in combat after he no longer had any use for it.

Ammunition for the AKs was often secured in the same

---

*In remembering that the most sought-after weapon by the Texas Rangers of the nineteenth century was also made by the Colt Company, it seems appropriate that the LRRPs preferred a rifle made by the same manufacturer.

manner as the rifle. However, in the latter years of the war, it became a practice in many infantry units to take captured AK rounds and carefully remove the powder and replace it with a bit of C-4. The booby-trapped ammunition was then left in the field in hopes it would be recovered by the enemy, blowing his rifle up in his face during the next fire fight.

Captured stocks of AK-47s eventually became so great that they were issued to various ARVN irregular units as well as other allies in Southeast Asia. Stories of altered ammo, either in fact or fiction, were so widespread that the 7.62-mm ammo had to be manufactured in the United States and so labeled before anyone would use it—including the LRRPs. Of course, in the midst of an ongoing battle exceptions to using captured rounds were readily made.

While the M-16 and CAR-15 were by far the most common LRRP weapons, virtually all teams, regardless of their SOP, carried at least one AK-47. A common signaling practice of the VC and NVA was to fire shots in the air. A recon team with an AK could answer the shots and move in on the unsuspecting enemy.

The standard infantry machine gun, the 7.62-mm M-60, was available to the LRRPs but was not ordinarily carried on patrol. Weighing over twenty-two pounds, the M-60 was too heavy and bulky for a team that had to move both quickly and quietly. Much more of the lightweight M-16 ammo could be carried than the heavy belts of machine-gun rounds. Unless a team was going on a specific mission of a raid or ambush, the M-60 remained at the company base.

Other rifles and automatic weapons used by the LRRPs at one time or another included M-2 carbines, M-3 ''grease guns,'' Thompson submachine guns, Sten guns, Swedish K-40s, and Smith & Wesson 76s. Because of the incompatibility between the ammunition of these weapons and the M-16 and CAR-15, they were normally included only to fulfill a special mission requirement.

The 40-mm M-79 grenade launcher, carried in every

infantry squad, was of little use in the close-in fighting preferred by the LRRPs. If used at all, it was usually cut down at both the stock and barrel and carried in a holster improvised from a one-quart canteen cover clipped to the web belt.

A variation of the M-79, the XM-148, was a grenade launcher mounted on an M-16. The "over and under"-type weapon was particularly popular with the LRRPs of the 9th Infantry Division and the 199th Light Infantry Brigade in their areas of operation in the Delta.

The M-79 and the XM-148 both fired a high-explosive grenade as well as various smoke and gas rounds. However, the most common ammunition used by the LRRPs was the buckshot round that, for all practical purposes, converted the launcher into a large-bore shotgun.

Real shotguns were used by recon point men at times. The most popular were pump-action 12-gauge commercial models manufactured by Remington, Winchester, or Stevens that held six buckshot rounds. Shotguns were somewhat effective in extremely thick vegetation; however, the weight of the ammunition and the tendency of the plastic shells to deteriorate rapidly and become unreliable minimized their use.

Pistols and revolvers of various types also found their way into the LRRP arsenal with the .45-caliber M-1911A1 being the most common. The .45 required little care and maintenance, ammo was plentiful, and the fact that it had been in use by the U.S. Army since 1911 with virtually no modifications spoke well for its reliability.

Other sidearms ranged from .38-caliber revolvers, either traded or stolen from aviators, to various civilian models mailed from family or friends back home. Because of its stopping power, a popular personal pistol was the Browning Hi-Power 9-mm. An added advantage of the Browning was its larger magazine, which held thirteen rounds as opposed to the seven in the .45. Captured pistols, usually only found on enemy officers, were also carried; however, their purpose was often as much for pride as in the weapon's firepower characteristics.

Single-shot Hi-Standard .22-caliber pistols that dated back to OSS usage during World War II were also available through supply channels for special missions. Fitted with a very effective silencer, the .22, loaded with hollow-point rounds, could kill silently when there was a need to take out a lone enemy sentry or rear guard.

Knives were a standard part of LRRP equipment although their use was more often for opening rations or cutting through the jungle than in actual combat. Preferred were thick blades at least six inches in length with a serrated upper ridge for sawing through larger objects. Handles were wrapped in thin strands of leather so a sweaty or bloody hand would not slip. Air force supply channels provided a popular K-Bar model, while those who could afford them highly praised the Randall knives commercially available from the States. If no other knife was available, the bayonet issued for the M-16 rifle worked well.

Usually the knife scabbard was taped with the handle facing downward on the web gear-carrying strap or attached to the web belt. Knives belted to the calf of the leg looked good in movies and on an air force–base security guard but were nonfunctional for a field soldier.

Grenades, explosives, and mines were as much a part of LRRP equipment as were rifles and rations. These included fragmentation grenades for killing and concussion grenades for stunning enemy soldiers marked for a prisoner snatch. White phosphorus or "Willie Peter" grenades were carried for their blast-and-burn effect and their additional benefit of providing a smokescreen to obscure the recon men from their prey. White phosphorus grenades weighed twice as much as frag grenades, but they offered a trade-off by the terror they struck in the enemy. A burning piece of white phosphorus could not be smothered or removed and had the nasty characteristic of burning through flesh and bone.

CS, a strong tear gas, was used to assist in breaking contact. A team could head upwind popping the gas canisters behind them in their flight. Some LRRP veterans recall carrying gas grenades of unknown content that contained stronger agents that would incapacitate a pursuing enemy. These agents were more than likely extremely concentrated forms of CS that caused nausea and disorientation. Neither official files nor former LRRPs reveal any evidence that these chemical agents exceeded the limits in the Laws of Land Warfare.

Smoke grenades, about the size of a soft-drink can, were used to mark pickup zones or to identify targets for gunships and tactical air support. Many colors, including purple, yellow, green, white, and red, were carried as the enemy often popped their own smoke in an effort to confuse the LRRPs' air support. By radio, the recon men and the pilots could confirm which color smoke was from the LRRPs by identifying it by color or combination of colors.

The M-18A1 Claymore mine was an essential part of all LRRP operations—either offensive or defensive. These plastic, rectangular, convex mines were packed with a pound and a half of C-4 and seven hundred buckshot-size ball bearings. Each mine came with a canvas carry-case and strap, one hundred feet of wire, a blasting cap, and a charging handle or "klacker." A push on the klacker exploded the C-4, blowing the ball bearings in a sixty-degree, fan-shaped pattern that was equally effective in springing an ambush or in breaking an attack against a LRRP defensive position.*

Claymores could also be positioned so that the back blast rather than the ball bearings hit the kill zone to disable but not kill an enemy so he could be taken prisoner. The mines could be used individually or be daisy-chained together with "det cord" so they could be fired in multiples. The mines proved to be one of the most useful weapons available, and every LRRP carried at least two on each mission. Some units increased this number to six or eight.

Another popular mine used by the LRRPs was the M-14 pressure or "shoe" mine. Made of plastic and about the size of a boot-polish can, the M-14 was used to cover

---

*The Claymore manufacturers had conveniently placed raised lettering on the convex side of the mine that stated "Front towards enemy" for the uninformed.

avenues of approach to an ambush or defensive position that could not be covered by direct fire. M-14s could easily be camouflaged by leaves, grass, or a thin covering of dirt. Although rarely fatal, the "shoe mine" did not receive its nickname because it was shaped like a shoe-polish can but rather because anyone who stepped on one would no longer need more than one shoe.

An added advantage of the "shoe mine" was that it was triggered by pressure and did not require the person that placed it to remain in the area. Also, the mine's explosion was not unlike mortar or artillery fire, further confusing the enemy as to whether opposing soldiers were nearby.

C-4 was the basic demolition material used throughout Vietnam. The claylike explosive was easily shaped, and a small amount could do much damage. LRRPs used C-4 to destroy enemy supplies that could not be extracted and to blow down trees and other obstructions to prepare helicopter extraction zones.

In the early years of the war, before C-4 was plentiful, two other explosives prevailed. One was C-3, a material similar to C-4 except not as pliable. The other was hard, round, tin-covered quarter-pound "blocks" of TNT. Regardless of the type of explosive employed, the recon men usually preferred caps ignited by time fuses cut to the needed length rather than electric caps that required the carrying of wire and a handcrank spark generator.

Communications for the LRRPs was provided by the PRC-25 radio or its improved version, which looked almost the same but had more range—the PRC-77. Weighing a little more than twenty-two pounds, the PRC-25 was sturdy and reliable. It was issued with a carrying pack; however, it was a general practice to strap the radio on the top of the rucksack frame with the sack itself secured below it. Each radio came with a short "whip" antenna and a spring-jointed, long antenna that could be folded for storage. A variety of field-expedient antennas, usually made of WD-1 commo wire, could nearly double the normal range of eight to twelve kilometers.

The major weakness of both the PRC-25 and 77 was a

handset that, if it got wet tended to short out the entire spectrum with a constant buzz. A simple, effective solution to the moisture problem was to wrap the handset in the plastic bag that packaged replacement radio batteries.*

As reliable as the PRC-25 proved to be, no team went on patrol without two of the radios. This redundancy not only provided communication within the team but also ensured they could reach the lifeline of support if one radio malfunctioned or was damaged in combat.†

Two radios also provided the team with multiple means of communication, enabling it to change frequencies on one to coordinate artillery or air support while maintaining commo with the company-operations section on the other.

A longer-range—but heavier—radio, the URC-68, was also available for teams committed on missions at great distances from friendly support. Used occasionally by the LRRPs, the URC-68 was more common in the Special Forces for their cross-border operations into Cambodia and Laos.

At times, LRRPs also carried small survival radios, procured from air force and army aviators. These ranged from transmitters-only, that were used to bring in extraction helicopters, to short-range, hand-size sets that allowed the recon men to communicate with aircraft overhead. The URC-10 was the most common model.

Communications were absolutely essential to LRRP operations. If a team was short of men, the team leader and assistant team leader carried their own radios. Without the capacity to report what they observed, and to call in support when necessary, the "eyes and ears" of the combat forces became blind and silent.

Communications within a patrol centered on silent com-

---

*Despite the general opinion that the military always uses complex, esoteric names for its equipment, this is not always true. For example, the rubber-covered activation switch on the radio handset was officially called the "push to talk, release to listen button."

†RTOs (radiotelephone operators) instinctively placed the radio in front of them in a fire fight. More than one radio stopped a bullet or shrapnel.

mands rather than verbal. Arm and hand signals were used extensively. Team leaders carried notepads to write instructions that could not be signaled. If voice commands were necessary, they were whispered. It was not unusual for a team member to go an entire seven-day patrol without uttering a word. Many a LRRP remembers that his first action aboard an extraction chopper was to yell at the top of his lungs—partially out of exhilaration at having survived another mission, but mostly just to use vocal cords that had not been exercised for days.

Recon men also used silent-communications devices, including signal mirrors to reflect the sun toward an orbiting helicopter and bright orange and white plastic panels to mark their positions in open areas.

Special equipment was available to the LRRPs on a mission-requirement basis. Rappel ropes, ladders, and McGuire rigs were provided if an LZ was unavailable for insertion or extraction. (For description of these devices, see the LRRP Tactical SOP in Appendix A.)

LRRPs did not carry special insertion and extraction devices in their already-overburdened packs; the devices were on the helicopters, and to use the equipment, the LRRPs carried tightly coiled, six-foot "sling ropes" connected to their web gear with a snap link. These ropes were used to tie "Swiss seats" around the soldier's hips and thighs and then attached to the rappel rope or McGuire rig with the snap link.

The sling ropes were also useful as safety lines in crossing streams and in securing prisoners. They also served as signaling devices when run from man to man in a night position.

Cameras were carried by the recon men on some missions to record terrain, enemy equipment and positions, or anything else that could not be physically brought back by the patrol. These cameras included the many types of 35mm available on the commercial market and the Pen EE, which was available through Special Forces supply channels.

Sensors capable of detecting movement or sound were

issued on some missions for the LRRPs to emplace in abandoned bunker complexes and along trails or pathways. Missions to emplace these sensors were not met with much enthusiasm as they meant added weight and often little results.

Because the enemy used wire communications between strongholds, particularly in the remote highland regions and near the borders of Cambodia and Laos, the LRRPs at times carried wiretap devices. These wiretaps were not monitored by the recon men, but were equipped with transmitters that relayed the enemy messages to receivers aboard C-130 airplanes known as "Batcats" or to fixed receivers at mountaintop fire bases.

A variety of night-vision devices were available to the LRRPs for increased observation in times of darkness and for night sniper missions. The most common was the AN/PVS-2, better known as a "starlight scope." With a four-power magnification, the PVS-2 intensified natural moon- or starlight, providing a clear, green-tinted field of vision out to four hundred meters.

Special weapons, sensors, night-vision devices, and other nonissue equipment were often not procured through normal supply channels or by "midnight requisition," but were delivered to the LRRP base camps by "tech reps" of various defense contract companies. Often these tech reps were actually Central Intelligence Agency officers posing as civilian businessmen. They seldom fooled the LRRPs, but no one questioned the source of the special equipment.*

Although it is significant to note what the LRRPs carried on patrol, what they did not carry is also noteworthy. Cigarettes were left behind at the company base, as no smoking whatsoever was allowed in the field. No letters, paperbacks, or any other reading material beyond the Signal Operating Instructions (SOI) was carried. The only

*Many LRRPs recall that a real tech rep and a CIA agent were easy to tell apart. Tech reps were friendly, modest, and always bought several rounds of beer during their visits. CIA officers were reserved, wore their egos on their sleeves, and expected the LRRPs to provide the beer.

identification worn was dog tags—either around the neck or in the boot laces. When a LRRP went to the boonies all he had with him was the equipment to accomplish the mission—and the skills and motivation of a professional recon man.

In summary, LRRP weapons and equipment were similar to that of any master craftsman. Only what was needed was taken. Everything carried had a specific purpose or objective. Teams within a company might be outfitted differently depending on mission requirements and individual preferences. What was carried on one patrol might be discarded, supplemented, or replaced on the next. Like an artist or a sculptor, the LRRPs used the tools that led to completion of their artwork—not a painting or a statue, but rather intelligence or enemy soldiers and equipment destroyed.

CHAPTER 9
●━●━●━●

Operations

I_T is difficult, if not impossible, to character-
ize a typical LRRP operation. The use of the recon elements varied in accordance with the period of the war, the
season of the year, the terrain in the area of operation,
enemy capabilities, and the LRRP units themselves.

Another critical factor, and possibly the most important, was that LRRPs worked not for themselves but for
the commander of the field force, division, or separate
brigade to which they were assigned—and these commanders changed as often as every six months. One commander might deploy his LRRPs strictly in the traditional
reconnaissance role and emphasize that, in the effort to
gain maximum intelligence, direct contact with the enemy
was to be avoided. Another commander would push for
body count and use his recon teams as hunter-killer units,
relegating reconnaissance to a secondary role.

Despite the frequent redirection of missions by senior
commanders and LRRP company or detachment commanders, the recon units followed similar operational procedures regardless of parent unit or location. These
methods are listed in the Tactical Standard Operating Procedures outlined in Appendix A.

Any military unit, regardless of size, begins its planning with an analysis of its assigned mission. LRRPs, by

organization and training, were first and foremost concerned with reconnaissance to gain intelligence on enemy
strengths, movement, equipment, and possible courses of
action. Sightings of the enemy led to commitment of other
forces or to the LRRPs' calling in artillery or air strikes.
If the hostile element was small, the LRRPs might take
direct action, through ambush, to kill the enemy and gather
important intelligence in the way of captured documents.
If an enemy could be captured alive, even greater intelligence could be gained during interrogation.

Reconnaissance patrols were also useful in assessing
past operations while gathering information for future
ones. The recon men frequently were inserted after B-52
high altitude bombing strikes (ARC LIGHT) to determine
their effectiveness. Other missions might include the emplacement of camouflaged sensing devices that could de-
tect sounds or movement in bunker complexes or along
the trails. These sensors were monitored from hilltop or
aerial platforms (such as the C-130 fixed-wing aircraft
mentioned in the previous chapter) and yielded information long after the LRRPs had moved on to other areas of
operations.*

LRRP teams on standdown between patrols were often
the most available and the best trained for rapid insertion
to remote sites to secure downed aircraft. This was one
mission where the careful planning steps, inspections, and
rehearsals were foregone in favor of speed. Many an air
crew owes a debt of thanks to the LRRPs for a rapid rescue
that prevented death or capture at some remote crash site.

Missions to locate downed aircraft and crews were not
limited to army assets. The LRRPs accepted recovery and
rescue tasks from all services. An operational report from
the American Division, dated November 10, 1969, states,

---

*Sensors were issued already painted in various shades of green and black shadow
camouflage. They could be buried in the ground with the antenna, designed to
look like a blade of grass or a vine extending into the air. Others resembled
branches or leaves so that they could be hung in the trees. One of the most
interesting sensors looked like a fresh pile of human or monkey dung, the idea
being that it would not appear out of place along a jungle trail and that it was
unlikely that anyone would deliberately step on the device.

"Inter-service coordination proved highly successful when Ranger teams Oklahoma and Georgia [G Company] were given a mission to find the wreckage of a Marine F-4B Phantom. One body was found and extracted. A more thorough reconnaissance of the area revealed the wreckage of a Marine CH-46 helicopter that had been missing in action. Because of successful coordination between USMC and USN personnel and Ranger teams, seven bodies were located that would have been otherwise continued missing in action."

LRRP support for aircraft and flight-crew recovery was certainly not one sided. Helicopter crews risked their machines and their lives on many occasions to extract patrol teams from the midst of hard-fought battles. A typical example occurred on February 24, 1969, in Tay Ninh Province. Ranger Patrol 34 of the 1st Cav Division's H Company ambushed and killed one enemy soldier only to be immediately attacked by a large force of NVA firing automatic weapons and rocket-propelled grenades. The Ranger patrol called for extraction as it hurriedly moved to the nearest landing zone. By the time Apache 33, a UH-1, from the 1st Squadron, 9th Cavalry, reached the LZ, the Rangers had four men wounded and were surrounded. Despite the circumstances, the helicopter, piloted by Lieutenant Robert D. Peterson and Warrant Officer Parker, with door gunners specialists Davis and George, landed amidst the fire fight. With bullets tearing through the thin-skinned aircraft, the door gunners dismounted and assisted the wounded Rangers on board. Taking off through a hail of fire, the pilots were able to nurse the severely damaged aircraft to a friendly airfield. All survived.

LRRP after-action reports are filled with reports of similar actions of extreme danger and hard-fought combat. Many of their sightings were, however, not as exciting but often far more valuable to the intelligence analysts. A typical report on recon missions was made by Rangers of G Company. Extracts from a patrol conducted from 0545 hours on 7 May to 1945 hours on 8 May, 1969, state, "Two trails running North and South, well used. Three

NVA, one with weapon spotted. Three NVA spotted, carrying AKs and light machine gun. Two sighted, one with heavy pack. Seven spotted, two with heavy packs, five with weapons."

The G Company report continues with similar entries along with grid-coordinate locations and additional descriptions of the enemy, weapons, and equipment. A summary sentence concluded the report stating, "Over 120 VC and NVA spotted in three hours."

Not all LRRP missions, of course, resulted in enemy sightings or contact. However, every patrol gathered important information of use for future operations. LRRP debriefing reports, forwarded to all levels of intelligence units, included detailed analysis of terrain, vegetation, possible landing zones, water sources, and map corrections and updates.

Lack of enemy sightings was often as important a bit of intelligence as actually finding the enemy. General Ellis Williamson recalls that in the first months his 173rd Airborne Brigade was in-country it hopscotched all over in pursuit of the enemy and to reinforce ARVN units and threatened Special Forces camps. In August 1965 the entire brigade, along with several ARVN units, was committed to the Kontum area to open the main road that had been held by the enemy for five weeks. Williamson began the operation be sending in the LRRPs, who soon discovered that the enemy had decided to withdraw across the border into Laos rather than stand and fight. Williamson states, "During these operations the greatest contributions of the LRRPs were providing negative information. Several times the friendly Vietnamese commanders were able to rapidly move large forces through areas that they had been reluctant to enter because we could assure them that there were no large enemy forces in the areas."

Another use of the LRRPs was not recon but rather strictly combat. At times, when a regular infantry unit had worked an area for an extended time and was being pulled out, a patrol team went in with the choppers and offloaded in the confusion of extraction. Assuming carefully camouflaged positions, they waited for the enemy, as it was common VC and NVA practice to sweep LZs after an extraction in seach of discarded or lost equipment or rations. "Stay behinds" also got body counts when artillery fire support bases were abandoned.

Raids and attacks on point targets were missions assigned to the LRRPs when specific intelligence was available on the exact location of small enemy elements. A prime source of this information was the CIA Phoenix Project, which sponsored agents and paid informants within enemy units or the local populace that supported them. Phoenix had its own operatives who carried out assassination missions on targeted individuals. When larger groups were identified and located, other units such as the LRRPs were called in for support. The recon men were often ordered to check out intelligence gathered by other agencies and sources, with mixed results. However, when information was received from Phoenix, the recon men could nearly always depend on the data's accuracy.

An adaptation of the raid mission employed by the E Company Rangers of the 9th Infantry Division was to air-assault into areas where helicopter gunships had engaged ground targets. Called Parakeet missions, these operations included a light observation helicopter (LOH) as a scout to find the enemy, a gunship to attack once a target was identified, and a utility chopper with a team of LRRPs to mop up, count the kills, and gather weapons and documents.*

A Parakeet-type mission into the Plain of Reeds southwest of Saigon by a team of E Company in August 1969

---

*Similar operations were conducted in all U.S. units. Most often each part of such teams was named after a color. LOHs were white, gunships red, and troop carriers blue. If men on the ground wanted support of a LOH and a gunship team, they called for a pink team rather than a red and white. If a LOH, gunship, and additional troop support were needed—red, white, and blue—an "All-American" team was requested. Divisional cavalry squadrons were assigned aerial rifle platoons that served as part of the teams full-time and were rarely referred to as anything other than the "blue platoon" or simply as "blues." LRRPs on occasion also worked as blues in support of a pink team; however, it was much more common for the LRRPs to be on the ground requesting help from the pinks and regular blues.

produced one of the highest-ranking NVA officers killed
in the war. Thomas P. Dineen, Jr., of Annapolis, Maryland, and a veteran of E Company Rangers, recalls "On
August 24, 1969, my company was working out of Tan
An in IV Corps. At about 1000 hours we were alerted to
provide a reaction team to an incident that had developed
earlier in the day.

"It seems that a routine mail chopper en route to Saigon
had spotted enemy personnel in the Plain of Reeds and
had requested gunships to investigate. The Cobras had
fired on a group of enemy and brigade wanted a team on
the ground for further surveillance and evaluation.

"Since no team was available, Sergeant 1st Class Jessie
Stevens went through the company area in search of volunteers. Sergeant Chris Valenti, Sergeant Rahamim Ba-
zini, Corporal Mike Kentes, Sergeant Bauza, and myself
quickly joined Stevens at the helipad for insertion. We
were accompanied by an indigenous mercenary by the
name of Kiet.

"Upon reaching the contact site we offloaded the chopper and began a sweep of the immediate area. There were
waist-high reeds and grass throughout the area, making it
difficult to see. We soon came across numerous NVA
corpses that obviously had been riddled by the attacking
helicopters. Next, we discovered a survivor who was taken
prisoner by Valenti. Shortly thereafter we came across another group of bodies with one individual off to one side.
As the 'corpse' began to move Stevens shouted 'Choi Hoi'
[surrender], at which point Kentes noticed that the man
was attempting to unfasten a grenade from his belt. Kentes
shot him with two bursts from his CAR-15. On searching
the body, we discovered a 9-mm Makarov pistol.

"Once we completed the search of the area, we were
extracted and returned to Tan An where we turned the
prisoner over to Military Intelligence. It was quickly
learned that the prisoner had been the personal medic for
Lieutenant General Hai Tranh, and that the man that
Kentes had killed was likely the general. We were immediately reinserted into the contact area to recover the gen-

eral's body. When we returned with it, it was confirmed that it was indeed the general.

"According to our custom, we gave the pistol to the mercenary, Kiet, as sale of captured weapons and equipment was his primary payment for working with us. I later learned that our company commander, Albert C. Zapanta, took the pistol from Kiet."

Zapanta, currently a lieutenant colonel in the Army Reserves and a resident of Dallas, Texas, adds to the story: "There were fourteen bodies and fourteen weapons. Three were women armed with M 1 carbines who must have been medics, as they were carrying aid bags. One of the bodies was armed with a beautiful Czech-made Makarov 9-mm pistol—the type carried only by senior officers and officials. Its previous, now dead, owner ended up being Lieutenant General Hai Tranh, the commander of Military Region 3. I understand it was the only pistol of its type captured in the war. Also recovered were the other weapons and twenty-five pounds of documents that included a mail sack."*

Dineen added a postscript that is relevant to another aspect of LRRP operations—cross-border, or out-of-country patrols. According to Dineen, "Although we were told that the general's party had initially been spotted by a 'mail chopper' from Saigon, I don't believe that. For one thing, we flew too far and too long to be 'in line' between Saigon or adjacent fire bases and the base camp in Tan An—we were probably in Cambodia. For another, the response time of the gunships to the sighting was too fast. I suspect that good intel intercepted the general's route. There was no need for us [the LRRPs] to know how brigade knew where the general was."

There is no doubt, but little proof, that the LRRPs did conduct cross-border operations into Cambodia and Laos. However, rarely were these missions recorded, and the

*The Makarov pistol remained in the possession of Zapanta until June 11, 1987, when he turned it over to the 75th Ranger Regiment at a retreat ceremony at Fort Benning, Georgia. Most appropriately, Kentes and Dineen were in attendance.

reports of those that were remain classified and unavailable. The recon men at the time were instructed not to discuss any out-of-country patrols, and the discipline and honor of the LRRPs remains almost unwavering despite the passage of well over a decade. When questioned about such operations, many LRRPs respond, "We never went out of country; it was not authorized." Others smile faintly and state, "I never saw a border out in the middle of the jungle, so I don't know if we crossed any or not."

The few who do discuss such missions do so on a non-attributable basis. One of the more interesting stories comes from a former LRRP company commander, who relates, "One of my teams was inserted a few klicks into Cambodia in late 1969. We had authorization from division, but I'm unsure of any above that. The team was supposed to only recon trails where NVA were coming across the border, but a target presented itself that was too good to pass up. A group of five NVA was spotted, accompanied by a huge Caucasian who was armed and seemed to be in charge. My team ambushed them and killed all six, including the Caucasian. When they reported what they had done, I instructed them to move to an LZ for extraction and to bring the body with them. When they returned they were met by some CIA folks. We later learned that the man was a Polish soldier who was an advisor to the NVA and that the body was flown to Vientiane, Laos, by the Agency and turned over to the Polish embassy. We were instructed that 'we had never been in Cambodia and knew nothing about any dead Poles.' "

Another LRRP recalls, "We did not do any cross-border operations—at least not very often. One time we were sent into Cambodia to pinpoint a bridge for an airstrike. Late one night I crawled out onto the Ho Chi Minh Trail and stood up—just so I could say I had done it. Of course I've never really got to tell anyone about it before now."

While LRRPs did, in fact, conduct missions outside of South Vietnam, it was not a regular practice, and when they did so it was rarely more than a few kilometers across the border. Most of these missions were strictly reconnaissance, gathering information on enemy buildups and possible future actions. On other occasions the missions were rescues of downed aircraft crews, and the LRRPs remained in the hostile territory the minimum possible time.

Cross-border operations were conducted in the same manner as those within Vietnam, with one exception. Insertion was often accomplished by aircraft of the CIA proprietary Air America, which flew routine rotor and fixed-wing flights throughout Southeast Asia. Air America supposedly only flew commercial missions, but they were certainly not in business to make a profit. One LRRP veteran recalls, "We went on a few missions out-of-country. Each time we were inserted by Air America helicopters that were on authorized flights between Saigon and various cities in Cambodia and Laos. It was kind of strange, as the choppers were painted silver and red and looked nothing like our combat birds. They just flew their regular route—with a brief stop at some out-of-the-way LZ to let us off. We were never extracted by the Air America choppers, as usually we walked back into South Vietnam and were picked up in the normal way."

The invasion of Cambodia by U.S. and ARVN forces in April to June 1970 was the only authorized and official recon action out-of-country. Before and during the operation, LRRP teams of the 1st Cavalry and 25th Infantry divisions were at the front and flanks of the offensive, providing intelligence and body count. An after-action report of the 1st Cav states that the Rangers of H Company "conducted 50 reconnaissance missions in Cambodia and provided the Division with numerous intelligence reports" during the operation.*

Despite the wide variety of LRRP missions, most operations were for reconnaissance or at least started out that

---

*Special Forces recon teams operated much more regularly out-of-country—often at extreme distances into neighboring countries as well as the southern parts of North Vietnam. As can be expected, most of their actions remain classified.

way. Patrols were planned for a duration of five to seven days with more than a week being the unusual. The reasons for limiting the length of patrols was both human and logistical. LRRPs slept little in the field, and the intensity of remaining constantly alert in territory where they were far outnumbered was extremely taxing. Everything needed on the mission had to be carried on teammembers' backs, as a resupply chopper would compromise their location.

A common patrol practice was for a team to recon an assigned zone of four square kilometers and on the fifth or sixth day establish an ambush at the best location. The LRRPs would then stay in position for twenty-four to forty-eight hours in the attempt to ambush an enemy element and then quickly move to an LZ for extraction.

In the early years of the war, the LRRPs tried many team sizes and organizations. Patrols were run with as few as three and as many as a dozen team members. During the days of provisional LRRP units, some commanders felt it was necessary to include Vietnamese soldiers or tribal mercenaries as part of the patrol teams, while still others thought scout dogs could play a role.

Although LRRP units continued to experiment throughout the war, their basic organization was consistent in all units as early as mid-1967. Companies and detachments varied from sixty-one to two hundred thirty officers and men, depending on the size of the parent unit they supported. Each LRRP unit, regardless of size, contained a headquarters, operations, and communications section, and from one to four patrol platoons. Each platoon contained from four to eight patrol teams made up of six men. (For an organization and manning diagram of a divisional LRRP company, see Annex I to Appendix A.)

Most of the organizational evolution and revolution centered on the composition of the teams. General Williamson's experience in the 173rd was typical of other units. Williamson recalls, "Initially we had ten-man patrols and invited the Vietnamese army to furnish two of those men. Many tries proved that two Vietnamese were not necessary, and we changed it to one and finally to all our troops.

The Vietnamese performed okay, but we found that the purpose for which we visualized them was not valid. At first we thought that we needed someone along who could understand and speak the language. That proved unnecessary, and we found that the patrols were more efficient when all American.''

Although ARVN soldiers rarely accompanied the LRRPs after the early days of the war, indigenous personnel of various backgrounds did serve with many of the recon units. These ranged from out-and-out mercenaries to Vietnamese of various backgrounds and military ties. An occasional Kit Carson scout, former VC or NVA who had rallied to the South Vietnamese government, was also attached to the LRRP units.

The use of scout dogs with the LRRPs was much discussed at various command levels but, with the exception of a few trials, never came to fruition. As late as 1968, USARV proposed that scout dog teams be assigned full-time to the LRRPs. On March 28 of that year, USARV held a conference of operations officers representing its major subordinate commands at Long Binh. In the summary of the conference, dated April 8 and signed by the USARV plans and operations officer, Brigadier General Frank H. Linnell, proposals for improving LRRP operations were listed.

One of these proposals stated: "A scout dog with handler should be assigned to the LRRP unit. The dog and handler should work with only one or two patrols to allow the dog to become accustomed to the patrol members. A well-trained dog, properly handled, can successfully warn the patrol of danger. In planning the use of dogs the following must be considered: The handler must volunteer to operate with the LRRP unit; food and water for the dog increases the load of patrol members; and the dog should be carefully selected to ensure he is suitable by temperament and training for performing under special conditions experienced by LRRPs.''

The fallacies of the proposal do not need to be elaborated, as they are listed within the idea itself. Volunteer handlers to go with the LRRP were as hard to find as were volunteer dogs—if anyone had been able or had gone to the trouble to ask the canines. The additional weight of food and water was unacceptable even if a dog "suitable by temperament and training" could be found. Finally, although LRRPs certainly had nothing personally against dogs, the general feeling was that neither ordinary man nor beast was better at accomplishing anything in the jungle than the recon men themselves.

Scout dogs, like many experiments with the LRRPs, was one that appeared better on senior headquarters paper than in the field. There is no evidence in official records or in the memory of the recon veterans of scout dogs ever playing a role of any significance in LRRP operations.

By the time the updated FM 31-18 was published in August 1968, the six-man team was so widely accepted that it became a formal part of LRRP doctrine. As in many cases, LRRPs had not followed any book—the books recorded what the LRRPs had proven in the field.

The selection of six as the size for a team was based on valid reasoning, the best and simplest being that it worked. Six men filled the essential positions of a leader and an assistant leader, two RTOs, a point man, and a "tail gunner" or rear security. The number was ample to provide enough firepower for security or offensive action against small enemy units while being small enough to move with a minimum amount of noise. It was also large enough to divide into two elements of three men each and small enough to hide itself easily along a trail. If casualties were taken, there were enough men for one to care for the wounded while those remaining continued the fight. Also very important was the fact that the normal load for a Huey transport chopper was six, allowing the LRRP team to be inserted or extracted with a single bird.

The patrol team was the heart of all LRRP units. Other members of the unit, including the operations and communications section—and even the commander and headquarters section—existed only to deploy, support, and control the teams. Although the LRRP teams could have not operated without these essential command and support elements, the fact remains that the recon units would never have achieved a bit of intelligence or a single body count except for the work of the six-man patrol teams.

The key to the success of the LRRP teams was that they were just that—teams. The six men worked, fought, and played together. They knew each others' capabilities, reactions to different situations, backgrounds, and weaknesses so well that the combined minds of the six could very nearly work as one. New team members, replacing casualties or those who rotated home, were taken on several trial patrols to see if they fit in with the team before being accepted. In the event a team member was on R&R or briefly hospitalized, a volunteer from another team on standdown between missions might join the team for a patrol. However, this was only done if the team leader approved and usually occurred only when the substitute was well known to the other members of the team. Platoon leaders or platoon sergeants or even the company commander occasionally filled in on teams short of soldiers. Despite the rank of these "fillers," they joined the team as teammembers and followed the instructions of the team leader.

LRRP teams were one of the few groups in the army where the person with the highest rank was not necessarily in charge. The team was run by the team leader regardless of rank. Manning documents called for a staff sergeant to fill the team leader position, but it was not unusual to find buck sergeants and at times a specialist four or corporal filling the job. If a higher-ranking NCO or officer joined a patrol to fill a temporary vacancy or to gain experience after first joining the unit, he did so in whatever capacity was assigned by the team leader.

If there was a shortage of volunteers or replacements, teams would deploy on missions with five or as few as four men. In these instances the team leader and/or the assistant team leader would carry his own radio, leaving the RTO position vacant.

Teams more often than not were a reflection of the team

leader. His personality was mirrored in his subordinates, and while each LRRP was certainly an individual, he was foremost a member of the team.

Patrol teams were normally designated by a two-digit number indicating unit and team number. For example, 21 stood for second platoon, first team, and 32 for third platoon, second team. Some LRRP units named teams after states such as Team Texas and Team Arizona. These state designations were usually in honor of the home of the present or a past team leader. Teams, especially within the unit, also were frequently known for their leader, such as Williams's Team or Brown's Team.

The general functions and duties of each team member are outlined in Appendix A. These responsibilities varied little from team to team and unit to unit. New men started out as RTOs or as rear security. Those who proved themselves able to move quietly while maintaining a general compass direction worked their way ''up'' to point man. Although point was one of the toughest and most dangerous jobs, it was one that was sought after by recon men. ''I walked point'' is still one of the first things a LRRP will proudly state when asked what his job was on patrol.

One such point man was Ed Beal of Greensboro, North Carolina. Beal, who was a scout dog handler in the 25th Infantry Division in 1967–68, returned to Vietnam in September 1969 and volunteered to be a LRRP in H Company of the 1st Cav. According to Beal, ''I liked to walk point. I felt that I was good at it and felt good doing it. In a way I kind of miss it.''

Point men who were good and who survived graduated to assistant team leader and, with more experience, to team leader. Although soldiers who had already earned their sergeant's stripes did join the LRRPs and eventually became team leaders, this ''grow your own'' system of increased rank and responsibility was much more common.

Teams remained under control of the team leader between missions at the company base in addition to when in the field. This was done not only for the sake of maintaining a chain of command and building teamwork but also because the team was never really off duty. A stand-down period of three to four days after each mission was not only for rest; it was also essential for the planning and preparation of the next patrol.

Upon return to the unit base camp, a patrol neither rested nor cleaned up before weapons and equipment had been maintained and everything was prepared for immediate deployment in case another team or a downed aircraft needed assistance. When all was ready for an emergency, then the LRRPs had time to take care of their personal care and comfort.

Planning for the next scheduled mission began within twenty-four hours of return from the field. The team leader reported to company operations, where instructions were waiting from the parent unit G-2 (intelligence) or G-3 (operations) officer. Just who the LRRPs worked directly for varied from unit to unit. The formal way of determining working relationships in the army is to identify who is responsible for writing the efficiency report of the subordinate unit's commander. In some recon units the parent field force, division, or separate brigade commander flatly stated that the LRRPs worked directly for him. Other parent-unit commanders preferred that the LRRPs work for their G-2 or G-3. Still other units attached the LRRPs to their subordinate cavalry squadron. These relationships changed over time and with change of commanders. Who the LRRPs worked for was often a good indication of their intended use. If assigned under the G-2, reconnaissance for the gathering of intelligence was the priority; if under the G-3, the combat role was emphasized.

Regardless of who the LRRPs worked for they did not do so in a vacuum. The G-2 and G-3 operated in close cooperation. Their boss was, of course, the parent-unit commander, and many of their mission assignments were the result of his guidance. The petty territorial fights that often result in peacetime had no place in the combat zone. Commanders, staff officers, and the LRRP units cooperated well together with mission accomplishment the only goal.

The LRRP unit operations officer, with guidance from his commander, planned for the employment of the patrol teams. From the parent-unit G-2 and/or G-3, he received the mission requirements and assigned areas of operations for individual teams.

After receiving the information from the higher headquarters, the LRRP operations officer and his staff began their planning procedures, including gathering intelligence, coordinating insertion assets, and securing any special equipment required. Since LRRP units strived to keep at least half of their teams in the field at all times, the operations section also was required to monitor ongoing patrols and plan for future extractions.

Two to three days of intense planning and preparation were required before a team or teams was committed on a mission. Intelligence data, maps, and aerial photographs of the assigned area of operations were collected and studied. A prime source of this information was the data base readout maintained by the parent-unit G-2 order of battle section. Included in the readout were weather and light data, after-action reports of all U.S. and allied operations in the area, ground and airborne sensor readings, agent reports, and information from prisoner interrogations.

Along with this raw data was a synthesized report, known as the order of battle, which contained the latest estimate of enemy unit identification, their strengths, locations, and possible courses of action. This information was compiled and analyzed by well-meaning staff officers, but, of course, if it had been accurate to any degree at all, it was unlikely that the LRRPs would have received the mission to check it out in the first place. Still, any information, no matter how old or doubtful in accuracy, was useful in mission planning.

Another primary source of premission information was the intelligence files the LRRPs kept themselves. Maintained by the intel sergeant in the operations section, these files contained the written debriefings and map overlays and corrections of all previous patrols in or near the same area.

As soon as enough information had been gathered, the operations officer, after approval by the unit commander, developed recon zones for each patrol. These zones were typically four square kilometers and were in the form of a two-by-two kilometer box or with irregular boundaries that followed the contours of stream beds or mountain ridges.

At this point in the planning process, the team leader of the patrol selected for each recon zone was issued a warning order containing as much information as was available and a time table counting down to the anticipated insertion. The team leader, after studying the information, gave his warning order to the team.

Many of the next steps went on simultaneously while the operations section, the team leader, and the team itself continued to prepare for the mission. The assistant team leader took care of ensuring the team secured and packed any special equipment and weapons required while the team leader went on an aerial recon of the assigned area of interest. On the aerial recon, flown by the same air crew that would be responsible for the insertion, the team leader observed the proposed LZ sites, looked for any evidence of enemy activity, and checked major terrain features for accuracy on his map. The aerial reconnaissance not only flew over the designated recon zone but also checked others on the same flight to confuse any enemy observers about the actual zone of future operations.

On return from the aerial recon, the team leader conferred with the operations officer to report his findings and to receive any updated information. After more study of the situation, the team leader issued his detailed patrol order to the entire team. This was followed by a question-and-answer period to ensure that each team member was thoroughly knowledgeable in all aspects of the mission and of his individual responsibilities.

After the team leader was satisfied that everyone understood the mission, he led the team through a rehearsal. The men walked through their actions during insertion, at halts, and during movement. Immediate action drills, which were designed to provide swift and positive reactions to visual or physical enemy contact, were rehearsed regardless of the time the team had been together or had previously conducted the same drills. (For details on re-hearsals and immediate action drills, see paragraphs 7 and 8 of the Tactical SOP in Appendix A.)

During the twenty-four hours prior to insertion, the LRRPs refrained from using soap, after-shave lotion, or any other substance that had an odor. Part of this proce-dure was valid in that the enemy's sense of smell was extremely acute after long periods in the boonies. Another reason was somewhat ritualistic in the LRRP's mental con-ditioning to prepare to depart the relative luxuries of the unit's base camp for the austere and dangerous environ-ment of the field. Some LRRP teams went so far as never to launder their field uniforms. When old fatigues wore out, new ones were held over smoldering fires to give them the same smell of smoke that was common of the enemy.

During the planning and rehearsal phases, the commu-nications plan was also prepared. Team RTOs updated their signal operating instructions (SOI) with current radio fre-quencies and call signs of friendly air, artillery, and ground units that might be able to support the operation. SOIs, about four-by-six inches in size and over an inch thick, also contained various codes for reporting positions and encrypting message data. As a part of each rehearsal phase, the team leader quizzed the RTOs to be sure they had memorized critical information. In the midst of a fire fight there would be no time to consult the SOI for a call sign or frequency that might mean the survival of the team.

Meanwhile the operations section was also studying the communications situation. By comparing distances and ra-dio ranges, the operations officer determined if a radio relay station would be required. If needed, a patrol team might be inserted onto a dominant terrain feature, such as a hilltop, to relay for one or more teams in their recon zones. If an artillery fire base was available near the re-quired sector, a team from the communications section could be inserted there to relay for the patrols. These teams planned and rehearsed for their mission in a fashion similar to the patrol teams.

LRRPs on radio-relay duty understood the importance of their mission. Joseph E. Rachten, then nineteen-year-old sergeant in H Company from Cleveland, Ohio, explains, "When you were on radio relay, you had to be good—you had the lives of your buddies in your hands."

Communications were critical to the LRRPs both for reporting their findings and requesting support and extraction if compromised. Still, it was common in virtually all the LRRP units to operate beyond the range of normal radio contact. Often a patrol team had no contact at all with its unit headquarters or other friendly units except for airborne helicopters or fixed-wing aircraft that overflew the recon zones at two-to-six-hour intervals. For obvious reasons, LRRPs never liked being without commo; however, their recon zones were at times so remote that only aerial relay platforms could reach them. In such cases the LRRPs avoided enemy contact at all costs and stuck strictly to reconnaissance.

In the final hours before the patrol's insertion, team members completed their personal preparation. Weapons were test-fired to ensure they were operating properly and ammunition was checked for cleanliness and defects. Any loose items of equipment were taped, and pieces of equipment that might rub together and make noise were padded. This process of "taping up" or "breaking tape" was validated on completion by the LRRP, in full equipment, jumping up and down to check for rattles or noise. If any resulted, more taping and repacking were done.

Before the final inspection by the team leader, camouflage was applied to equipment and to the recon men themselves. Thin strips of olive-drab burlap were wrapped around weapon stocks and rucksacks. Any shiny pieces of metal were spot-painted or covered with still more tape. Natural foliage was added to the camouflage once the team arrived in the recon zone.

Greasepaint from camouflage sticks was applied to the face, hands, and other exposed skin. Army-issue camouflage sticks came in tin tubes about an inch in diameter and three inches long. Each end of the tube had a cap that protected the two-color stick. One end of the stick was black, which was applied to tone down dominant features such as the cheekbones, the nose, and the forehead. Grease from the green end of the stick was smeared on the areas in between until all exposed skin was covered. A bit of insect repellent added to the camouflage grease assisted in its application and durability. Camouflage sticks were carried on the mission to reapply the greasepaint as it wore or was sweated off.

Some of the "men with painted faces" had additional camouflage challenges due to their light-colored hair. Sergeant Lee Roy Pipkin recalls that in the 74th Infantry Detachment (LRP) he and others with blond or red hair used boot polish on their heads and pulled their boonie hats down low to add to their camouflage.

When all premission preparations were completed, the team moved to a final inspection area called the pad or platform. This protected area was usually no more than a large wooden deck where the team leader checked each of his men a final time. When he was satisfied, the platoon leader and/or the company commander conducted a final inspection before the team was cleared for insertion.

Several of the LRRP units had one last ritual before deployment. A team picture was made to be added to the unit's records. Unfortunately, few of these pictures were ever included in the official files, and the only ones still in existence are in the hands of LRRP veterans. The camouflage is so detailed in the surviving photos that it is often difficult to recognize individuals. What is obvious in the pictures is the cockiness and total self-confidence of the subjects—along with a youthfulness that belies the image of tough, hardcore combat recon men.

One of the most interesting of these premission photos is in the possession of Kregg Jorgenson, an H Company Ranger veteran. The picture of Jorgenson's team was taken in late 1969 and by accident of a double exposure shows the ghostlike image of the team taken before his. Jorgenson states that the only two recognizable LRRPs in the double exposure were killed on patrol before the picture was developed.

Methods of insertion of the patrol teams included every available means of transportation. Teams entered their recon zones by boat from both inland waterways and the open surf, by land transportation including truck and tracked vehicle, and by the traditional, all-weather-capable foot power that infantrymen know too well.

While all those sources were used at one time or another, the principal means of insertion on the vast majority of missions was the transportation resource that dominated the war—the helicopter. Whether the chopper delivered the LRRPs on the LZ by touchdown or by hovering so they could jump, rappel, or ladder to the ground, insertion from the air was the way most missions began.

Insertion assets included a Huey carrying the patrol team and either a LOH or another Huey carrying the operations officer who supervised the insertion. In case the LZ proved to be hot, one or more gunships flew cover.

The Huey carrying the team streaked over the countryside, making fake passes at LZs both near and far from the designated landing site. These false insertions were again conducted several times after the actual landing to confuse the enemy as to the real site. Other efforts were made to deceive the enemy, such as preparatory artillery fire and other aircraft making false insertions at other LZs. One of the more interesting deceptions tried in several recon units was propping cardboard silhouettes in the troop compartment of the choppers making false insertions. In the Huey making the actual insertion, the dummies were mounted on a board with a spring where the LRRP sat en route to the LZ. When the LRRPs exited the aircraft, the dummies sprang up, filling the aircraft doors with silhouettes of men. For an enemy watching the LZ from a distance, the chopper would appear to approach the touchdown area with troops on board and take off the same way. It was hoped the unwary enemy would assume his LZ had only been the target of a false insertion.

Once off the helicopter, the LRRPs moved into the jungle as quickly as possible. After several hundred meters the team halted and remained in place for up to a quarter of an hour listening for sounds of enemy activity. Once satisfied that the team had not been detected, a quick communications check was made and the patrol moved out on their mission.

The team moved through the jungle on a predetermined compass azimuth, avoiding open areas and other locations where they might easily be observed by the enemy. Making himself a part of the vegetation rather than fighting it, the point man carefully picked his pathway to minimize noise while remaining alert for any sign of hostile activity. The team leader followed close behind, directing the point man by arm and hand signals when he varied from the compass heading or if a new direction needed to be taken. At intervals of five to ten meters, in file, the senior RTO followed, then the assistant team leader, and the junior RTO. Each carefully scanned his assigned sector to the flanks. At the end of the formation was the rear security man, or "tail gunner," who guarded the team from any force following their trail while doing his best to cover any evidence that the team had passed through at all.

With five to seven days to cover their assigned recon zone, the team had plenty of time to move slowly and observe frequent security halts. Any time the patrol halted for more than a few minutes, the team members assumed defensive positions, added to their camouflage, and emplaced their Claymore mines in a 360-degree protective circle with additional mines concentrated on likely avenues of approach.

The team covered its zone in zigzag routes so as not to establish any pattern. At times they would cloverleaf out from a dominant terrain feature until all directions had been covered. If instructions needed to be given that could not be accomplished by arm and hand signals, the team leader quietly whispered into hand-cupped ears or wrote on a pad and passed it around. As night fell, the LRRPs crawled into thick vegetation and circled into a "wagon wheel'' with their feet meeting at the center and weapons oriented outward. In teams of two they took turns eating and, if the situation warranted, they rested or caught a few minutes of sleep.

If the patrol discovered a path or trail showing recent use, the men took a hidden position nearby, waiting and watching. Lying nearly motionless for days at a time, the patrol would break silence only to make regular situation reports and spot reports of enemy sightings. When the enemy was observed, the LRRPs had the option of merely reporting the sighting to add to the intelligence data on hostile activity, calling in air or artillery strikes, or engaging the enemy with their own firepower. The latter technique was useful in gaining body count and the possibility of a prisoner or valuable documents, but it also compromised the remainder of the mission. Once the recon men revealed to the enemy that they were in an area, they had to be extracted because they were too few for sustained combat.

These extended trail watches yielded far more observations than just of the enemy. The LRRPs were so good at noise discipline and camouflage that the jungle wildlife was often as unknowing of their presence as the VC and NVA were. Every recon veteran recalls seeing monkeys, an occasional tiger or elephant, and snakes, lizards, and reptiles of all types walk or slither by their positions. The wildlife offered interesting breaks to the otherwise tedious and often terrifying duty.

During the entire mission, the team leader and his assistant kept notes on the terrain, vegetation, and water sources in their recon zone, along with map corrections and any sign of enemy activity. They also took a good look at areas that might be used as future LZs as well as those that could be used for a hasty extraction. The entire team was always aware of the closest area where a chopper could land or drop McGuire Rigs or ladders to pull the team out in case of emergency or enemy pursuit.

Precautions were also taken in case members of the patrol became separated due to temporary disorientation or enemy contact. Every several hundred meters the patrol leader designated rally points where the team would reassemble and reorganize if dispersed during movement.

A recon zone was the exclusive territory of the patrol team assigned to it. The areas were designated at all command level headquarters as "no fire, no fly," meaning that no friendly artillery could fire into or aircraft fly over the zone without a request or permission from the LRRPs on the ground. The no fire, no fly designation protected recon men from "friendly" fire, which was particularly important when they were using enemy uniforms and equipment. It also assured them that anyone in their zone besides themselves was an enemy.*

When the LRRPs did make visual or physical contact with hostile forces, there were a variety of fire support assets on which to call. Coordination had been made with all artillery batteries within range of the recon zone during the planning phase prior to insertion. Preplotted artillery concentrations were planned at likely spots of enemy contact. With data already computed by the artillery-fire direction center, the artillery could have steel on target within minutes of a request. If the artillery support was needed at a location other than at one of the preplotted targets, adjustments could be made from the known point, which was much faster than requesting an entirely new fire mission.

Naval gunfire was also preplotted by those LRRP units that operated near the South China Sea. Air support from both army and air force assets was available in addition to artillery and naval fire support. These assets were critical at all times, but especially when the LRRPs operated outside the range of the artillery. Although it was extremely desirable for the LRRPs always to be in the range of artillery fans, many of their missions were so distant from

---

*It was rare for the LRRPs to work in or near populated areas where civilians lived and worked. Their recon zones were usually far from villages, in remote jungles regarded as no-man's-land and belonged to the enemy until the LRRPs challenged their claim.

friendly units that air power was the only support that could reach them.

Time and location for the patrol's extraction were established during the mission-planning phase prior to the insertion. However, alternate plans for emergency extraction were devised during the entire mission. If the patrol was compromised, it had to be extracted immediately or reinforced with additional troops. To accomplish this, a lift chopper and a gunship were on constant strip alert. In addition, an infantry company, usually one on fire base security or on standdown in a rear area, or a cavalry squadron "blues" platoon was on standby to assist in the team's extraction. Still other infantry units were on call to divert from current operations to the nearest LZ to reinforce or exploit the LRRP's contact. As a final backup, patrol teams working other recon zones and those teams between missions could be assembled under the leadership of the company commander and inserted to assist their fellow LRRPs.

On some missions, such as raids on known enemy targets and prisoner snatches, extraction assets were not on call but rather already on station. Orbiting just out of sight and sound of the recon box, the chopper could be at a pickup zone within seconds of the team leader's request.

Regardless of the mission's length or intensity or the casualties sustained, a mission did not end on extraction. As soon as a team returned to the company base, they were immediately debriefed by the operations officer and/ or intel sergeant. If the mission had been particularly productive, intelligence officers from the parent unit and other higher echelons would also be present to get firsthand reports.

The debriefing included a team session and individual questioning. What had been seen and heard by each man was important and often different—especially those observations made in the midst of a fire fight. Men only a few meters apart often viewed a battle quite differently.

As a part of the debriefing process, the team leader completed written forms with detailed information on the recon zone and any enemy activity. These forms were forwarded to all echelons of higher headquarters, and a copy went into the unit's file along with a map overlay of the mission.

Not until the team leader signed the debriefing form was the mission complete. After a brief cleanup and rest period, the team began preparation for its next mission. The only reward for doing well was more of the same—and the pride that came in being a recon man.

CHAPTER 10
□□□□□□□□□

Results and Accolades

Measuring the results of any military organization or operation is difficult at best. Tet of '68 was a resounding victory by the ARVNs and Americans on the battlefield, yet it was a catastrophic defeat back home. Although American forces never lost a major battle or campaign, Saigon today is Ho Chi Minh City, and the Vietnam conflict is now taught in the classroom as the United States' only defeat.

As the years have passed since the fall of Saigon, the realization that Vietnam was lost in the conference room and through lack of national support rather than in the paddies and jungle has finally resulted in the recognition, at least in part, of the men who fought. The recon men, like their fellow soldiers of all branches of service, were little different from any of the warriors sent to foreign lands by the nation's leadership over the last two centuries. The major difference is best summed up by Lieutenant General (Retired) Stanley R. Larsen, who commanded II Field Force from August 1965 to August 1967. Larsen states, "More needs to be written about the Vietnam War, but unfortunately, these studies must consider that they are covering a 'lost' war run by politicians determined to beat out a no-win war, who were afraid to make difficult decisions, and certainly never aimed at MacArthur's famous truism, 'There is no substitute for victory.' ''

In that vein, it must certainly be admitted that any view of the accomplishments of the LRRPs has to be tempered by the knowledge that they were done in a lost cause. Yet the efforts of the recon men may have been one of the most positive aspects of the war. In relation to resources expended, the LRRPs' techniques of out-guerrillaing the guerrilla yielded far more contact with the enemy than any other organization. The intelligence they gathered led to many of the major battles and operations of the war. While their assignment was usually reconnaissance, not direct combat, LRRP units attained incredible enemy body counts and seized large quantities of weapons and equipment with very low friendly losses.

The Department of the Army has not yet compiled an official history of the Vietnam War. The closest it has come is a series of pamphlet-size works called ''Vietnam Studies'' that were written by major commanders and staff officers in the early '70s. In each, only brief mention is made of the LRRPs, but what is there is extremely positive.

Lieutenant General John Hay's comment in ''Tactical and Material Innovations,'' published in 1974, called the LRRPs ''one of the most significant innovations of the war.'' In another part of the same book Hay states, ''The long range patrol (LRP) was a particularly significant aspect of US operations in Vietnam.''

Hay also quotes Major General William Peers, who, as the commander of the 4th Infantry Division, was a leader in establishing LRRP units. According to Hay, Peers said, ''In 1967, before we had any form of surveillance such as the people sniffer [an airborne heat sensor] and the air cav with the scout unit, every major battle that the 4th Infantry Division got itself into was initiated by the action of a Long Range Patrol; every single one of them. That included the battle of Dak To, for the Long Range Patrols completely uncovered the enemy movement. We knew exactly where he was coming from our Long Range Patrol actions.''

More recently, Hay adds to his published comments on the LRRPs by saying succinctly, ''The information they provided was most useful; they produced well; all in all I give them high marks.''

In another of the Department of the Army's ''Vietnam Studies,'' entitled ''The Role of Military Intelligence 1965 to 1967'' and written in 1974 by Major General Joseph A. McChristian, LRRPs are again lauded. McChristian, who was General Westmoreland's intelligence officer from July 13, 1965, to June 1, 1967, writes, ''The importance of ground reconnaissance cannot be overemphasized. Ground reconnaissance can not only provide timely and accurate information on all aspects of the enemy and the area of operations, but also can report on where the enemy and his influences do not exist.''

McChristian concludes, ''Long range reconnaissance patrols were employed at almost every echelon of command in Vietnam. These teams were good sources of intelligence for tactical commanders.''

In the massive work titled *Infantry, Part I. Regular Army* by John K. Mahon and Romana Danysh, only ten pages are dedicated to the war in Vietnam, but almost a full page is about the LRRPs. The book, published by the army's Office of the Chief of Military History in 1972, reports, ''LRPs were small teams especially trained to penetrate deep into enemy-held territory. From there they reported detailed, accurate, and timely information concerning troop concentrations, installations, and activities needed for planning future operations, or they called in and adjusted artillery fire or air strikes.''

Praise for the LRRPs also is readily given by those commanders who saw the recon men firsthand. Lieutenant General Larsen, in addition to his comments about studying Vietnam in the context of a ''lost war,'' states, ''I had much respect for the courage and difficult missions performed by the men in the LRRP/Ranger operations. They were an essential element contributing valuable intelligence information.''

General (Retired) Michael S. Davison, who commanded the II Field Force from April 1970 to June 1971, adds, ''I can only tell you that I believe that the LRRPs represented a very valuable intelligence asset.''

Colonel (Retired) Dave Hackworth, in reference to his early days in Vietnam with the 1st Brigade of the 101st Airborne, perhaps gives the highest accolade, and the briefest, to the LRRPs by saying, ''They were tigers; real studs; professionals.''

Despite the unique mission of the LRRPs and their contributions to the war effort, little was written at the time or since about the recon men. The legendary reputation, the wide recognition of the name of ''LURPs,'' and the professionalism, fighting abilities, and stealth associated with them has been attained more by word of mouth than by print. Less than a dozen articles of any consequence have been published, and most of those appeared in professional journals such as *Infantry* and *Army* magazines during or shortly after the war. (See Bibliography for a complete list.)

The most detailed report on LRRPs and Rangers appeared in a special issue of the somewhat pulpy *Gung Ho* magazine in October of 1984. *Gung Ho*, however, focused more on the history of the Rangers and devoted a total of only three pages, mostly photos, to the Vietnam-era recon men. In the editors' introduction to the LRRP story, they state, ''There is little or nothing on the Vietnam era US Rangers. A comprehensive history, as was done about the WWII Rangers, doesn't exist, as far as we know.''

Why so little has been written about the Vietnam LRRPs/Rangers was best explained in the Spring 1972 edition of *First Team*, a semiannual authorized but unofficial magazine published by the 3rd Brigade of the 1st Cavalry Division. In ''Silence Is Their Only Advantage,'' an article about the Rangers of H Company written by Sergeant Doug Sterner, an editor's note states, ''Little has been written of the Rangers in Vietnam, the teams of men who creep through the jungle living the proverbial 'life of danger,' seeking out the enemy in a silent and deadly fashion and meeting him with the same terms and tactics he has employed against us. It isn't that Rangers are publicity shy, but to effectively tell their story one must live with them, hump with them, and fight with them. Seldom is the privilege of sharing their lives extended to a correspondent, or for that matter, any outsider. The Ranger Team is an elite team, specially trained to do a special job, and an untrained man can mean disaster.''

It can be speculated that the reputation of the recon men was enhanced by the little that was known of their operations. Maybe so and maybe not. Perhaps the legend would have been larger if more had seen and reported the LRRPs at work. Sterner was certainly convinced, as he included in his article, "No one made a noise. Quietly, I unsnapped my camera, focused it, and pushed the button to release the shutter. It sounded like a bomb dropping in a soundproof room, and everyone turned quickly to look at me. A little embarrassed, I put up my camera and resolved my pictures would have to wait a little longer.''

Regretfully, the official accounts of LRRP/Ranger operations are nearly as deficient as the public writings. In 1984, the analysis branch of the U.S. Army Center of Military History published a pamphlet titled "Researching the Vietnam Experience," by Ronald H. Spector. According to Spector, "In terms of sheer volume, the records relating to the Vietnam War appear to dwarf those of any previous American conflict. The war was the first to be fought in the age of the copying machine and the computer, and the influence of these innovations is reflected in the massive paper trail left by that conflict. There can be no debate about the quantity of documentation. Quality is another matter.''

Spector continues, "During the early years of the war, unit commanders, overworked and understaffed, often neglected or ignored Army requirements concerning the preparation and preservation of reports and records.''

When the army realized later in the war that proper

documentation and records management was not taking place, Spector notes, "The result was the rapid accumulation of masses of trivial and ephemeral material."

Spector also quotes from the 1974 publication by the army, "Report of the Preliminary Investigation Into the My Lai Incident," that found so much fault with the overall records of Vietnam that a special annex was published concerning the problem. According to the report, filing of historical records was complicated by the "tendency of units to destroy records rather than to retire them."

Another important point made by Spector is that "documentation of the Vietnam War is also extremely one-sided. At the end of World War II, American historians had available to them masses of captured enemy documents from which they were able to reconstruct the decision making process of the German, Italian, and to a lesser degree, the Japanese governments. Former high-ranking officers of those nations were available for questioning and often were utilized as research assistants in the preparation of the official Army and Navy histories. Nothing remotely similar exists for Vietnam. Although large numbers of captured Communist documents are available, the overwhelming majority are of a routine and low-level nature."

One area that Spector does not explore is the loss of records due to combat operations. Vietnam was a war without lines. Despite elaborate security measures, no area in the war zone was completely safe from enemy attack—even the compounds of the LRRPs. For example, the daily staff journal of K Company Rangers of the 4th Infantry Division for June 7, 1969, states, "At 0045 hours, all past records were destroyed. An unknown number of enemy made their way through the perimeter wire and into the company area. Explosions erupted throughout the area. The orderly room, operations room, supply room, and three troop billets were heavily damaged. Three Rangers were wounded. Enemy casualties are unknown."

Another problem in verifying information on LRRP activities is that most official reports and histories were not required at the separate company level. Because the

LRRPs, and later the Rangers, had no overall command headquarters, their reports were included as a part of the parent unit's when forwarded to the various archives.

One of the prime sources for researching combat actions is the operations report/lessons learned (ORLL) prepared by all major units on a quarterly basis. However, the ORLL, which was an historical summary and a brief description of major fights, was required to be submitted only by units down to separate battalion level. This, of course, did not include any requirement for separate companies or detachments. As a result, any report in the ORLLs on the recon men was usually only a brief paragraph included in the intelligence section.

Another source that should yield information on the recon units is the daily staff journal or duty officer's log that is required by regulation to be forwarded to the historical archives. Unfortunately, many of these reports were never forwarded out of Vietnam, and some of those that were are yet to be catalogued and made available to the public. In many cases, those which can be dug out are woefully lacking in specific information beyond the sketchiest details. For example, a team's successful ambush and subsequent extraction may at best be recorded in a two- or three-line summary, stating to the effect, "Team 42 made contact at 0245 hours; 3 enemy body count; 1 probable, 2 weapons captured; Team extracted at 0320 hours."

Some of the LRRP and Ranger units did make an effort to submit annual historical summaries. However, with change of commanders, casualties, and the tendency of the recon men "to prefer to fight than write," the ones that do exist are lacking in detail. Units that did do a fair job of submitting these summaries, at least in comparison to the others, were the LRRPs of E Company, 20th Infantry; Company E, 52nd Infantry; Company F, 58th Infantry; and the Rangers of G, H, and L Companies.

Despite the records available in the various official sources and those in the hands of the veterans and other private individuals, it is impossible to assemble a complete record of the accomplishments of even a single LRRP or Ranger unit's service in Vietnam. Enough information is available, however, to offer a good snapshot of the actions of the recon men.

For example, Company E, 50th Infantry (LRP), conducted 202 patrols in the three months of August through October 1968. The enemy was sighted on 127 of those missions with 71 of those resulting in contact for a body count of 47. In the first three months of 1969, the same company (redesignated E Company Rangers on February 1) conducted 244 missions with enemy sightings on 134. There were 111 contacts and a body count of 169.

During the first eight months of 1969, Rangers of Company G conducted 220 patrols, spotting the enemy on 124 of them. The Rangers killed 140 confirmed by body count and captured 7 prisoners. During the period of operations many more enemy were killed by artillery and air strikes but could not be confirmed because the recon men were extracted. Total friendly losses were three killed and seventeen wounded by hostile fire. Three others were injured in accidents—one each by rappeling, falling off a cliff, and being hit by lightning.

A more detailed report on actions from March 1 to July 15, 1969, was made by the Rangers of Company H. During that period, they deployed 328 patrols with 143 enemy sightings resulting in 118 contacts. Of those contacts, 99 were initiated by the recon men with the enemy firing first on only 9 occasions. The LRRPs killed 128 of the enemy with 56 more listed as possibles while capturing 16 prisoners and 28 inches of documents. Also captured were 101 weapons of which the majority (88) were AK-47s.

The report of the actions for four and a half months by H Company also shows the excellent support received by the recon men. Of the 143 sightings, 61 resulted in artillery being called in on the enemy's positions. Gunships, firing 2.75-inch rockets known as aerial rocket artillery, responded on 113 occasions, and regular gunships firing rockets, automatic grenade launchers, and machine guns supported 121 times. Fixed-wing aircraft of the U.S. Air

Force flew 29 missions in support of the Rangers' sightings.*

In addition to the artillery and air support, many of the findings by the recon men produced larger battles as the result of senior commanders' committing more units to exploit the actions initiated by the LRRPs. Of the 118 occasions during the reported period that the men of H Company were in physical contact with the enemy, ground troops were sent in to reinforce on 59, exactly one-half, of the fights.

The recon men paid a price in blood and lives for these impressive numbers, but on a much smaller scale than the enemy. During the reported period, six LRRPs were killed by hostile action and forty-two were wounded. However, thirty-two of the injured were returned to duty after brief hospitalization.

Although it is impossible to compile a completely accurate numerical account of the total LRRP effort in Vietnam for the reasons previously mentioned, by using the records that were kept, and are available, a fairly good estimate can be made. Difficulties in accounting are also complicated by the fact that few records were made or kept when the LRRP units were in a provisional status in the early years of the war. Fluctuating strengths, both authorized and on hand, provide further problems in compiling numbers.

Despite these difficulties, it can be reasonably estimated that over 23,000 LRRP patrols were conducted during the war. Of those, in excess of 14,500 resulted in sightings of the enemy with nearly 10,000 hostiles killed. When studying these numbers, it must be kept in mind that the recon men's mission was not, at least most of the time, to kill but to find and report. These reports yielded many more enemy casualties as the result of artillery and air strikes called in by the LRRPs or by regular infantry units that

*The total number of the various fire-support missions exceed the number of sightings because often air, artillery, and gunships were used during the same contact.

reacted to the recon men's observations. Also, many missions that did not yield direct observations of the enemy still gathered important information about terrain, vegetation, and other useful data of great value for future operations.

In no war could such results be attained without friendly casualties. However, the LRRPs were utterly fantastic in their ability to out-guerrilla the guerrilla, inflicting well over twenty-two enemy deaths for every recon man killed in combat. During the entire war fewer than four hundred fifty recon men made the ultimate sacrifice for unit and country.

One of the units hardest hit was the LRRPs of the 101st Airborne Division—Company F, 58th Infantry (LRP) and L Company, 75th Infantry (Ranger)—which suffered forty-six killed by hostile action over the nearly five years they were in-country. Compared to an infantry or any other unit of the same size, the figures are extremely small—and a true testament to the abilities and professionalism of the men with painted faces.

It might be expected that teams of only six men operating far from friendly support and often in the midst of enemy strongholds would be vulnerable to the loss of the entire team. Although rumors abound of LRRP teams that "disappeared, never to be heard from again," most are just that, rumors. As has been shown, LRRPs sustained relatively few casualties. When a team was in trouble, assets from all over were committed to their support.

One of the few instances where an entire team was lost was on May 11, 1970, when a patrol of L Company was overrun while in a night defensive position. Despite the fact that the enemy was victorious, they showed their respect for the LRRPs. Although all six members of the team were killed and their weapons and equipment removed, the bodies were not mutilated and were left where they had died so that their remains could be recovered by their fellow recon men.

The respect for the dead LRRPs of L Company was

apparently not unusual. However, as has been previously noted, it is impossible to interview enemy witnesses and search their records in a war that was not won. Nonetheless, both prisoners and documents at the time attest to the respect the enemy had for the LRRPs.

Although the enemy is often depicted as an almost superhuman jungle fighter, the fact is that many were urban-born and raised in the Hanoi area or in open rice-farming regions. The jungle was often as foreign and forbidding to the enemy, particularly the NVA, as it was to the greenest American replacement.

The psychological impact of the LRRPs beating the enemy, on what was supposed to be their own turf while using their tactics and methods, was tremendous. A body count ratio of over 22 to 1 had to add to their respect and fear of the men with painted faces. It was occasionally confirmed through captured documents and prisoner interrogations that many enemy units established bounties on LRRPs. Most often this was in the way of cash paid in amounts as high as the equivalent of $1,000—the same bounty for killing a U.S. colonel.

On at least one occasion, the NVA trained and sent south a special team with the specific mission of countering the recon men. Interestingly, the team was composed of six men—just like their prey. In this case, however, the hunter became the hunted. In February 1972 a patrol of H Company ambushed the NVA counter-LRRP team. Among the documents captured was one detailing the NVA team's mission and a picture of the six men taken in the North holding their country's flag. According to the documents, they would each receive a small rice farm for killing or capturing an entire LRRP team. Again the LRRPs out-guerrillaed the guerrilla; the only farm the NVA team earned was one that measured six feet deep.

CHAPTER 11

■□■□■□■□■

The Nonbelievers

*I*T would be neither fair nor accurate to portray LRRP operations in Vietnam as being totally supported and respected. There were those, including some in high positions of authority, who were against forming recon units to begin with and continued to oppose their existence after they were organized. Still others were positive or neutral toward the LRRPs initially but later became disenchanted with the recon forces.

Some of these negative feelings toward the LRRPs were based on preconceived notions about elite units in general, while others were the result of honest evaluations and theories about how a successful army should operate. A few, unfortunately, resulted from a simple lack of understanding of the LRRPs and perhaps the war itself.

The impact and contributions of the LRRPs during the war as detailed in the preceding chapters speak for themselves. Their influence on the army of today will be chronicled in the next. Yet, like any military operation or unit, the LRRPs were not perfect by any means, and there are certainly legitimate criticisms of their actions.

Throughout the history of the U.S. Army, and those of other nations, elite units have shared many of the criticisms that were common to the LRRPs. A basic concept in the training of all successful fighting forces is the "de-individualizing" of the recruit. From shorn hair and sameness in dress to drill and ceremonies, consistency of the group is demanded, rather than emphasis on individuality. There is far more than just a name in calling all military clothing "uniforms," for uniformity has long been understood as an important link in converting a self-oriented civilian into an order-following soldier.

The time-proven and near-universal requirement of consistency naturally leads to resentment when certain units are considered superior to the rest of the force. The resentment is compounded when "special" units are awarded such visible privileges as the right to wear berets, patches, and bloused jump boots.

Tradition-minded commanders and NCOs are reluctant to accept elements of their "uniform" service who act or are treated differently. This resentment extends to the remainder of the troops when they see their fellow soldiers enjoying the benefits and publicity of the elite units.

Nevertheless, warfare over the ages has proved that there is a requirement for units composed of specially trained volunteers who are motivated to take on the most hazardous assignments. Regardless of the demonstrated need, resentment—often mixed with respect and envy—has often been the response.

Another negative perception of elite units, one at times applied to the LRRPs, is that they are composed of misfits and malcontents who cannot fit in with traditional units and that they are "undisciplined renegades" because of their tendency to disregard orders and rules dictated by officers and NCOs who were not of the elite "brotherhood." And it is true that many LRRP units in Vietnam had to establish their own clubs and recreational facilities because of the altercations that occurred when the recon men mingled with conventional troops.

Other complaints about the LRRPs are common to all elites. The most prevalent was that special units create a leadership drain by attracting critically needed individuals from the conventional ranks. Superior soldiers who would have been squad leaders or platoon sergeants in regular

units might only be team members in a LRRP unit. This
attitude is best summed up by General (Retired) Frank T.
Mildren, who as a lieutenant general was the deputy commander of USARV from June 1968 to July 1970. "With
respect to LRRP units and their evolution to Ranger companies, [it] was a waste of superb manpower—the individuals could have been used better in combat units of the
Infantry and Armor."

One of the most common criticisms of the LRRPs,
shared by even the staunchest supporters of the recon men,
was the enormous amount of assets that were required to
directly support patrol operations or to be in a standby
posture for commitment to assist. Despite the large number of troop units, army aviation assets, and air force close
air support aircraft dedicated to the conflict, the war zone
was expansive and the enemy force quite formidable.
Commanders were constantly competing for limited assets
to fight the enemy in their areas of responsibility, and the
LRRPs, by the very nature of their operations, required
far more support than many thought was their fair share.

The single asset that was most in demand and often the
shortest in supply was the helicopter. Although the chopper was perhaps the most distinctive contribution to warfare of the Vietnam period, it did have its shortcomings.
As with any sophisticated piece of equipment, the helicopter required extensive maintenance. Safety restrictions
required that the pilots have sufficient rest between missions. Finally, the helicopter was limited in its survivabil-
ity on the battlefield because it could be shot down by
small-arms fire. As a result, helicopter assets were closely
controlled and monitored. It is not surprising that the sight
of lift birds and gunships being held on strip alert to support LRRP teams was upsetting to staff officers and commanders who were desperately in need of air assets.

Even those commanders who were the most supportive
of the LRRPs during the war, and in their writings since,
see the number of assets dedicated to the recon men critically. Lieutenant General John Hay, while flatly stating,
"the LRRPs had no shortcomings," reluctantly adds,

"however, they did tie up the limited number of air assets such as lift and gunships as we had to keep them available so they had support any time they were needed."

A direct relationship exists between complaints of overuse of assets by LRRPs and the parent unit to which they belonged. In the separate brigades and the regular infantry divisions, where helicopters were always in short supply, the feelings about LRRPs requiring too much support were common. In divisions that were structured for heavy helicopter use, in particular the 101st Airborne and the 1st Cavalry Divisions, the recon units were rarely criticized.

Another widespread complaint was based partly on a lack of understanding of what LRRP operations entailed, and largely on the uniqueness of the war itself. Commanders and soldiers alike were critical of the sustainability of the recon patrols. The typical infantrymen resented the fact that the LRRPs rarely stayed in the field for more than a week while he frequently measured his operations in months without a break. Commanders, who, due to the rapid rotation system, were in their positions for only six months or so, wanted maximum results during their tenure. LRRPs sitting in their unit base, despite the need for mission planning and preparation, were seen as gaining neither body count nor intelligence.

Even commanders who were supportive of the recon men found fault in their inability to remain in the field for extended periods. Major General (Retired) Robert C. Forbes, who served from 1966 to 1968 as an assistant division commander in the 9th Infantry, chief of staff of II Field Force, commander of the 199th Light Infantry Brigade, and as a MACV staff officer, says today that the LRRPs "did outstanding jobs in the circumstances in which they performed." Forbes adds that one of their major shortcomings was their "lack of staying power" but adds that this was more a "function of [their] size and composition" rather than a lack of motivation.

Major General (Retired) Salve H. Matheson, who commanded the 1st Brigade of the 101st Airborne in 1967, agrees with Forbes, saying that the greatest weakness of the LRRPs was their "inability to maintain themselves when threatened or under attack."

Harsher criticisms are offered by General (Retired) Frederick J. Kroesen, who commanded the 23rd Infantry Division (Americal) in 1971. Kroesen finds fault in the LRRPs' "willingness to stay in the field for protracted periods" and states that too many called for early recovery. He adds that the LRRPs "expected prima donna treatment" and were "never committed enough—too many days off." Despite his feelings, Kroesen concludes, "I am heartily in favor of LRRP companies and Rangers in the army force structure."

Out-guerrillaing the guerrilla was the principal mission of the LRRPs, and they did it well. However, LRRPs were few and the guerrillas many. Conventional units, despite their organization and previous training, also had to resort to many of the same tactics of the recon men to find the elusive enemy. The effectiveness of the LRRPs was questioned by commanders whose regular infantry was operating in many of the same ways. This was particularly true in areas of operation occupied primarily by Viet Cong rather than main force NVA regulars. General Forbes says, "A major reason that LRRPs were not used effectively and to a greater extent, at least in my area of operations, was that my companies and battalions were doing—on a larger scale, of course—many of the same activities as those which in any other environment other than Vietnam would have been assigned to LRRP units."

So the LRRPs, like every other elite and innovative unit in the annals of military history, had their critics. Some of the barbs were well founded. Nearly all were well meaning, their intent being improvement rather than idle complaint. As for the LRRPs themselves, they cared little at the time and care little today if they received rocks or flowers—for they did right as they saw right with no regrets or apologies.

CHAPTER 12
━━━━━━━━━

Legacy of the LRRP/Rangers

As U.S. involvement in the war wound down, combat units were withdrawn along with their assigned LRRPs. Many of the divisions and brigades were stood down and left the active rolls of the army. The units that did return to their stateside posts changed back to peacetime organizations that did not include recon units. Although the war was not won and the conflict left unresolved, the LRRPs had done their best. With little fanfare, they folded their flags, turned their equipment over to the ARVNs, and transferred to LRRP units still in-country or returned home.

By the end of 1970 only six of the original thirteen Ranger companies in Vietnam were still in existence. Further pullouts and unit standdowns continued so that by the beginning of 1972 only one recon unit remained—H Company Rangers of the 1st Cavalry Division. H Company was gradually reduced in strength until by June 1972 it could field only five teams. Although they were the last of their breed, and American units were being encouraged to leave the fighting to the ARVNs, the LRRPs continued business as usual. On June 9 the last recon men were killed in action on patrol. H Company's Team 76 was inserted into the Tan Uyen area and soon discovered an enemy bunker complex. The team—composed of team leader

Sergeant Elvis Osborne, assistant team leader Sergeant Robert Roy, and team members Sergeant Thomas Heiney, SP4 Jeffrey Maurer, SP4 Mike Spratt, and Sergeant Donald Schellinger—called in helicopter gunships to hose down the area. As the gunships departed, Osborne took two men back into the complex to assess damages while the remainder of the team stayed in a security position.

Osborne, Maurer, and Schellinger almost immediately encountered heavy small-arms and machine-gun fire. The three Rangers, rather than withdrawing, pushed forward, firing their weapons and throwing grenades. Their advance was stopped by a massive explosion of a command-detonated, 250-pound bomb. Schellinger, realizing his companions were dead, knowing that the rest of the team would soon come to investigate, and despite suffering extensive wounds and loss of blood, dragged himself through the dense terrain to intercept his teammates and prevent their advance into the enemies' trap.

A reaction force airmobiled into a nearby LZ to reinforce Team 76, and after several more hours of fighting secured the bunker complex and recovered the bodies of the two fallen Rangers. Few except the LRRPs of H Company were aware that Osborne was on his last mission and was scheduled to rotate home after nearly two years in Vietnam. Although not due for an insertion, Osborne had volunteered for one last patrol. Jefferey J. Cole, a SP4 in H Company at the time and now living in Gig Harbor, Washington, talked to members of Team 76 just before their insertion and to the survivors who returned. "There was no pullback by the LRRPs just because we were about to go home; no one was worried about being the last to die in Vietnam. Everyone had a good self-image, not bulletproof, but confident. We felt we could take care of ourselves."

At the same time Team 76 was experiencing its difficulties, teams of H Company were patrolling other recon zones in the same area. One of these, Team 72, led by Sergeant John Lebrun, had as a patrol member the company's newly assigned commander, Captain Robert J.

Hoffman. Hoffman's unenviable task was to close down the last LRRP unit in Vietnam; however, he did so as much from the jungle as from the company base, participating as a team member on several patrols.

Lebrun, a native of British Columbia, Canada, attended OCS after the war and is at this writing still on active duty as a major at Fort Leavenworth, Kansas. He recalls, "Hoffman's first mission was as a member of my team on a patrol from 6 to 10 June, 1972. We covered a lot of territory. I decided to 'walk the ass off' of the new CO to check him out. It was not a very good idea, as at end of the patrol I was the one who was dragging and Hoffman was still driving on. It was not until later that I found out that he was a former long-distance runner and still in excellent shape."

The last enemy fell to the LRRPs on June 21, 1972. Team 71 of H Company engaged from ambush four NVA in the Xa Gian Kiem area, killing one and recovering an individual weapon, a pack, ammunition, and a half-pound of documents. The mission was composed of team leader Staff Sergeant Clifford Price; assistant team leader SP4 David Hanson; and team members Sergeants Robert Sablan and Fred Griffis and SP4 Rory Selterman. Hoffman accompanied the team.

On July 16 the final LRRP patrol in Vietnam was conducted in the area of Tan Uyen in support of the 1st Cavalry Division's Task Force Garry Owen. Team 72 was led by Corporal John E. Roessler with Sablan acting as the assistant team leader. Others in the five-man team were Hoffman and Sergeant James Rogers and SP4 Timothy Dailey. On August 15, H Company was stood down. The proud service of the recon men in Vietnam had come to an end.

As in all previous wars the United States had fought, special or elite units had been formed to conduct the toughest missions, only to be disbanded as the nation returned to peace. Although the Vietnam LRRP/Ranger companies had been disbanded, two Ranger companies remained on the active rolls at stateside posts. For the first time in U.S. military history, Rangers would be a part of the peacetime army. Although the LRRPs were gone, they had left a legacy that outlived over two hundred years of tradition.

The LRRP legacy was in the form of A and B Companies (Ranger) of the 75th Infantry that had been organized on February 1, 1969, when the Vietnam LRRPs had been redesignated Ranger companies. At war's end, A Company, originally organized at Fort Benning and later moved to Fort Hood, Texas, and B Company, formed at Fort Carson, Colorado, and moved to Fort Lewis, Washington, were the only Rangers on the active rolls. With a TO&E strength of 198, they were assigned stateside to train for a wartime mission supporting the V and VII U.S. Corps in Germany. Both companies often deployed in the early 1970s for the annual European war games known as Reforger. Many Vietnam-era LRRP vets filled their ranks.

At the outbreak of the Middle East War of 1973, the Department of the Army became concerned that during the post-Vietnam period forces had concentrated on heavy mechanized and armored divisions and that there were no longer any light, mobile forces that could quickly be moved to any trouble spot. As a result, the chief of staff of the army, General Creighton W. Abrams, who also had followed Westmoreland as commander of USARV and MACV in Vietnam, sent a message to the field in January 1974 directing formation of Ranger battalions. "This elite Infantry unit is to be composed of highly trained and motivated Airborne, Ranger qualified personnel." He was also aware that elite units are not quickly formed. "Organizing the Ranger battalions must be done right, there is no timetable for the effort."

As an armor battalion commander in the European theater during World War II and during his time in Vietnam, Abrams had become well acquainted with LRRPs and Rangers and was aware of previous shortcomings of, and complaints about, the elites. Abrams accompanied his directions for the formation of Ranger battalions with a stern warning. "The Ranger battalions will contain no hoodlums or brigands, and if the battalions are formed from such persons or degenerate to this, they will be disbanded.''

On January 25, 1974, Headquarters, United States Army Forces Command, published General Order 127 directing activation of the 1st Battalion (Ranger), 75th Infantry, with an effective date of January 31, 1974. The new battalion was to be stationed at Fort Stewart, Georgia. On October 1, 1974, the 2nd Battalion (Ranger) was activated at Fort Lewis, Washington.

Upon establishment of the two Ranger battalions, A and B Companies were inactivated. While some of the personnel did transfer from the companies to the battalions, neither A nor B Company played any role in the formation of the new units. The reason was that the new Ranger battalions had a far larger mission than that of reconnaissance. Rangers were no longer dedicated to tactical battlefield missions but rather to national strategic objectives. Members of the battalions would still be able to operate in small teams for recon work, but their main purpose would be to act as a strike-force battalion. Patrol teams would no longer be the center of the organization. The basic unit of the Ranger company would be the squad with a battalion organization similar to that of a light infantry battalion, with three rifle companies and a headquarters company. To increase mobility, a combat support company would not be present, and all equipment in the battalion would be man-portable.

The mission of the Ranger battalions remains ''to conduct special military operations in support of the policy and objectives of the United States of America.'' Typical Ranger missions include special operations against deep targets; operations in conjunction with conventional forces; airborne and airmobile operations in support of larger units; rescue operations; safeguarding U.S. lives, property, or investments, or U.S. citizens and embassies abroad; and deployment worldwide to show U.S. resolve and readiness.

The requirements for joining the Rangers were established with elitism in mind at the time of the battalions' organization and remain so today. As in the days of the Vietnam LRRPs, each man must be a volunteer. Each volunteer must have a high school diploma and a clean civilian and military criminal record. Just as the LRRPs conducted unit training that had to be successfully completed before joining the patrol teams, the present Rangers do likewise. The tough, four-week course, known as the Ranger Indoctrination Program (RIP), has an attrition rate of about fifty percent. Once the volunteer has successfully completed RIP, he is assigned to a squad. If he further proves his leadership abilities, he is sent to the Ranger Course at Benning after about a year.

Rangers of today take their jobs as seriously as those in the past. At every ceremony and important event they recite in unison the Ranger Creed, in which they swear, "Never shall I fail my comrades" and to "uphold the prestige, honor, and high 'esprit de corps' " of their battalion. The words of Abrams's warning that the battalions were to "contain no hoodlums or brigands" are also not forgotten, as the creed includes, "My courtesy to superior officers, my neatness of dress and care of equipment shall set the example for others to follow."

The creed, while certainly in line with the legacy of Rangers of the past, is a new tradition. Written in 1974 by Neil R. Gentry, the command sergeant major of the 1st Battalion, it is now used in all Ranger battalions. Most appropriately, Gentry is a Vietnam LRRP veteran and the former 1st sergeant of L Company (Ranger) of the 101st Airborne Division. (For the complete Ranger Creed, see Appendix G.)

To maintain readiness for their variety of missions, the Rangers spend little time at their home stations. Europe, Korea, the Mideast, North Africa, Canada, and Central America are visited frequently by Rangers on deployment exercises and training missions.

The first real combat operation by the Rangers was in support of the abortive hostage rescue operation in Iran in 1979. Although the Rangers were not a part of the Delta

Force strike element that met disaster in the desert, they were deployed at various airfields in the Mideast where the hostages were to be brought for transfer to friendlier territory. Much of the actual Ranger part of the operation is still classified.

The ultimate proof of the effectiveness of the Ranger battalions came during the liberation of the island of Grenada on October 25, 1983. During the operation, code named URGENT FURY, the 1st and 2nd Ranger Battalions led the attack with a daring, low-level parachute assault from a mere 500 feet to seize the Cuban-held airfield at Port Salines. In training, airborne operations are conducted at 1000 to 1200 feet, with the lowest level recommended for combat operations being 800 feet. This minimum is a necessity to give time for a jumper to deploy his reserve chute in case the main canopy malfunctions.

The Rangers in Grenada were well aware of these restrictions; however, intelligence sources had revealed that the airfield was heavily defended by Soviet-made antiaircraft guns. It the Rangers jumped at 500 feet, the guns would be unable to depress their trajectory enough to engage the aircraft or the jumpers. Without hesitation the Rangers agreed to the low-level drop. As Lieutenant Colonel Ralph Hagler, commander of the 2nd Battalion, would later explain, "Since the drop was too low to have time to deploy a reserve chute, we discarded them and carried more ammunition instead."

After securing the airfield, the Rangers regrouped and pressed on to rescue isolated American medical students at the True Blue campus and later conducted heliborne assaults to eliminate pockets of resistance.

The demonstrated effectiveness of the Rangers in Grenada convinced the army to increase the size of the force. On October 3, 1984, the 3rd Battalion (Ranger) was activated at Fort Benning. At the same ceremony the Headquarters and Headquarters Company (Ranger), 75th Infantry, was formed. The additional battalion brought the size of the Ranger force to the largest it had been in forty years. More important, the Headquarters Company organization marked the first time that U.S. Rangers had a parent headquarters.

The final step in formalizing the Rangers as a continuing part of the U.S. Army occurred on February 3, 1984. On that date Secretary of the Army John O. Marsh ordered the redesignation of the 75th Infantry (Ranger) as the 75th Ranger Regiment. Rangers were at long last official rather than parenthetical. At the same time, Marsh directed that the lineage and honors of former Ranger units be transferred from the Special Forces to the new regiment. The Ranger Regiment of today now carries the lineage and honors not only of Merrill's Marauders but also of the Vietnam LRRPs and Rangers, and the Rangers of World War II and Korea.

Although the Ranger battalions that have evolved are difficult to compare to the LRRPs, the Vietnam recon men had sown the seeds and nurtured them with their sweat and blood to begin the process that bore the fruit of the current Rangers. LRRPs have become a part of history and legend, but the passage of time has not negated the need for timely battlefield intelligence that can only be gathered by men on the ground.

In 1986 the army published a new version of FM 100-5, *Operations*, which reorganized and defined combat doctrine. Officially known as the "Airland Battle doctrine," the manual outlines an approach to fighting intended to develop the full potential of U.S. forces.

The airland battle concept is defined as "nonlinear battles which attack enemy forces throughout their depth with fire or maneuver. They require the coordinated action of all available military forces in pursuit of a single objective. Air and ground maneuver forces; conventional nuclear and chemical forces; unconventional warfare, active reconnaissance, surveillance, and target acquisition efforts, and electronic warfare will be directed against the forward and rear areas of both combatants. Successful Airland Battle operations are characterized by initiative, depth, agility, and synchronization."

In the development of the Airland Battle doctrine during the early 1980s, the planners recognized that the army did not have a formal organization dedicated to reconnaissance and surveillance. In an effort not to reinvent the wheel, it would seem logical that the army planners would turn to the concept of the Vietnam LRRPs, who had performed a similar mission so well. They, in fact, did—and did not, at the same time. Vietnam is still a controversial issue both within and without the armed forces. Much effort has been made to distance the present army from what is now commonly referred to as the only war the United States ever lost. No one was particularly interested in re-forming recon units and labeling them with a name almost synonymous with the unpopular war.

At the army's Training and Doctrine Command (TRADOC), located at Fort Monroe, Virginia, some staff officers, including the commander, General William R. Richardson, are quoted as going a step further in saying that they wanted nothing to remind anyone of the "unsavory LRRP experience in Vietnam."

Interestingly, TRADOC is the successor to the old CONARC headquarters of the Vietnam era. Although they would call the new recon units Long-Range Surveillance Units (LRSU) rather than LRRPs, their pamphlets and circulars, and ultimately the field manual, closely resemble the CONARC documents of the 1960s that established the LRRPs—so much so that many phrases and even entire paragraphs are identical.

The first official document published on the LRSU, pronounced "Lursue," was issued by TRADOC on October 25, 1984. Titled TRADOC Pamphlet 525-42, *Long-Range Surveillance Units*, the pamphlet resembled the CONARC Directive 525-4 on LRRPs dated May 26, 1961, in more ways than just its number. Whatever the irony, the Airland Battle doctrine study had accomplished the same thing as the ROAD-65 study of a quarter-century previous. The army was once again recognizing the need for recon units and the groundwork for their reality was well on its way.*

Just as in the original concepts for LRRPs, the assignment of LRSUs was initially recommended at only corps level. Again, like the planning for LRRPs, this concept eventually broadened to include LRSUs at division level as well.

The return of the LRRPs/LRSUs was well received. In a message to TRADOC and other senior training and combat headquarters on April 18, 1986, the United States Army Infantry School (USAIS) at Fort Benning echoed the rest of the army. "USAIS has the lead per TRADOC CG guidance in the implementation, equipping, training and fielding of the Division and Corps long range surveillance units. There is no single project the Infantry School is now working where we can make such a giant step in combat capabilities for minimal expenditure of resources. The Airland battle demands near real time HUMINT [human intelligence] for maneuver tactics and fire power targeting: LRSUs will be a major step forward in this intelligence capability."

A little over a month later, one of the most important decisions in the planning process for LRSUs was made. The problems and inconsistencies that led to LRRPs in Vietnam often being used as much in a combat role as for reconnaissance would not plague the LRSUs. On May 20, 1986, TRADOC transmitted a message to the field stating, "the long range surveillance units will be organic to the MI [Military Intelligence] Brigade at Corps and the MI Battalion at Division."

In the spring of 1986, TRADOC published a draft edition of Field Circular 7-93, "Long Range Surveillance Unit Operations," and forwarded it to corps and divisions

---

*Other nations, including allies and potential future adversaries, have also concentrated on the organization of LRRP-type units. Two of the most formidable are the Special Operations Forces of North Korea and the Spetsnaz of the Soviet Union. Other recon units are found in the armies of the United Kingdom, West Germany, Denmark, Belgium, The Netherlands, France, East Germany, Czechoslovakia, and Greece.

for comment before its publication as an official document. FC 7-93 would look very familiar to the Vietnam-era LRRP, as it closely resembles the series of FM 31-18 manuals published between 1962 and 1968.

Although FC 7-93 and related documents have not been officially published at the time of this writing, the army has already moved ahead and is establishing LRSUs at divisions and corps. Their organization closely resembles the LRRPs of old, with the six-man "surveillance" team, as it is now called, being the center of the unit.

The fact that the present LRSUs are a legacy of the LRRPs has not been lost on the present recon men. On the activation of the 101st Airborne Division (Air Assault) LRSU company at Fort Campbell, Kentucky, a reunion was held for LRRPs and Rangers who had served with the division in Vietnam. Former recon men of the division's 1st Brigade Provisional LRRPs, Company F, 58th Infantry (LRP) and L Company (Ranger) were on hand for the ceremony. The presentation of the LRSU guidon was by Lieutenant Colonel David H. Ohle, who, as a captain, had commanded the Rangers of L Company from August 1970 to July 1971. Regardless of the official name, a new era of LRRP operations had begun.

CHAPTER 13
========

Conclusions

*F*ROM 1959 to 1975, more than 2.7 million Americans served in Vietnam. Over 58,000 died; 300,000 were wounded; 2,436 remain missing in action. It was the first war in United States history that was recorded as a defeat.

The reasons for the lack of victory are fairly well agreed upon today. No U.S. national objective was ever clearly articulated for the involvement in Vietnam. Neither was a strategy ever developed to accomplish that objective—whatever it was. Soldiers, sailors, airmen, and marines were committed to the conflict by presidential order and without the support of the Congress or the American people. Finally, the enemy was a determined one. Neither time nor the catastrophic loss of over 600,000 dead—the equivalent to the United States losing ten million—deterred him from fighting on.

The LRRPs were an important though small part of the U.S. war efforts. With few exceptions, they would be organized out of wartime necessity rather than peacetime forethought. The fact that the recon teams were formed on the battlefield rather than in stateside safety would cost in frustration, blood, and lives. Perhaps, just perhaps, if created before the war and used with a better understanding of their capabilities and in greater numbers, they might well have turned defeat into victory. At the very least, magnified LRRP operations would have minimized the number of Americans who never got the chance to grow old because of their deaths in Vietnam.

However what "might have been" is, in reality, "never was." The significant accomplishments of the LRRPs in Vietnam can only be described as a valiant effort in a lost cause.

Although the Vietnam War is now history, the LRRPs can look at the present with pride, for their efforts in the conflict directly led to the formation of the largest numbers of Rangers and LRRPs (now LRSUs) ever on the army's active rolls. The LRRPs' most important contribution may very well be the modern warriors and recon men who maintain the peace through their readiness for war.

During the mid-1980s, Secretary of the Army John O. Marsh would make many of the decisions that led to the increase of Ranger units and the formation of the LRSUs. In 1971, Marsh was a fourth-term congressman from the state of Virginia and a member of the House Appropriations Committee. At that time he made a visit to various military installations, including the Florida Ranger Camp of the Fort Benning Ranger School. Speaking to the camp's instructors, who were all Vietnam veterans—many with the LRRPs—Marsh said, "The test is men, not armament. Battles have always been decided by the soldier on the ground. The best weapon—yesterday, today and tomorrow, on any battlefield—is the American Ranger. Our country is in his debt."

APPENDIX A

━━━━━━━━

Tactical Standard Operating Procedures, LRRP Company

(NOTE: The following is a combination of several SOPs that were used by LRRPs and Rangers in Vietnam. It also includes guidance as outlined in the various editions of FM 31-18, "Long Range Reconnaissance Patrols," and the United States Army Infantry School Ranger Handbook of the period. The SOP is based on the standard table of organization and equipment for a LRRP company assigned to an infantry division. Except for number of assigned patrol teams, the SOP is applicable to any LRRP unit that saw service in Southeast Asia.)

1. PURPOSE

This SOP standardizes routine, recurring procedures of the company, thus eliminating the need for lengthy recitation of these items in patrol orders. It includes the organization, employment, support, and coordination essential to the tactical operation of the company and applies to all operations and to all assigned and attached personnel.

2. MISSION

The mission of the LRRP company is to enter specified areas within enemy-held or contested territory to observe and report enemy dispositions, fortifications, and activities. Specific missions include:

  a. Determine and report the strength, equipment, disposition, organization, and movement of enemy forces
  b. Locate reserves, command posts, and key facilities
  c. Perform reconnaissance and surveillance of specific sites, routes, or areas, and determine enemy movement patterns
  d. Maintain surveillance over suspected infiltration routes and avenues of approach
  e. Locate targets for air strikes, artillery, and ground attack
  f. Conduct tactical damage assessments of air strikes and artillery
  g. Conduct ambush or combat patrols or raids on specified targets
  h. Capture prisoners
  i. Emplace and monitor sensor devices
  j. Recover downed aircraft and crewmen
  k. Provide information on possible landing zones for airmobile operations
  l. Advise and train other units in recon operations
  m. Perform other missions as assigned

3. ORGANIZATION

The company is organized with a headquarters section, an operations section, a communications section, and two patrol platoons. (Annex I)

  a. The headquarters section consists of the company commander, executive officer, 1st sergeant, company clerk, supply sergeant, supply clerk, and mess personnel.

b. The operations section consists of an operations sergeant, intelligence sergeant, and operations specialist.

c. The communications section consists of a head-quarters section and three base radio stations to be employed as radio relays. In the headquarters section is a section sergeant and a field radio re-pairman.

d. Each patrol platoon is composed of a platoon leader, platoon sergeant, and seven LRRP teams. Each team is made of six personnel with the following assignments:
   (1) Team leader
   (2) Assistant team leader
   (3) Senior scout observer
   (4) Junior scout observer
   (5) Senior radio-telephone operator
   (6) Junior radio-telephone operator

4. COMMITMENT

The tactical commitment for the company is a minimum of fifty percent of the operational teams deployed at all times. Normally teams will be deployed in six-man teams as described in paragraph 3d. At no time will a team be committed with less than four men.

5. CONCEPT OF EMPLOYMENT

a. The company or team will normally receive its missions two to three days prior to the planned insertion. This time span is required for all the necessary coordination to be accomplished. The company or individual teams may react more quickly, however; a minimum notice of twenty-four hours is required.

b. LRRP teams should be employed recognizing these limitations:

(1) Team composition and armament
(2) Communications
(3) Limited mobility once on ground
(4) Support requirements

c. The following sequence of events will be followed prior to execution of a LRRP mission:

(1) Company receives mission
Missions for patrols are received from the Division G-2 (intelligence). These missions are assigned in coordination with the Division G-3 (operations) to gather or confirm intelligence.

(2) Request data base readout
The data base readout is obtained from the Order of Battle section of the G-2. It contains all intelligence information available concerning the proposed area of interest as reported by all previous units in the area.

(3) Landing zone (LZ) selection
At least one day prior to the scheduled insertion, the company operations officer will make an aerial recon of the proposed area to select at least two LZs for the insertion.

(4) Selection of the recon box
Upon completion of the aerial recon, the operations officer will select and designate on the map the area in which the team will operate. This box will normally be four grid squares (one thousand meters square each); however, when dictated by terrain, the boundaries may conform to stream lines or mountain ridges.

(5) Request aircraft for the mission
The division air cavalry squadron will normally provide all LRRP air support. If aircraft is not available through the squadron, assets will be requested through Division G-3. Aircraft required for each mission include

UH1H utility helicopter(s) and AH1G gun-
ship(s) for the overflight, and the same type
aircraft plus a command and control ship for
both the insertion and extraction.

(6) Overflight
An overflight will be conducted so that the
team leader and assistant team leader can
make a visual recon of the area of interest
(AI) prior to the insertion. The operations officer who made the LZ selection will accompany and point out the possible primary and
alternate LZs, the recon box, and recommended routes of march. The aircraft commander who will fly the actual insertion will
also fly the overflight and will determine
whether or not the team will touch down, ladder, or rappel into the LZ. During the overflight the operations officer and the aircraft
commander will also determine possible areas for false insertions prior to and after the
actual landing.

(7) Overflight debriefing
Upon return to the company tactical operations center (TOC), the operations officer will
debrief the team leader and assistant team
leader on the overflight. The debriefing will
include:
  (a) Primary and alternate LZs
  (b) Routes of march, to include escape and
      evasion
  (c) Significant terrain features
  (d) Emergency extraction locations
  (e) Observed signs of enemy activity
  (f) Locations of preplotted artillery targets
  (g) Locations of false insertion LZs

(8) Emplacement of radio relay
A radio relay will normally be positioned at
the artillery fire base (FB) nearest to the area

of interest. It will consist of three men and the necessary equipment to establish communications between the teams in the field and the company TOC. When no FB is located near enough to the AI to provide the necessary relay, a heavy team of six to nine men will establish and secure a relay site near the AI on high ground. This mission may also be performed by a patrol team positioned between the primary AI and the TOC.

(9) Presentation of the company operations order and intelligence briefing

The operations officer or sergeant will present the operations order to the team leaders in the briefing room of the TOC. Intelligence obtained from the order of battle section will also be disseminated at this time.

(10) Signal operating instructions (SOI) preparation

The operations section will update all SOIs with current call signs, frequencies, and codes. The team leader will sign for the SOI. RTOs will be required to memorize critical items of the SOI.

d. LRRP team activity prior to insertion:

(1) Receive alert for mission and pick up necessary maps

(2) Study mission, plan use of time, study terrain and situation

(3) Team leader issues warning order

(4) Conduct overflight

(5) Overflight debriefing

(6) Prepare ammo and equipment list

(7) Draw and issue ammo, rations, explosives, and special equipment. Uniform and weapons designated by team leader. Minimum additional equipment will include:

(a) 6 M-26 fragmentation grenades per member
(b) 1 concussion grenade per member
(c) 2 CS grenades per member
(d) 2 Claymore mines per member
(e) 3 strobe lights per team
(f) 2 signal panels and 2 signal mirrors per team
(g) 3 lensatic compasses per team
(h) 3 pen-gun flare sets per team
(i) 3 smoke grenades per member
(j) 2 penlights per team
(k) 1 SOI per team
(l) 1 poncho liner per member
(m) 1 can foot powder per member
(n) 1 pair extra socks per man
(o) 1 first-aid kit per member
(p) 1 first-aid bag per team
(q) 1 sling rope and snap link per member
(r) 2 radios per team (PRC-25 or PRC-77)
(s) 1 emergency radio per team (URC-10 or URC-68)
(t) 2 extra batteries per radio
(u) 1 extra handset per 2 radios
(v) 1 field expedient antenna per team
(w) 5 days rations per man (8 during monsoon season)
(x) 5 quarts of water per member with one bottle water purification tablets
(y) 1 camouflage stick per member

e. Communications
As prescribed in the minimum equipment list, each team will carry two PRC-25 or -77 FM radios as their primary means of communications. At the team leader's discretion the team may also carry a PRC-74 AM radio. Radio relays will be employed if the teams are deployed out of range of the TOC radios. Each team will also carry a URC-68 or -10 as an emergency FM backup.

6. INSERTION

The method of insertion of the patrol team depends upon the mission, enemy situation, support available, weather, terrain, and the location of the AI in which the team will operate. Insertion will be accomplished by helicopter, foot, vehicle, boat, or stay behind.

a. Helicopter
   All helicopter operations are controlled by the operations officer.
   (1) Prior to the insertion, the operations officer will brief the aircraft commander on the following:
      (a) Actions on the LZ if the aircraft takes enemy fire and all personnel are still on board
      (b) Actions on the LZ if the aircraft takes enemy fire and one or more men are off the aircraft and cannot reboard
      (c) Actions if the helicopter is hit on the LZ and cannot fly (team leader becomes ground commander of air crew and team)
      (d) Actions taken if the insertion is not a touchdown
      (e) Duties of the "belly man" who will assist in rappel and ladder insertions
      (f) Flight route
      (g) Location of false insertion(s)
      (h) Type of insertion (low or high level)
      (i) Order of insertion if more than one team is going into the same AI
      (j) Whether or not the LZ will be prepped with artillery and/or gunships
      (k) Enemy situation in the AI
      (l) Radio call signs and frequencies of all elements involved in the operation

- (2) The four types of helicopter insertions that will be employed are:
  - (a) Touchdown: The aircraft, once at the LZ, rests its skids on the ground and the team rapidly exits.
  - (b) Jump: The aircraft hovers as near the surface of the LZ as possible, and the team jumps from the skids to the ground. It is the responsibility of the team leader to determine if it is safe for the team to exit. If the aircraft is too high, the team leader will abort the primary LZ and instruct the aircraft commander to proceed to the alternate LZ.
  - (c) Ladder: The aircraft hovers between ten and fifty feet above the LZ and the belly man drops the ladder. The team then climbs down the ladder to the ground. The belly man is responsible for the team's safety in dropping the ladder at the proper time and in giving instructions to the aircraft commander.
  - (d) Rappel: Insertions by rappelling will be conducted with two ropes, each one hundred twenty feet in length. Prior to take-off, team members will coil their ropes, tie their Swiss seats, and hook their snap links into the rope. The belly man will direct the aircraft commander to the proper position above the LZ and, once the correct hover is maintained, instruct the team to drop their ropes. After checking for entanglements and insuring the ropes reach the ground, he will order the team to rappel to the ground.

b. Foot
   Insertion by foot will be conducted when the AI is near a friendly fire base or secure area. The

company operations section will coordinate with
friendly units for passage of lines and to ensure
that no other friendly units are in the recon box.
Insertion by foot, especially during hours of
darkness, is the most clandestine method of entering the recon zone.

c. Vehicle

Vehicle insertions are conducted along roads or
paths by either track or wheeled vehicles. The
company operations section will coordinate with
adjacent friendly units for passage. Overhead
gunship support for the convoy will be provided
if deemed appropriate. When the vehicles reach
the designated dropoff point they will dismount
and enter the AI by foot. Vehicles will make false
stops before and after the actual dropoff so as not
to compromise the operation.

d. Boat

Water-borne operations for inserting LRRP teams
consist of movement on and landings from both
rivers and surf. Teams will receive briefings at
the staging area from the naval officer in charge
and then load the boats and proceed to the AI.
The team will exit the boat when it nears the shore
or beach. Both prior to and after the actual insertion, the boat will make false insertions to deceive the enemy.

e. Stay Behind

The team will link up with a friendly unit at
least two hours before its scheduled departure
from an area. When the unit departs, the team
remains in place and assumes responsibility for
the area to see if enemy troops will reoccupy
the area in belief that friendly troops have departed.

7. GROUND MANEUVER

a. Formations

Teams will normally move in a file formation due to the thick terrain in which operations can best be conducted. In more open areas, the file can be modified into a cigar-shaped column formation. Distance between each team member will ordinarily be five to ten meters apart, but never farther apart so as not to be within visual observation of the man immediately to the front and rear.

b. Order of and individual responsibilities during movement

(1) Senior scout observer: Will act as point man and is responsible for front security, early warning of enemy activity, and maintaining a general compass direction of the route of march. In the event the team leader and assistant team leader become casualties, assume command of the team.

(2) Team leader: Responsible for all actions of the team. Will be second in order of march and will direct the point man by arm and hand signals to maintain the specific route of march. With help of the assistant team leader, will assign team equipment, uniform, and weapons.

(3) Senior RTO: Will be third in order of march and is responsible for maintaining communications with company TOC or relay station. Also will observe designated flank for security and will maintain a pace count to assist the team leader in land navigation.

(4) Assistant team leader: Will be fourth in order of march and will monitor compass heading and pace count to maintain a constant awareness of the team's exact map location. In the event the team leader becomes a casualty, as-

sumes leadership of the team. Will carry the
team aid bag and is the team medic.

(5) Junior RTO: Will be fifth in order of march
and is responsible for security of designated
flank. Responsible for communications as
designated by team leader.

(6) Junior scout observer: Will be sixth in the
order of march and is responsible for rear
security and to sanitize the team's route of
march by ensuring nothing is left behind to
alert the enemy to the team's passage. This
will include straightening branches, covering
skuff marks, etc.

(NOTE: On extended missions, the team
leader may adjust the order of march and individual responsibilities to maintain alertness. In the event that the team is short of
personnel, the team leader and/or assistant
team leader may carry his own radio and assume the additional duty of RTO. The team
leader is not confined by this portion of the
SOP if the situation dictates otherwise.)

c. Actions at halts

(1) For short halts, the team will "herring bone"
with the point man facing forward, the rear
security man covering the rear, and the other
team members facing in alternate directions
down the file.

(2) For longer halts, including night positions,
the team will "wagon wheel" with their feet
to the center and weapons facing outward. If
terrain or situation so dictate, the team may
set up in a linear position within arm's reach
of each other. In any position occupied for
more than a few minutes, Claymores will be
emplaced to provide 360-degree protection
with concentration on likely avenues of enemy approach.

    d. Actions at danger areas
      (1) Danger areas are defined as those areas where the terrain offers increased chances for detection of the team by the enemy. They are usually in the form of open areas, road or trails, or streams.
      (2) The best way to handle a danger area is to avoid it. The team should go around the area or wait for the hours of darkness before crossing. If the danger area must be crossed during daylight, the point man will cross and recon the far side before directing the remainder of the team to cross. Rally points will be designated by the team leader at both the near and far sides before the crossing in case the team is engaged by the enemy and becomes temporarily separated.

8. IMMEDIATE ACTION DRILLS (IAD)

Immediate action drills are defined as drills designed to provide swift and positive reactions to visual or physical contact with the enemy. They are single courses of action which require a minimum of signal or command to initiate and may be initiated by any member of the team. IAD may be defensive or offensive in nature. They must be simple and capable of quick execution. Common IAD include:

    a. Chance contact
      First man to spot the enemy freezes and signals the rest of patrol to do the same. The team remains motionless until the enemy passes. If spotted by the enemy, the team immediately opens fire.
    b. Hasty ambush
      A team members spots the enemy without being detected. He signals the rest of the team of the spotting and the direction of the enemy. The team leader signals orientation of the team to engage

while the enemy is allowed to proceed as far as possible into the kill zone. Any ambush formation may be used; however, linear will most often be employed due to simplicity, time available, and ease of control. Team leader initiates the ambush with well-aimed shots.

c. Immediate assault

The team and the enemy sight each other simultaneously. Nearest team member fires as rest of team swiftly moves on line and assaults.

d. Counter-ambush

(1) If part of the team is caught in the killing zone, they return fire and attempt to withdraw. The remainder of the team supports by fire or maneuvers to assault the flank of the enemy ambush.

(2) If the entire team is caught in the kill zone, return fire and attempt to withdraw. If in extremely close quarters, the only option may be to attempt to assault through the ambush. (NOTE: Smoke or CS grenades will assist in covering the team's withdrawal.)

e. Withdrawal by fire

In most chance contacts the best course is to withdraw as rapidly as possible until the strength of the enemy can be determined. It is not the recon team's mission to stand and fight. Withdrawal by fire may best be accomplished by a leapfrog method of bounds while one part of the team covers the other.

f. Reaction to enemy mortar fire

If the team is engaged by mortar fire it can be assumed that the fire is being adjusted by direct observation. The team should hit the ground on hearing incoming rounds and after impact move at a right angle to the direction of march as rapidly as possible. These same actions will be taken if hit by accidental friendly artillery or mortars with the addition of the RTOs immediately calling for an emergency "check fire" on all radio nets.

9. EXTRACTION

a. The LRRP team may be extracted by helicopter or by walking out of the AI upon completion of the planned duration of the patrol.

b. Normal helicopter extraction will be conducted by either touchdown, ladder, or McGuire Rig. Prior to the extraction the company operations officer will notify the team of the time for the extraction and will request a LZ report from the team leader. The report will include:

   (1) Type (touchdown, ladder, or McGuire Rig)
   (2) Location (map grid coordinates)
   (3) Size (dimensions of the LZ in meters)
   (4) Vegetation (height, type, density, etc.)
   (5) Slope (degree and direction)

c. After submitting the LZ report, the team will conduct a thorough recon of the LZ to ensure it is secure and report their findings. As the command and control and lift ships near the LZ, the team will display the prescribed marking panel, signal mirror flash, smoke, or strobe light. When the lift chopper is on final approach, the team leader will consolidate the team from their security positions and prepare to be extracted.

d. Actions taken by the team during extraction include:

(1) Touchdown: As the helicopter sets down on the LZ, the team boards as rapidly as possible. As soon as all are on board the crew chief will notify the aircraft commander to lift off.

(2) Ladder: As the helicopter hovers above the LZ, the belly man will drop the ladders to the team. The team will approach the ladder in threes, attach their packs to the bottom of the ladder with snap links, and ascend the ladder. After all are

aboard, the aircraft will take off to a higher altitude where the ladders and packs will be pulled on board.

(3) McGuire Rig: As the helicopter hovers above the LZ, the belly man will drop the McGuire Rigs. Normally, a helicopter will lift out only three men on the McGuire Rigs requiring two aircraft per team extraction. Once the three men are in the rigs the team leader will signal the belly man and the helicopter will make a vertical ascent until all personnel are clear of the trees. The second aircraft will then repeat the process. Once the aircraft have flown to a friendly fire base, they will make a slow vertical descent until the team reaches the ground. The aircraft will then land so the team can load inside and return to the company base.

(4) Walk-out: In a walk-out extraction the team will follow a planned route of march to a linkup with friendly units. On reaching the designated area, the team will notify the company TOC for further transportation.

(5) Vehicle or boat: The team will move to and secure the pickup position at the edge of the road or stream. The vehicle or boat will proceed to and beyond the pickup point. As the transportation passes the team they will make the appropriate signal. Upon verification of the team's position by the operations officer the vehicle or boat will turn around and return to the pickup point where they will briefly stop while the team loads.

10. EMERGENCY EXTRACTION

Emergency extractions are those that are conducted when in or anticipating enemy contact. They will be conducted in the same manner of normal extractions except for emergency night pickups by McGuire Rig and emergency walkouts. In all instances the team will keep the operations officer informed of the developing enemy situation. Procedures for emergency night McGuire Rig and walk-out extractions are as follows:

   a. Night McGuire
     The team will use one strobe light to mark the LZ. A second strobe will be turned on when the first load of three men is ready to be lifted from the LZ. A third strobe is lit when the second group is prepared to be lifted out. Each group of three will keep a strobe lit while in flight to assist the aircraft pilot in lowering the team to the ground once they arrive at a secure area.

   b. Emergency walk-out
     The team follows a predesignated escape and evasion (E&E) route when in contact with a superior enemy force. The team leader informs the operations officer of the enemy situation and that they are moving on their E&E route. The team may also decide to perform an emergency walk-out in the event communications are lost and all efforts to contact the TOC, radio relay, or other friendly elements has failed.

11. REPORTING

LRRP teams will report to the company TOC, which will relay appropriate messages to higher headquarters. Reports include:

   a. Insertion report
     On reaching the insertion point the team will report:
     (1) Location of the insertion
     (2) Time of insertion
     (3) Enemy situation (hot or cold)

   b. Situation report
     Current situation reports will be rendered at 0600, 0900, 1200, 1500, and 1800 hours and

hourly on the half hour during hours of darkness. This schedule may vary in the event the team is beyond normal radio communications and must relay through aircraft. At no time will the team be without radio relay support for more than four hours. Situation reports (Sit-reps) will include:

(1) Team location
(2) Enemy situation

(NOTE: Reports at night or when designated by the team leader will be initiated by the TOC or radio relay rather than by the team. To maintain as much silence as possible the TOC will call requesting a sit-rep. The RTO can answer by a predetermined set of keying the radio handset to break squelch. Other questions can be answered in similar manner with one squelch meaning yes, two for no, and three for ask again.)

c. Spot report

Spot reports will be made immediately when a significant sighting or enemy contact is made. The spot report will follow the acronym SA-LUTE:

(1) Size of enemy force
(2) Activity
(3) Location
(4) Unit or uniform description
(5) Time
(6) Equipment observed

(NOTE: In the event contact is made, remarks should be added as to results in body count and weapons and equipment captured.)

d. Other reports will be make in accordance with other paragraphs of this SOP (LZ, extraction, etc.) or as designated by the company commander or operations section.

12. DEBRIEFING

a. Patrols will be debriefed immediately on return to the company base. Debriefings will be conducted by the company intelligence NCO or by the company commander. Intelligence officers of higher commands may attend and participate in the debriefing if approved by the company commander. Debriefings will take place in the company debriefing tent or in another location that is secure and free of interruption or distractions. A formal, written report of the debriefing will be made and signed by the team leader and the debriefing official. Copies of the report and appropriate maps and map overlays, which will be classified at least at the confidential level, will be filed in the company intel section with copies forwarded to division and to units operating in or near the AI.

b. Debriefing will include:

(1) Name, rank, and position of each team member

(2) Mission

(3) Time, location, and method of insertion and extraction

(4) Routes of movement by the team

(5) Terrain (vegetation, height of canopy, trails, water sources, LZs)

(6) Enemy (strength, location, activity, equipment, weapons, morale, estimate activity)

(7) Results of enemy contact (body count, captured weapon description and serial number, description of documents and equipment)

(8) Map corrections

(9) Communications

(10) Condition of patrol (including time needed before next mission)

(11) Conclusions and recommendation

13. FIRE SUPPORT

Coordination and planning with fire support elements is essential to the success of LRRP operations. Fire support includes:

a. Artillery

  Artillery fire support will be coordinated with the division and the artillery battery in range of the AI through the company operations section. A fire support plan will be prepared with pre-planned targets and numbers so that the data can be preplotted by the artillery fire direction center. On the mission the team leader will communicate directly with the supporting battery on the artillery radio net. Artillery fires may be used to:

   (1) Destroy or neutralize enemy personnel or equipment
   (2) Deceive the enemy as to the patrol's location or intention
   (3) Deny the enemy freedom of movement
   (4) Defend the patrol while in contact or withdrawal
   (5) Direct the patrol during movement by firing navigation rounds at preplotted locations
   (6) Delay enemy reinforcements and pursuit

b. Naval gun fire

  When in range, naval gun fire can be used similarly to artillery. Naval gun fire will be coordinated through the naval liaison officer at Division.

c. Air Support

   (1) Army: AH-1 Cobra gunships will be employed in support of all team insertions and extractions. During missions gunships will be on strip alert or in the air near the AI and will be able to support in no more than ten minutes from the time requested by the team through company operations.

(2) Air Force: The patrol teams will be supported by the Air Force forward air controller (FAC) of the brigade headquarters nearest the AI. Company operations section will also inform the division Air Force liaison of planned missions. Tactical air support will generally be available within fifteen minutes of request.

(NOTE: All AIs, while patrols are in the zones, will be no fire/no fly zones to all other elements. No fires of any type will be put into the AI without the coordination and approval of the team leader. The same rules apply to a one thousand meter buffer area around the AI.)

14. COORDINATION

A LRRP liaison from the operations section will conduct the coordination with all supporting units. Coordination will include:

a. Artillery
   Coordination will be made with all batteries within range of the recon zones.

b. Air Force
   Coordination will be made with the division Air Force liaison officer when the teams are deployed outside the brigade operational areas. When patrols are within a brigade's sector, coordination will be made with the brigade Air Force liaison officer.

c. Ready Reaction Force (RRF)
   An RRF of either an infantry platoon or company will normally be on ten-minute alert to reinforce teams in contact that cannot withdraw under their own firepower or to exploit a finding by the recon team or to assist in an emergency extraction. Coordination will be made directly with the commander of the RRF and with the RRF's unit-higher headquarters.

(NOTE: Operations orders, including map overlays, will be distributed to the Air Force liaison, supporting artillery, the division G-2, the division G-3, the RRF, and to the brigade(s) next to or near the recon zones. Radio call signs and frequencies and the exact location and dimensions of the recon zones will also be provided.)

15. FINAL COMMENTS

All users of this SOP are reminded that while this document sets standard procedures, measures should be taken in the field to avoid set patterns that, if detected, would favor the enemy. Lastly, this SOP is only as effective as those LRRPs who follow it.

Signed
Captain, Infantry
Commanding

ANNEX I

To TAC SOP: LRRP/Ranger Company
Organizational Diagram

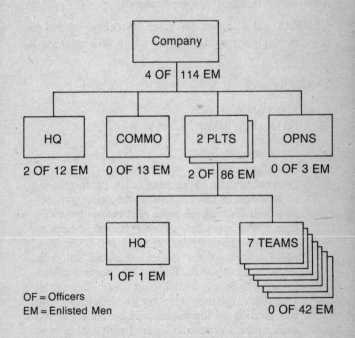

```
                      ┌──────────────┐
                      │   Company    │
                      └──────────────┘
                       4 OF │ 114 EM
        ┌──────────────┬─────┴──────┬──────────────┐
   ┌────────┐     ┌─────────┐  ┌─────────┐    ┌────────┐
   │   HQ   │     │  COMMO  │  │ 2 PLTS  │    │  OPNS  │
   └────────┘     └─────────┘  └─────────┘    └────────┘
  2 OF 12 EM     0 OF 13 EM    2 OF │ 86 EM   0 OF 3 EM
                            ┌────────┴────────┐
                       ┌────────┐        ┌─────────┐
                       │   HQ   │        │ 7 TEAMS │
                       └────────┘        └─────────┘
                       1 OF 1 EM         0 OF 42 EM
```

OF = Officers
EM = Enlisted Men

ANNEX II

To TAC SOP: Rigging of Helicopters

GENERAL: This annex describes the techniques and procedures employed in rigging the UH-1 helicopter for the following:

1. Ladder

    a. Materials required
        (1) 1 cargo ladder 30 feet long
        (2) 6 snap links
        (3) 2 sling ropes
    b. Procedures
    Depending on the vegetation of the landing zone, as reported in the LZ report, the operations officer will instruct the belly man on the length of ladder that must be available for the insertion/ extraction. The standard method will be to have equal lengths of the ladder extending out both sides of the aircraft. The middle portion of the ladder will be connected to the floor rings of the aircraft's cargo area with the six snap links. The free portion of the ladder will be coiled to the sides of the aircraft and secured with a sling rope tied with a slip knot for quick release. If high vegetation requires, a maximum length of twenty-eight feet may be achieved by extending all the ladder out of one side of the aircraft. At least two ladder rungs must be inside the aircraft so they can be connected with all six snap links.

2. Rappelling

   a. Materials required

      (1) 2 nylon ropes per station, each 120 feet by $7/16$ inch

      (2) 1 donut ring (composed of 10 feet of $1/2$ -inch cable with the ends overlapping and connected by 4 u-bolt clamps)

      (3) 1 floating safety ring composed of two snap links taped together with gates opening in opposite directions connected to a 12-inch-long, $5/8$ -inch-diameter steel cable.

      (4) 1 log or board 2 feet in length and 4 inches in diameter per station

      (5) Each rappeller will have a sling rope for tying a Swiss seat with a snap link and leather gloves

   b. Procedures

      (1) The donut ring will be connected in a circular pattern to the floor of the aircraft and connected by six snap links. The floating safety ring will be connected to a different ring in the floor at the center of the ring with the twelve-inch cable running from the floating safety to the donut ring and connected with a snap link.

      (2) A middle-of-the-rope bowline with a bight will be tied eighteen inches from the end of the rope. At the end of the rope, an end-of-the-rope bowline will be tied. A snap link will then connect the end-of-the-rope bowline to the donut ring with another snap link connecting the middle-of-the-rope bowline to the floating safety ring.

      (3) The rappel rope is then rolled onto the board or log.

      (4) Individuals will snap link their Swiss seat to the rappel rope, and the aircraft is prepared for departure.

3. MCGUIRE RIG

a. The interior aircraft donut ring and floating safety ring are prepared in the same manner as for rappelling.

b. At the ground end of the rope a bowline with a bight is tied eight feet from the end of the rope. At the end of the rope is tied an end-of-the-rope bowline which connects to a rope harness or one made from a parachute harness. A safety line will connect the harness to the upper bowline with a snap link.

ANNEX III

To TAC SOP: Handling of Enemy POWs and KIAS

1. POWs

Enemy POWs will be handled according to the five S's, which are:

- a. Search
- b. Silence
- c. Safeguard
- d. Segregate
- e. Speed

2. When a prisoner is taken, an immediate request for evacuation will be made. If the POW is wounded, he will be treated and all efforts will be made to keep him alive. If more than one POW is taken, they should be separated and not allowed to communicate. They should be blindfolded and secured against escape. A POW may be a tremendous source of intelligence—a POW is far more valuable than a body count—they will be brought in alive if at all possible.

3. Enemy KIA

Dead enemy will be stripped of all weapons and equipment, including their uniforms and footgear, which will be extracted with the team. Bodies should not be mutilated.

ANNEX IV

To TAC SOP: Ground Radio Relay Stations

1. GENERAL:

This annex describes the composition, equipment, and duties of the ground radio relay.

2. COMPOSITION:

A radio relay will consist of a team of three made up of one chief radio operator and two assistant radio operators. The chief radio operator is in charge of the team and is responsible for all actions of the radio relay team.

3. EQUIPMENT:

   (a) 2 PRC-25s or PRC-77s
   (b) 1 PRC-74 (AM)
   (c) 1 RC-292 antenna
   (d) 1 extra handset per radio
   (e) 6 extra batteries per radio
   (f) Maps and operational overlays of the AIs
   (g) Signal operating instructions (SOI)
   (h) Individual weapons and equipment
   (i) Rations and water for six days
(NOTE: If the radio relay is not to be located at a fire base or other secure area, a patrol team of six men will accompany the relay to provide security.)

4. DUTIES:

The company radio frequencies will be monitored twenty-four hours a day. All reports from the teams to the TOC or the TOC to the teams will be relayed exactly as received. All reports will also be logged in the daily journal along with the correct time. Each member of the radio relay will receive periodic classes from the company commo NCO to include employment and care of radios and antennas, artillery adjustment, air support, and other subjects as directed by the company commander.

(NOTE: While performing radio relay at fire base and other secure areas, you will be representatives of this company. Your actions, appearance, and professionalism will at all times meet the LRRP standard.)

ANNEX V

To TAC SOP: Tactical Operations Center

1. The function of the company TOC is the responsibility of the operations sergeant, with supervision by the operations officer. The TOC will be operational twenty-four hours a day with at least two personnel on duty at all times. All messages and reports will be recorded in the daily staff journal with the proper time and initials of the person recording the data.

2. Situation reports will be submitted to the TOC by teams in the field at 0600, 0900, 1200, 1500, and 1800 hours and hourly on the half hour during the hours of darkness. These reports will be forwarded to Division and those units operating near the AIs. If any team is more than thirty minutes in making these required reports, the company commander will be notified immediately.

3. Teams will make spot reports on any enemy sighting or for other significant findings. Enemy sightings will be immediately passed to the company commander.

4. Radio traffic to teams in the field will be kept to a minimum to prevent interception by the enemy and to assist in maintaining silence. Reports at night will originate with the TOC asking for Sit-reps. Negative responses may be reported by merely breaking squelch the number of times as outlined in the team's operation order.

APPENDIX B
○□○□○□○□○

Standing Orders—
Rogers's Rangers, 1759

1. Don't forget nothing.

2. Have your musket clean as a whistle, hatchet scoured, sixty rounds powder and ball, and be ready to march at a minute's warning.

3. When you're on the march, act the way you would if you was sneaking up on a deer. See the enemy first.

4. Tell the truth about what you see and what you do. There is an Army depending on us for correct information. You can lie all you please when you tell other folks about the Rangers, but don't ever lie to a Ranger or officer.

5. Don't never take a chance you don't have to.

6. When you're on the march we march single file, far enough apart so one shot can't go through two men.

7. If we strike swamps, or soft ground, we spread out abreast, so it's hard to track us.

8. When we march, we keep moving till dark, so as to give the enemy the least possible chance at us.

9. When we camp, half the party stays awake while the other half sleeps.

10. If we take prisoners, we keep 'em separate till we have time to examine them, so they can't cook up a story between 'em.

11. Don't ever march home the same way. Take a different route so you won't be ambushed.

12. No matter whether we travel in big parties or little ones, each party has to keep a scout twenty yards on each flank and twenty yards in the rear, so the main body can't be surprised and wiped out.

13. Every night you'll be told where to meet if surrounded by a superior force.

14. Don't sit down to eat without posting sentries.

15. Don't sleep beyond dawn. Dawn's when the French and Indians attack.

16. Don't cross a river by a regular ford.

17. If somebody's trailing you, make a circle, come back onto your tracks, and ambush the folks that aim to ambush you.

18. Don't stand up when the enemy's coming against you. Kneel down, lie down, hide behind a tree.

19. Let the enemy come till he's almost close enough to touch. Then let him have it and jump out and finish him up with your hatchet.

APPENDIX C

●●●●●●●●

LRRP and Ranger Units in Vietnam

LRRP Units

Unit	Service	Parent Command
Co E, 20th Inf (LRP)	25 Sep '67 to 1 Feb '69	I Field Force
Co E, 50th Inf (LRP)	20 Dec '67 to 1 Feb '69	9th Inf Div
Co F, 50th Inf (LRP)	20 Dec '67 to 1 Feb '69	25th Inf Div
Co E, 51st Inf (LRP)	20 Dec '67 to 1 Feb '69	23rd Inf Div (American)
Co F, 51st Inf (LRP)	25 Sep '67 to 1 Feb '69	II Field Force
Co E, 52nd Inf (LRP)	20 Dec '67 to 1 Feb '69	1st Cavalry Div
Co F, 52nd Inf (LRP)	20 Dec '67 to 1 Feb '69	1st Inf Div
Co E, 58th Inf (LRP)	20 Dec '67 to 1 Feb '69	4th Inf Div

Co F, 58th Inf (LRP)	10 Jan '68 to 1 Feb '69	101st Airborne Div
*70th Inf Det (LRP)	19 Dec '67 to 15 Jan '68	11th Inf Bde
71st Inf Det (LRP)	20 Dec '67 to 1 Feb '69	199th Light Inf Bde
74th Inf Det (LRP)	20 Dec '67 to 1 Feb '69	173rd Airborne Bde
78th Inf Det (LRP)	15 Dec '68 to 1 Feb '69	3rd Bde, 82nd Airborne Div
79th Inf Det (LRP)	15 Dec '68 to 1 Feb '69	1st Bde, 5th Inf Div (Mech)
†Co D, 151st Inf (LRP)	30 Dec '68 to 1 Feb '69	II Field Force

*The 70th Inf Detachment (LRP) combined with Company E, 51st Infantry (LRP), when the 11th Infantry Brigade was reassigned from a separate infantry brigade to come under the 23rd Infantry Division (Americal).
†Company D, 151st Infantry (LRP) was an Indiana National Guard unit activated for service in Vietnam.

Rangers

Unit	Service	Parent Command
Co C, 75th Inf (Rgr)	1 Feb '69 to 25 Oct '71	I Field Force
Co D, 75th Inf (Rgr)	1 Feb '69 to 10 Apr '70	II Field Force
Co E, 75th Inf (Rgr)	1 Feb '69 to 23 Aug '69	9th Inf Div
*Co E, 75th Inf (Rgr)	1 Oct '69 to 12 Oct '70	3rd Bde, 9th Inf Div
Co F, 75th Inf (Rgr)	1 Feb '69 to 15 Mar '71	25th Inf Div

Co G, 75th Inf (Rgr)	1 Feb '69 to 1 Oct '71	23rd Inf Div (Americal)
Co H, 75th Inf (Rgr)	1 Feb '69 to 15 Aug '72	1st Cavalry Div
Co I, 75th Inf (Rgr)	1 Feb '69 to 7 Apr '70	1st Inf Div
Co K, 75th Inf (Rgr)	1 Feb '69 to 10 Dec '70	4th Inf Div
Co L, 75th Inf (Rgr)	1 Feb '69 to 26 Dec '71	101st Airborne Div
Co M, 75th Inf (Rgr)	1 Feb '69 to 12 Oct '70	199th Light Inf Bde
Co N, 75th Inf (Rgr)	1 Feb '69 to 25 Aug '71	173rd Airborne Bde
Co O, 75th Inf (Rgr)	1 Feb '69 to 20 Nov '69	3rd Bde, 82nd Airborne Div
Co P, 75th Inf (Rgr)	1 Feb '69 to 31 Aug '71	1st Bde, 5th Inf Div (Mech)
†Co D, 151st Inf (Rgr)	1 Feb '69 to 20 Nov '69	II Field Force

*Company E is credited with two tours in Vietnam. Two brigades of the 9th Infantry Division stood down and returned to the States in August 1969 leaving only the 3rd Brigade in country. Company E reorganized from a 118- to a 61-man company at that time. Although the company was off the official rolls for over a month before being reactivated, in reality it was a paper drill and the company never ceased operations, albeit at a reduced scale.

†Since Company D, 151st Infantry, was to return to control of the Indiana National Guard at the completion of their tour, they were not redesignated as a company of the 75th Infantry. Their only change was to redesignate the parenthetical LRP to Ranger.

Assets Used to Form Ranger Companies
and Assigned Strengths

RANGER COMPANY	ASSETS DERIVED FROM	STRENGTH*
Co C	Co E, 20th Inf (LRP)	230
Co D	Co F, 51st Inf (LRP)	198
Co E	Co E, 50th Inf (LRP)	118
Co F	Co F, 50th Inf (LRP)	118
Co G	Co E, 51st Inf (LRP)	118
Co H	Co E, 52nd Inf (LRP)	198
Co I	Co F, 52nd Inf (LPR)	118
Co K	Co E, 58th Inf (LRP)	118
Co L	Co F, 58th Inf (LRP)	118
Co M	71st Inf Det (LRP)	61
Co N	74th Inf Det (LRP)	61
Co O	78th Inf Det (LRP)	61
Co P	79th Inf Det (LRP)	61

*Authorized strengths of Ranger and LRP units varied slightly at different stages of the war. Strengths listed are for February 1969, when the LRP units were redesignated Rangers.

APPENDIX D
□□□□□□□□

LRRP Medal of Honor Recipients

PRUDEN, ROBERT J., staff sergeant, Company G
(Ranger), 23rd Infantry Division (Americal). Born September 9, 1949, in St. Paul, Minnesota. Entered the service at Minneapolis, Minnesota.

Staff Sergeant Pruden was serving as reconnaissance
team leader on November 29, 1969, in Quang Ngai Province. His six-man team was inserted by helicopter into
enemy-controlled territory to establish an ambush position
and to obtain information on enemy movements. As the
team moved into the preplanned area, Pruden deployed
his men into two groups on the opposite sides of a well-used trail. As the groups were establishing their defensive
positions, one member of the team was trapped in the
open by heavy fire from an enemy squad. Realizing that
the ambush position had been compromised, Pruden directed his team to open fire on the enemy force. Immediately the team came under heavy fire from a second
enemy element. Pruden, with full knowledge of the extreme danger involved, left his concealed position and,
firing as he ran, advanced toward the enemy to draw the
hostile fire. He was seriously wounded twice but continued his attack until he fell for a third time, in front of the
enemy positions. Pruden's actions resulted in several enemy casualties and withdrawal of the remaining enemy

forces. Although grievously wounded, he directed his men into defensive positions and called for evacuation helicopters, which safely withdrew the members of the team. Pruden died of his wounds.

RABEL, LASZLO, staff sergeant, 74th Infantry Detachment (Long Range Patrol), 173rd Airborne Brigade. Born September 21, 1939, in Budapest, Hungary. Entered service at Minneapolis, Minnesota.

Staff Sergeant Rabel was serving as a team leader in Binh Dinh Province on November 13, 1968. At 1000 hours Rabel's team was in a defensive perimeter conducting reconnaissance of enemy trail networks when a member of the team detected enemy movement to the front. As Rabel and a comrade prepared to clear the area, he heard an incoming grenade as it landed in the midst of the team's position. With complete disregard for his own life, Rabel threw himself on the grenade and, covering it with his body, received the complete impact of the immediate explosion. Rabel averted the loss of life and injury to the members of his team at the cost of his own life.

LAW, ROBERT D., specialist 4, Company I (Ranger), 75th Infantry, 1st Infantry Division. Born September 15, 1944, in Fort Worth, Texas. Entered service at Dallas, Texas.

While on a long-range reconnaissance patrol in Tinh Phoc Province on February 22, 1969, Specialist Law and his five comrades made contact with a small enemy patrol. As the opposing elements exchanged intense fire, he maneuvered to a perilously exposed position flanking his team and began placing suppressive fire on the hostile troops. Although his team was hindered by a low supply of ammunition and suffered from an unidentified irritating gas in the air, Law's spirited defense and challenging counterassault rallied his fellow soldiers against the well-equipped hostile troops. When an enemy grenade landed in his team's position, Law, instead of diving into the safety of a stream behind him, threw himself on the grenade to save the lives of his fellow soldiers at the cost of his own.

APPENDIX E
ooooooooo

Unit Awards, Citations, and Commendations

L_{RRP} and Ranger detachments and companies were among the most decorated units of the war and recognition included awards, citations, and commendations from both the United States and the Republic of Vietnam. The decorations and an explanation of the basis of eligibility follows:

PRESIDENTIAL UNIT CITATION

The Presidential Unit Citation is awarded to units of the armed forces of the United States for extraordinary heroism in action against an armed enemy. The unit must display such gallantry, determination, and esprit de corps in accomplishing its mission under extremely difficult and hazardous conditions as to set it apart and above other units participating in the same campaign. The degree of heroism required is the same as that which would warrant award of a Distinguished Service Cross to an individual.

VALOROUS UNIT AWARD

The Valorous Unit Award is awarded to units of the armed forces of the United States for extraordinary heroism in action against an armed enemy. The award requires a lesser degree of gallantry, determination, and esprit de corps than that required for the Presidential Unit Citation. Nevertheless, the unit must have performed with marked distinction under difficult and hazardous conditions in accomplishing its mission so as to set it apart from other units participating in the same campaign. The degree of heroism required is the same as that which would warrant award of the Silver Star to an individual.

MERITORIOUS UNIT COMMENDATION

The Meritorious Unit Commendation is awarded to units for exceptional meritorious conduct in performance of outstanding services for at least six continuous months during the period of military operations against an armed enemy. The unit must display such outstanding devotion and superior performance of exceptionally difficult tasks as to set it apart and above other units with similar missions. The degree of achievement required is the same that which would warrant award of the Legion of Merit to an individual.

REPUBLIC OF VIETNAM GALLANTRY CROSS UNIT CITATION

The unit citation of the Gallantry Cross was awarded by the Vietnamese government for valorous combat achievement.

REPUBLIC OF VIETNAM CIVIL ACTIONS MEDAL UNIT CITATION

The unit citation of the Civil Actions Medal was awarded by the Vietnamese government for meritorious service.

Awards Received by Unit and Dates

Company E, 20th Infantry (LRP)

Republic of Vietnam Civil Actions Medal
15 Oct 67 to 10 Oct 68

Company E, 50th Infantry (LRP)

Republic of Vietnam Gallantry Cross
1 Dec 66 to 30 Jun 68
1 Jan to 31 Jan 69
Republic of Vietnam Civil Actions Medal
20 Dec 67 to 31 Jan 69

Company F, 50th Infantry (LRP)

Valorous Unit Award
1 Jan to 30 Jan 69
Republic of Vietnam Gallantry Cross
20 Dec 67 to 31 Aug 68
1 Jan to 31 Mar 69

Company E, 51st Infantry (LRP)

Meritorious Unit Commendation
18 Jun 68 to 30 Jan 69

Company F, 51st Infantry (LRP)

Valorous Unit Award
31 Jan to 19 Feb 68
Republic of Vietnam Gallantry Cross
1 Feb to 19 Feb 68

Company E, 52nd Infantry (LRP)

Republic of Vietnam Gallantry Cross
20 Dec 67 to 31 Jan 69

Company F, 52nd Infantry (LRP)

Republic of Vietnam Civil Actions Medal
20 Dec 67 to 1 Jul 68

Company E, 58th Infantry (LRP)

Republic of Vietnam Gallantry Cross
20 Dec 67 to 31 Jan 69
Republic of Vietnam Civil Actions Medal
20 Dec 67 to 31 Jan 69

Company F, 58th Infantry (LRP)

Republic of Vietnam Gallantry Cross
19 Jul 68 to 31 Jan 69
Republic of Vietnam Civil Actions Medal
18 Mar 68 to 1 Feb 69

71st Infantry Detachment (LRP)

Valorous Unit Citation
31 Jan to 19 Feb 68
Meritorious Unit Commendation
31 Jan to 31 Dec 68
Republic of Vietnam Cross of Gallantry
31 Jan to 19 Feb 68
19 Jun 68 to 1 Feb 69
Republic of Vietnam Civil Actions Medal
1 Feb 68 to 1 Feb 69

74th Infantry Detachment (LRP)

Presidential Unit Citation
6 Nov to 23 Nov 67

Company C, 75th Infantry (Ranger)

Valorous Unit Award
23 Jul 69 to 28 Feb 70
Republic of Vietnam Gallantry Cross
1 Feb 69 to 26 Sep 70

Republic of Vietnam Civil Actions Medal
15 Apr 69 to 16 Mar 71

Company E, 75th Infantry (Ranger)

Republic of Vietnam Gallantry Cross
1 Feb 69 to 30 Jun 69
29 Jul 69 to 20 Jun 70
Republic of Vietnam Civil Actions Medal
26 Jul 69 to 20 Jul 70
1 Feb to 28 Jun 70

Company F, 75th Infantry (Ranger)

Valorous Unit Award
1 to 22 Feb 69
Republic of Vietnam Gallantry Cross
1 Feb to 31 Mar 69
1 Sep 69 to 30 Sep 70
Republic of Vietnam Civil Actions Medal
17 Feb 69 to 21 Jan 70

Company G, 75th Infantry (Ranger)

Meritorious Unit Commendation
1 Feb to 31 Aug 69
Republic of Vietnam Gallantry Cross
24 Aug to 31 Dec 69
31 Mar to 30 Jun 70

Company H, 75th Infantry (Ranger)

Valorous Unit Award
1 Oct to 31 Dec 69
1 May to 29 Jun 70
10 Apr to 1 Oct 71
Republic of Vietnam Gallantry Cross
1 Feb to 19 May 69
1 May 69 to 1 Feb 70
21 Feb 70 to 28 Feb 71
Republic of Vietnam Civil Actions Medal
1 Feb 69 to 2 Feb 70

Company I, 75th Infantry (Ranger)

Republic of Vietnam Civil Actions Medal
1 Feb 69 to 7 April 70

Company K, 75th Infantry (Ranger)

Republic of Vietnam Gallantry Cross
1 Feb to 28 Jul 69
Republic of Vietnam Civil Actions Medal
1 Feb to 31 Oct 69

Company L, 75th Infantry (Ranger)

Valorous Unit Award
7 Dec 69 to 16 Feb 70
Republic of Vietnam Gallantry Cross
1 Feb to 14 Mar 69
2 Dec 69 to 8 Jan 71
18 Apr to 31 Aug 71
6 to 19 Sep 71
1 Mar to 9 Oct 71
Republic of Vietnam Civil Actions Medal
1 Feb 69 to 2 May 70

Company M, 75th Infantry (Ranger)

Meritorious Unit Commendation
1 Jan 69 to 10 Jun 70
Republic of Vietnam Gallantry Cross
19 Jun 68 to 31 Jul 70
Republic of Vietnam Civil Actions Medal
1 Feb 69 to 31 Aug 70

Company N, 75th Infantry (Ranger)

Republic of Vietnam Gallantry Cross
1 Feb 69 to 26 Sep 70
Republic of Vietnam Civil Actions Medal
15 Apr 69 to 16 Mar 71

Company O, 75th Infantry (Ranger)

Republic of Vietnam Cross of Gallantry
1 Feb to 11 Nov 69

Company P, 75th Infantry (Ranger)
Republic of Vietnam Cross of Gallantry
8 Feb 69 to 30 Apr 71

APPENDIX F
●●●●●●●●

Long Range Reconnaissance Patrol Unit Replacement Training Schedule

DAY	SUBJECT
1	
0500–0600	Physical Training
0800–1000	LRRP Orientation and History
1000–1130	Equipment Issue and Use
1300–1400	Combat Intelligence
1400–1530	VC/NVA Tactics and Organization
1530–1615	Landing Zone Selection
1615–1730	Pathfinder Techniques
1900–2000	Review and Quiz
2	
0500–0600	Physical Training
0800–0830	Combat Intelligence
0830–0940	Geographic Coordinates
0940–1130	Military Grid System
1300–1400	Wiretapping
1400–1530	Introduction to Map Reading
1530–1700	Map Orientation
1900–2000	Review
3	
0500–0600	Physical Training
0800–1000	Radio Use and Maintenance

1000–1130	Field Expedient Radio Antennas
1300–1400	Map Scale and Distance
1400–1530	Map Elevation and Relief
1530–1700	Map Practical Exercise
1900–2000	Review

4

0500–0600	Physical Training
0800–0900	Points of Origin for Reporting Locations
0900–1000	Radio Procedures
1000–1130	Emergency Radio Procedures
1300–1400	Use of the Compass—Direction
1400–1500	Intersection and Resection
1500–1700	Map Practical Exercise
1900–2000	Review

5

0500–0600	Physical Training
0800–0900	Signal Operating Instructions (SOI) Usage
0900–1000	Jamming and Bogey Radio Traffic
1000–1130	Communications Practical Exercise
1300–1430	Communications Review
1430–1630	Communications Test
1900–2000	Map Reading Review

6

0500–0600	Physical Training
0800–0900	Map Practical Exercise
0900–0930	Map Review
0930–1130	Map Test
1300–1400	Medical Life Saving Steps
1400–1530	Pills and Special Medication
1530–1700	Treatment of Wounds
1900–2000	Review

7

0500–0600	Physical Training
0800–1000	Medical Training
1000–1130	Medical Practical Exercise
1300–1400	Emergency Signal Devices
1400–1530	Patrol Tips and Techniques
1530–1600	Escape and Evasion and Survival

| 1600–1700 | Commander's Orientation |
| 1900–2000 | Review, Escape, and Evasion Quiz |

8

0500–0600	Physical Training
0800–1000	Medical Review and Test
1000–1040	Stream Crossing Techniques
1040–1130	McGuire Rig (Helicopter)
1300–1400	Introduction to Rappelling
1400–1700	Rappelling (Tower)
1900–2000	Review

9

0500–0600	Physical Training
0800–1130	Rappelling (Helicopter)
1300–1400	Stealth and Security
1400–1500	Immediate Action Drills
1500–1700	Immediate Action Practical Exercise
1900–2000	Review

10

0500–0600	Physical Training
0800–0900	Artillery Orientation
0900–1130	Artillery Forward Observer Procedures
1300–1430	U.S. Weapons Familiarization
1430–1530	Individual Weapon Zero
1530–1730	Allied and Enemy Weapons Familiarization
1900–2000	Starlite Scope (Night Vision)

11

0500–0600	Physical Training
0800–0930	Artillery Review and Test
0930–1030	Helicopter Gunships
1030–1130	Tactical Air Support
1300–1400	Patrol Warning Order
1400–1600	Patrol Order
1600–1730	Patrol Debriefing Procedures
1900–2000	Patrol Review and Quiz

12

| 0800–1130 | Final Exam |
| 1130–2400 | Preparation for First Mission |

APPENDIX G
⚌⚌⚌⚌⚌

Ranger Creed

RECOGNIZING that I volunteered as a Ranger, fully knowing the hazards of my chosen profession, I will always endeavor to uphold the prestige, honor, and high "esprit de corps" of my Ranger Battalion.

Acknowledging the fact that a Ranger is a more elite soldier who arrives at the cutting edge of battle by land, sea, or air, I accept the fact that as a Ranger my country expects me to move further, faster, and fight harder than any other soldier.

Never shall I fail my comrades. I will always keep myself mentally alert, physically strong, and morally straight, and I will shoulder more than my share of the task whatever it may be. One hundred percent and then some.

Gallantly will I show the world that I am a specially selected and well-trained soldier. My courtesy to superior officers, my neatness of dress, and care of equipment shall set the example for others to follow.

Energetically will I meet the enemies of my country. I shall defeat them on the field of battle for I am better trained and will fight with all my might. Surrender is not a Ranger word. I will never leave a fallen comrade to fall into the hands of the enemy and under no circumstance will I ever embarrass my country.

Readily will I display the intestinal fortitude required to

fight on the Ranger objective and complete the mission, though I be the lone survivor.

(NOTE: The first letter of each paragraph of the Creed forms the word RANGER.)

BIBLIOGRAPHY
●○●○●○●○●○●

Periodicals

Carroll, Robert C. "Six Men Alone." *Infantry*, Jan–Feb 1975.

Darragh, Shaun M. "Rangers and Special Forces: Two Edges of the Same Dagger." *Army*, Dec 1977.

Gable, Tom. "LRRP." *Infantry*, Jan–Feb 1969.

Garlock, Warren D., and Michael L. Lanning. "Ranger Training." *Infantry*, Nov–Dec 1972.

Gole, Henry G. "Bring Back the LRRP." *Military Review*, Oct 1981.

Halloran, Barney. "Pros at the Survival Game." *Soldiers*, May 1972.

Hamrick, Tom. "The Black Berets." *Army*, May 1977.

Ivers, Larry. "Rangers in Florida—1818." *Infantry*, Sept–Oct 1963.

James, Richard D. "Delta Team Is in Contact." *Infantry*, Nov–Dec 1970.

Johnson, Gerald W. "Aquabush." *Infantry*, Jan–Feb 1972.

Johnson, Thomas M. "Montagnards Become Rangers." *Infantry*, July–Aug 1971.

Lyde, William, Jr. "LRSU Course." *Infantry*, Nov–Dec 1986.

Shaughnessy, Thomas J. "Rotors for the Rangers." *Army*, May 1972.

Soehngen, Rick. "The Blackhawks Return." *Army Digest*, July 1970.

Sterner, Doug. "Silence Is Their Only Advantage." *First Team*, Spring 1972.

Van Houten, John G. "The Rangers Are Back." *Army Information Digest*, Aug 1951.

Voyles, James E. "Vietnam Rangers (LRRP)." *Gung Ho*, Oct 1984.

Published Works

Altieri, James J. *The Spearheaders*. New York: Popular Library, 1960.

Beaumont, Roger A. *Military Elites*. New York: Bobbs-Merrill, 1974.

Beckwith, Charlie A. *Delta Force*. New York: Harcourt, Brace, Jovanovich, 1983.

Bass, Robert D. *Swamp Fox: The Life And Campaigns of General Francis Marion*. New York: Henry Holt and Co., 1959.

Bourke, John G. *An Apache Campaign in the Sierra Madre*. New York: Charles Scribner's Sons, 1958.

Callahan, North. *Daniel Morgan, Ranger of the Revolution*. New York: Holt, Rinehart and Winston, 1961.

Collins, James Lawton, Jr., and Stanley Robert Larsen. *Allied Participation in Vietnam*. Washington: Department of the Army, 1975.

Collins, John M. *Green Berets, Seals, and Spetsnaz: U.S. and Soviet Special Military Operations*. McLean, VA: Brassey's International Defense Publishers, 1987.

Cuneo, John R. *Robert Rogers of the Rangers*. New York: Oxford University Press, 1959.

Danysh, Romana, and John K. Mahon. *Infantry Part I: Regular Army*. Army Lineage Series. Washington: Office of the Chief of Military History, 1972.

Eckhardt, George S. *Command and Control, 1950–1969*. Washington: Department of the Army, 1974.

Ewing, Joseph H. *29 Let's Go, A History of the 29th Infantry Division in World War II*. Washington: Infantry Journal Press, 1948.

Fehrenbach, F.E. *Lone Star*. New York: American Legacy, 1983.

Fulton, William B. *Riverine Operations*. Washington: Department of the Army, 1973.

Garland, Albert N. *Infantry in Vietnam*. Fort Benning, GA: Infantry Magazine, 1967.

Hamersly, Thomas H. S. *Complete Regular Army Register (1779–1879)*. Washington: T. H. S. Hamersly, 1880.

Hay, John H., Jr., *Tactical and Material Innovations*. Washington: Department of the Army, 1975.

Heitman, Francis B. *Historical Register and Dictionary of the United States Army*. Washington: Government Printing Office, 1903.

Huie, William Bradford. *The Execution of Private Slovik*. New York: Delacorte, 1954.

Hymoff, Edward. *Fourth Infantry Division in Vietnam*. New York: M. W. Ladds, 1968.

Jones, Virgil Carrington. *Ranger Mosby*. Chapel Hill: University of North Carolina Press, 1944.

Karnow, Stanley. *Vietnam, A History*. New York: Viking, 1983.

Kelly, Francis J. *Army Special Forces, 1961–1971*. Washington: Department of the Army, 1973.

King, Michael J. *William Orlando Darby: A Military Biography*. Hamden, CT: Archon Books, 1981.

Mahon, John K. *The War of 1812*. Gainesville: University of Florida Press, 1958.

Miller, Kenn. *Tiger the Lurp Dog*. Boston: Little, Brown and Co., 1983.

Mosby, John S. *The Memories of Colonel John S. Mosby*. Bloomington: Indiana University Press, 1959.

McChristian, Joseph A. *The Role of Military Intelligence 1965–1967*. Washington: Department of the Army, 1974.

Ogburn, Charlton, Jr. *The Marauders*. New York: Harper & Brothers, 1956.

Palmer, Bruce, Jr. *The 25-Year War: America's Military Role in Vietnam*. Lexington: The University of Kentucky Press, 1986.

Palmer, Dave Richard. *Summons of the Trumpet*. Navato, CA: Presidio Press, 1978.

Pearson, Willard R. *War in The Northern Provinces*. Washington: Department of the Army, 1975.

Rogers, Robert. *Journals of Major Robert Rogers*. New York: Corinth Books, 1961.

Scott, Leonard B. *Charlie Mike*. New York: Ballantine, 1985.
————*The Last Run*. New York: Ballantine, 1987.

Sharp, U. S. G., and William C. Westmoreland. *Report on the War in Vietnam (As of 30 June 1968)*. Washington: U.S. Government Printing Office, 1968.

Spears, James R. H. and William G. Watt. *Indiana's Citizen Soldiers*. Indianapolis: Indiana State Armory Board, 1980.

Stanton, Shelby L. *Green Berets at War*. Navato, CA: Presidio Press, 1985.

———*Order of Battle U.S. Army World War II*. Navato, CA: Presidio Press, 1984.

———*The Rise and Fall of the American Army*. Navato, CA: Presidio Press, 1985.

———*Vietnam Order of Battle*. Washington: U.S. News & World Report, 1981.

Vietnam Odyssey, The Story of the 1st Brigade, 101st Airborne Division in Vietnam. Texarkana: Southwest Printers and Publishers, 1967.

West, Francis J., Jr. *Small Unit Action in Vietnam: Summer 1966*. New York: Arno Press, 1967.

Westmoreland, William C. *A Soldier Reports*. Garden City, New York: Doubleday, 1976.

Wolf, Duquesne A. *The Infantry Brigade in Combat*. Manhattan KS: Sunflower University Press, 1984.

Interviews and Corresondence

The following men and women gave freely of their knowledge, recollections, personal papers, and research time. Without their support, candor, and hard work, this book would not have been possible.

William F. Atwater	Fort Campbell, KY
Jerry R. Ballantyne	Tacoma, WA
Ed Beal	Greensboro, NC
COL (Ret) Robert W. Black	Carlisle, PA
John W. Blake	Yorktown, VA
GEN (Ret) George S. Blanchard	McLean, VA
MG (Ret) Alexander R. Bolling, Jr.	Richardson, TX
Harvey Brough	Portland, CT
CPT William H. Buck	Fort Benning, GA
William B. Bullen	East Greenville, PA
Robert Busby	Racine, WI
George D. Clark	Sun City, AZ
Jeffrey J. Cole	Gig Harbor, WA
LTC Ed Constantine	Fort Lewis, WA
SFC Lawrence Dand	Fort Bragg, NC
GEN (Ret) Michael S. Davison	Arlington, VA
Thomas P. Dineen, Jr.	Annapolis, MD
CSM (Ret) Warren Divers	Steilcoom, WA
SFC Don W. Dupont	Rockford, IL
LTG (Ret) Julian J. Ewell	McLean, VA
Herb Farrow	Burton, OH
MG (Ret) Robert C. Forbes	Atlanta, GA
CPT William A. Gawthrop	Huntsville, TX
Phil Gioia	San Francisco, CA
Louis R. Gonzales	Merced, CA
COL (Ret) Dave Hackworth	Queensland, Australia
COL Ralph Hagler	Fort Lewis, WA
Thomas R. Hargrove	Los Banos, Philippines
Ric Harrison	Newport, WA
Roy D. Hatfield	Tazewell, TN
LTG (Ret) John H. Hay	Ridgway, CO
MG Kenneth W. Himsel	Indianapolis, IN
Dave Hogan	Guinea, VA
1SG Marshall C. Huckaby	Warner Robbins, GA
Susan Jaworski	Fort Hood, TX

Kregg P. J. Jorgenson	Seattle, WA
Michael Kentes, Jr.	Falls Church, VA
1LT Cathi A. Kiger	Indianapolis, IN
GEN (Ret) Frederick J. Kroesen	Arlington, VA
SGM James W. Kraft	Alexandria, VA
LTG (Ret) Stanley Larsen	San Francisco, CA
Craig L. Learberg	Colorado Spings, CO
MAJ John LeBrun	Victoria, Canada
John Leppleman	Moscow, ID
COL (Ret) Dandridge M. Malone	Lake Placid, FL
MG (Ret) Salve H. Matheson	Carmel, CA
Roxanne M. Merritt	Fort Bragg, NC
GEN (Ret) Frank T. Mildren	Beaufort, SC
LTC William J. Morrow	Coeur d'Alene, ID
LTG (Ret) William J. McCaffrey	Alexandria, VA
C. A. McDonald	French Lick, IN
George C. McGarrigle	Washington DC
1SG (Ret) William E. Nuckols	Milton, FL
George A. Paccerelli	Colville, WA
Joe Parker	Atlanta, GA
LTG (Ret) Willard Pearson	Wayne, PA
Lee Roy Pipkin	San Jose, CA
Joe Rachten	Clevelan, OH
Cal Renfro	Ballard, WA
MAJ William F. Reynolds	Schofield Barracks, HI
GEN (Ret) W. B. Rossen	Roanoke, VA
Thomas L. Roubideaux	Rosebud, SD
Bob Schroder	Fort Campbell, KY
LTC Leonard B. Scott	Carlisle Barracks, PA
MG (Ret) Paul F. Smith	Satellite Beach, FL
Sid Smith	Miami Beach, FL
Barb Springer	Fort Carson, CO
Shelby L. Stanton	Bethesda, MD
GEN (Ret) Richard G. Stilwell	Arlington VA
CSM (Ret) Walter D. Stock	Philadelphia, PA
LTC Robert K. Suchke	Fort Lewis, WA
LTG (Ret) Orwin C. Talbott	Annapolis, MD
BG (Ret) James S. Timothy	Longboat Key, FL
Lawrence W. Thomas, Jr.	Baltimore, MD
BG (Ret) Joseph R. Ulatoski	Bellevue, WA
SGT Robert J. Warsinske	Carlisle Barracks, PA
GEN (Ret) William C. Westmoreland	Charleston, SC

MG (Ret) Ellis W. Williamson   Arlington, VA
Ray Wittiker   Fort Benning, GA
COL (Ret) Duquesne A. Wof   Falls Church, VA
LTC Albert C. Zapanta   Dallas, TX

About the Author

MICHAEL LEE LANNING was born and educated in Texas and recently retired from the United States Army as a lieutenant colonel after over twenty years of active duty. He served in infantry, airborne, ranger, armor, and public affairs asssignments in Europe, Vietnam, and throughout the United States. Among other awards and decorations, Lanning earned the Bronze Star for Valor with two oak leaf clusters and the Combat Infantryman's Badge. He is ranger qualified and a senior parachutist. His previous books include *The Only War We Had, A Platoon Leader's Journal Of Vietnam* and *Vietnam 1969-1970: A Company Commander's Journal.* Lanning now writes full time, dividing his time between Tacoma and Eastsound in the state of Washington and San Jose, California.